The More the Merrier

Celebrating Seventy

Judy Pollard Smith

Archway Publishing books may be ordered through booksellers or by contacting:

Archway Publishing
1663 Liberty Drive
Bloomington, IN 47403
www.archwaypublishing.com
1 (888) 242-5904

ISBN: 978-1-4808-7204-2 (sc)
ISBN: 978-1-4808-7203-5 (e)

Library of Congress Control Number: 2018966765

Print information available on the last page.

Archway Publishing rev. date: 02/20/19

These thoughts I dedicate to little Hoàng Thị Lan Phương, Beautiful Orchid, who is forever tucked into a corner of my heart.

Late Summer

AUGUST 23RD, 2017 ~ It was wonderful to wake up to seventy this morning, wonderful for many reasons all of which will tumble out, one after the other, like socks from the dryer once I get going on this journal.

Many of my friends are turning seventy themselves. None of us can quite believe it.

Diane called from Halifax. "Seventy is all very well but it's such a high number," she said in a plaintive voice. We both laughed.

Journals, letters and memoirs have been my favourite reading for years, most of them about writers or people of fame. I've wondered if the journals of ordinary people are worth reading and I've decided that, yes, since most of us *are* ordinary people, they might have their own friendly value. My seventieth birthday has provided the perfect excuse to write an entry a day for the year. I'm not promising an exciting read. I'm promising only that I'll make good use of my days and that I'll try be observant of the life that unfolds around me.

On my book shelves are the journals and letters of Barbara Pym, Diana Athill, British playwright Alan Bennett, poet Philip Larkin, Susanna Moodie and her sister Catharine Parr Traill, Penelope Fitzgerald,

Henry Beston whose classic, The Outermost House, chronicled a year of living on a Cape Cod beach and E.M. Delafield's hilarious fictional Diary of a Provincial Lady, published in 1947, the year of my birth. In fact, I see that a few of my many books are circa that same year. Did I have a craving even then to know what to expect from the quotidian as I entered stage left?

Favourite of all my journals is that of the late Canadian Diplomat, Charles Ritchie. (Ritchie, 2008, 271). He had me the moment I read his words of February 1st, 1947 when he wrote, "Elizabeth Bowen is here." A reading of Love's Civil War, the letters and diaries of Ritchie and Bowen, had me hooked forever on hearing stories from the source.

I was twelve years old when I read The Diary Of Anne Frank. Her words stung like needle on bone. I vowed eternal loyalty to the Annes of this world. Words have purpose. String them together in a meaningful ribbon and they can change world views. At twelve years of age my own future mindset was informed by Anne's story.

I've called this journal The More the Merrier for a reason. I recently learned how to say it in Vietnamese, a language that has its own powerful place in my life. The more the merrier; Càng đông càng vui.

In this divided world we need more than ever to stand together, to be merry with friendships from every culture, from every creed and with every condition of life.

I bring my birthright, the cultural landmarks I've inherited from my English and Irish grandparents and my parents, along to this birthday. I cherish the guideposts that were taught me from my early childhood.

Seventy is indeed a high number. It's my "three score years and ten" to quote from both Moses's prayer in Psalm 90 and the card from Rob and Helen in Dumfriesshire that arrived today.

I'll do my best.

THURSDAY AUGUST 24TH, 2017 ~ Chilly. I need my navy sweater this morning in my reading corner on the back porch. Am enjoying a book about the Hanoverians (A Royal Experiment ~ The Private Life of King George 111, by Janice Hadlow. In spite of the emotional turmoil he suffered near the end of his life, it seems that George the 111 was the authour of a new form of kingship, one that would be welcomed and inform future generations of the British monarchy. He was determined that his own family would spend time together and be kind to one another, heralding a kind of household joy that was foreign to the Hanoverian line. King George 111 and Queen Charlotte were credited with trying to introduce a fresh code of authentic morality to the kingdom. History has proven that it didn't always work.

On the deck I can hear a host of birds twittering as they hold their annual avian convention about when to head south. Overhead a hawk floats on a thermal, the vast blue sky above him. The air is clear.

Indian food and birthday cake last night at Drew and Ely's with Jock and two of our little granddaughters, one of whom helped me to blow out the candles as the other did the salsa from the waist up in tune to Despacito, a salute to her South American roots. She is walking on her knees a minute to the mile and scoots around gathering up toys in her wake and tossing them hither and yon.

An annoying questionnaire from the public gardens today asked for information about our income, car, educations and professions and if we would like to buy tickets for one hundred dollars a pop for music nights. Yes, we would, but no, we won't. I have to wonder where the public part comes in. Several years ago, John was the City member on the board of the gardens. They never did grasp the concept that the gardens were publicly funded, and so, belonged to the citizens, who had the democratic right to a voice. He held them accountable for that fact. For the stance he took I nicknamed him the Bolshevik. And all of these years later we get a survey today asking questions about the model of our car and our income. Can't be a good thing to bargain nature, horticulture, lilacs and roses in exchange for catering to the monied class, of which we are not members, although the survey hopes we are.

FRIDAY, AUGUST 25TH, 2017 ~ How is it that I can remember every word, every bit of musical phrasing, every nuance of every song from my early years - Mitch Ryder and The Detroit Wheels, Abba, The Band, Credence Clearwater Revival's Bad Moon Rising, Judy Collins's rendition of Joni Mitchell's Both Sides Now - but had a bit of a time recalling the last four digits of our phone number for someone who asked me for it last night? My most beloved song was Up on Cripple Creek by The Band from 1969. As that tune blasted throughout the now defunct Sam the Record Man on Yonge Street in Toronto, I knew that

I had to have that music in my life. I think it was two dollars for the 45 rpm.

Every day brings much. It's a matter of capturing it before it flies off.

Another clear day. Charlotte stayed with us for two hours this afternoon. We walked to the bottom of the hill and she chatted the whole time. Now *she* remembers details, but then so did I when I was four. It struck me on the way back up the hill that this might be our last little daytime walk for some time as she will start junior kindergarten next week. There is a tinge of sorrow in my excitement for her about that. When our own three started school I knew that the umbilical cord was being given the final ditch. Can it be four years since I was pushing her in the stroller? Today I held her sweet soft hand as we walked and chatted.

John and I dropped off a salmon sandwich and a fruit salad for our friend J who is recovering from surgery. I tell her that she is my inspiration about living well and staying young. She reads, she exercises, she is social and she eats well. She said today "I never drink Coke but it polishes up brass nicely and does wonders for shining shoes."

On the news front there is a cry to remove the statue of Sir John A. Macdonald, the founding Father of Canadian Confederation, from downtown, to be followed by removing the statue of Queen Victoria and other statues across the country to cleanse us of our colonial past. Mackenzie King turned back nine hundred Jewish souls who sought refuge on the SS St. Louis, all of whom died in the Nazi gas chambers. Wilfrid Laurier goes down now as a racist. This is the truest version of Canadian history, all of its shames still firmly attached. How can the past be erased for all its faults? If the current vein continues Canada will end up with a revisionist history, without truth. We will become a country with a fake past. Never in school did we learn the truth. That is what must change. Valid versions of history must be taught, not the rinsed and sparkling versions.

Twilight already at 7:43 p.m.

SATURDAY, AUGUST 26TH, 2017 ~ The Globe And Mail crossword comes on Saturdays. I finished it on the porch. I feel I'm doing my brain elasticity a favour when I do crosswords although the new wisdom declares that if you are a regular crossword-lover you should switch to Sudoku to give your brain a different type of jolt. Fat chance of me and Sudoku getting on well.

Down the hill to the bridge and back. Haven't gone far all summer; too hot, too wet. The trail is now re-opened after the heavy spring rains washed it out.

Am trying to love coffee. I've missed out on the pleasure that I see other people have over it. I'm starting to like it so a trip to the coffee shop this morning for a cuppa and a muffin. The coffee shop's name has been replaced with something fancier. It's comfy worn-out seats and homey atmosphere have been refurbished. It's been beautified and beatified, as has the other coffee shop down the street; shiny, metallic, antiseptic. It's lost its personality. But the same good people, the same blueberry-cranberry muffins remain *in situ*.

Met a friend in there today. He said how in this present political dystopia he has returned to reading Jane Austen *et al* to preserve a bit of quietude. Me too. I've spent this summer reading about Augustus John and his tribe, and about the Sackville-Wests, and about the English summer of 1911 before WW 1 began. Now *there's* dystopia for you. I wonder why those books appeal to me when that time period and those Bohemians were alarming in their own right?

Lunch; a tomato sandwich and raspberries, plump, ruby gems in the white bowl.

SUNDAY, AUGUST 27TH, 2017 ~ A Wedding ~ *"When you love someone, all your saved-up wishes start coming out."* (attributed to Elizabeth Bowen but unsubstantiated)

How naïve that statement seems to me but whenever I'm at a wedding I get lost in the charm of the idea that two people from disparate backgrounds can find in one another their match, their alter-ego.

When we conquer ourselves first and then meet our match it fills us, emboldens us.

A sunny cool afternoon for an outside wedding at The Mill. John Officiated. The couple are dear friends, the bride with a remarkable history.

The union of these good young people pleases us. They have worked hard towards this beginning. It's time for all their *"saved-out wishes"* to start coming out.

MONDAY, AUGUST 28TH, 2017 ~ *"…as for her mother's heart, that might have been a railway terminus, so many shining threads ran up into it out of sight –threads of pride and love and relief and maternal agitation…"* (Sackville-West, 1983, 156.)

I shed a tear of love for our granddaughter E this morning. Hayley emailed to say how emotional she

felt as she watched our tiny girl walk into the huge auditorium with the masses. First day of Kindergarten means that we give our children up to the world. Good teachers have importance beyond measure.

On the day she was born, Epiphany, January 6th, 5 years ago, I went out for an early morning walk to try to forget that our daughter was in labour miles away. The sky was lit up with pink sunrise as I came back to John at the open door. "She's here!" he grinned.

We hopped in the car with our pre-packed cases and off we went for a ten hour journey. At the end of it there she was, a dear little human all rolled up like a burrito. We drove to Old Town to La Madeleine Bakery and bought an Epiphany Cake which had a tiny pink plastic baby on top. John asked me "Why is the Christ Child always portrayed as being pink, considering His eastern Birthright?"

JH and FH for coffee here this morning. As always, some good chatter including ideas about ripping down statues everywhere in the world. The latest suggestion is to remove Lord Nelson from Trafalgar Square, London. If they start on Belgium, King Leopold on his horse will "come a cropper" as my Grandmother used to say, and all the gilt on buildings in Brussels that was garnered by the sweat of Congolese slavery

will go with it. Leopold The Second is a reminder as to how base we can be, how open to corruption. We need to keep these conversations lively. It might help us to decide just who should be cast in bronze from here on in. Maybe no human is worthy of a statue. Now there's a thought.

Conversely, a blue historical plaque will soon be unveiled in Frome, Somerset, England. I have been pressing for it for a few years and am thankful that The Frome Society for Local Study has undertaken the project as they have done in the past for Christina Rossetti *et al.* The plaque is in honour of Lady Harris, Alice Seeley, the British missionary to Congo in 1899. As my research of a few years ago concluded she was a heroine to many and an anti-heroine to others. That's what life is like. And that's what humans are like. We, none of us, are omnipotent. We toil for one group and often get muddled about whom to serve first. We are flawed.

I amused Self this morning while John was in the bank. Sat in the car and read the Personal Ads in The London Review of Books. An anonymous woman is seeking a man with "a complicated mind." Please tell me she's kidding.

TUESDAY, AUGUST 29TH, 2018 ~ To grocery store early to pick up some Multigrain Salad which is made fresh every morning. En route out of the near empty parking lot a burly young fellow stopped me, leaned into the open window and asked if I could "give him a boost." His battery was dead, he claimed. My first instinct was to help but my more newly developed instincts wondered if he wanted to grab my purse.

I said "Could you ask somebody else?" to which he replied "No problem."

I drove off knowing that I'd let him down. Perhaps he thought that I was the dodgy one, not helping him in a crisis. But I do have my Multigrain Salad. And my purse.

Following battery/purse episode came home to make generous bouquets from our garden; roses and pink cosmos with white snapdragons in the antique blue and white pot on the bookcase, the clay jug in the kitchen filled with hydrangeas which have this week tinged themselves all over in a shade of dusty pink.

Autumn is approaching on quiet but swift feet. Darker mornings. Long golden shadows in the afternoons.

WEDNESDAY, AUGUST 30TH, 2017 ~ The flooding in Houston, Texas breaks hearts. Television news overwhelms. Race riots. Anger. Blaming.

John at the funeral in Burlington this afternoon for Hiền Quang Võ. Hiền's tribulations and his successes have our admiration and respect. Phư gave the eulogy. I want to write his name here, as a sort of well deserved honouring and to mark his place as a good Canadian man.

THURSDAY, AUGUST 31ST, 2017 ~ How the days do fly. Another perfect weather day with little jolts of Autumn in place. Crickets, cicadas, sparrows; all of them chirping. And it's cool. I'm wearing a sweater and a scarf.

Friendship; the word itself should be cast in bronze. One of the endowments of aging is that inside this arc in the circle of life, this section that includes muscle spasms and bifocals, is the renewal of old friendships.

We had dinner here last night with Lynn and Andrew. No words for how enjoyable, fulfilling, warming it was to be together with LB whom I have known since I was twelve and AB whom I have known since I was nineteen. I think that this was the first time that we have, all four, sat down together. I was with LB the very night that she met AB in the university cafeteria. Tonight we talked about all manner of things, asked one another questions about family, from whence our parents had come, things that wouldn't have interested us when we were young but which now seem to be our markers, our buoys in the water. They brought along their gentle black Labrador, Killick, who laid on the floor, paws stretched out in front of him. He did what I do in the night; put a concerted effort into finding a more comfy spot, a cooler place on which to rest my head. We had chicken and the aforementioned Multigrain Salad and creamed cauliflower, green beans and sliced tomatoes and tiramisu cake chased with a few cups of Typhoo tea.

My Letter to the Editor was in the National Post this morning. I was defending Emily Carr against as an accusation made in 2005 of "cultural violence" based on the idea that she was getting name recognition through painting Indigenous topics as a non-member of that group; *"To accuse Emily Carr of cultural violence is in itself verbal violence against a great Canadian artist. She respected First Nations people and they returned the favour by welcoming her benign presence into their communities. Were it not for her wonderful*

swirls of rich oils we would be missing a huge chunk of the historical record of our West Coast Peoples. They named her Klee Wyck (Laughing One) for good reason."

Now maybe to read a bit on the back porch in the fresh air. Or, instead, doze? Didn't sleep much last night; happy remembrances chasing their tails around in my head.

FRIDAY, SEPTEMBER SEPT 2nd, 2017 ~ Lunch with JB and RB at The Beverly on Locke Street for a catching-up after a summer of not seeing one another. Lunch consisted of the most delicious grilled cheese sandwich I have ever eaten. Ditto for the salad. Was fun to celebrate our 70th birthdays over lunch.

Tonight at the bottom of the hill to Princess Point, John's favourite white goose was sitting on the grass with a man who was talking to him and smiling at him (at the goose, not at John). We stopped and waved and the man waved back. Nice to think of man and beast having a special friendship like that. And then, three deer, a family we think. The baby came out, his spindly legs on the road, saw us and leaped back into the underbrush, disappearing into dense thicket in a flash of bobbing white tail.

Very chilly tonight so winter housecoat.

SUNDAY, SEPTEMBER 3RD, 1017 ~ A dripping, read-a-book sort of a morning. Not yet time to herald this entry with a quote from Keats's Ode To Autumn as much as I'm tempted. It will have to wait until the trees put on their bright and shining clothing.

The plan was for me to teach the Sunday School children about the gracious Queen Esther and her doing what was right in the face of the nasty Haman who set about to kill all the Jews. Haman The Evil was his nickname. The few children who were there today were happy to stay upstairs so next week we'll have their lesson. Since the Bible stands as historical record (see Josephus) with every reading of things I learn a new item. In my bag of tricks I have a dollar store crown for sweet little Esther who never misses.

Yesterday morning had a walk to the bridge. It's downhill all the way and I love the downhill bit; cool breeze, leafy branches overhead, birds darting. It's the trek back uphill that isn't as much fun.

Sat yesterday in fresh air on the porch with King George and Queen Charlotte and The Globe And Mail Crossword. Still can't get the word for 111 Across (mathematical subgroup). If I could find 94 Down (large mackerel) it would work itself out.

I re-hung our yellow winter curtain in the kitchen

window. Cosier as the evenings darken. Mornings too. I don't want next-door to have to see us boiling our eggs, rinsing the plates.

N and H dropped in this afternoon with a bag of sweet navel oranges for us. I've put them in the wooden bowl and I ate one after dinner. N and H came to Canada thirty-five years ago, started over, went to work pronto and raised two of the best children on earth in Paul and Rebecca.

MONDAY, SEPTEMBER 4TH, 2017 ~ A steamy Labour Day. My hill-walk. Sore leg muscles coming back up but then I remind Self of my dad who did this in his nineties down Highway 8 where he lived in an apartment above mom's nursing home. He did it after two hip replacements and with February winds blowing against him. Engagement in World War Two taught people perseverance.

I think of him every day. His philosophies have pulled me up and out of the quagmire on many occasions. He taught us that if something didn't seem right then it probably wasn't. When we were teenagers they took us camping to Florida. He insisted that we do our laundry in the laundromat that said Coloureds Only over the door because there was no sane reason

to divide people up into groups. He was an admirer of Martin Luther King. His unshakeable faith guided his principles. He believed in setting goals and going for them, in the oneness of the human family, in fair play and in standing up with courage for your ideals. He entreated us to do everything according to his mantra; "Put a little gumption into it." I was never sure just what gumption was but I knew it must be a good thing. He had a dry sense of humour and knew how to laugh. He made up preposterous bedtime stories complete with the character's voices.

My mom was a pragmatist but a romantic one. She bought me a book of Keats's poetry when I was a teenager in heart-break mode. She raced right down to the only bookshop in town and bought me back something of beauty. I have it now in pristine condition. Her sense of the appropriate is one of the things I loved and miss most. If I were to create a list of things I learned from her it would look like this: Notate the things you want to remember; bits of poetry, quotes, music. Do not "gush". Things, situations and sometimes people are often not what they appear to be. Buy good shoes because healthy feet are a must. And never trust a man who doesn't polish his shoes. Keep yourself to yourself. Don't tell all you know. Don't gossip. Set a proper table. Use your cutlery properly. Iron your sheets. (Her sheets had knife-pleat edges. We could have sliced our toes off on the edges of her sheets.) If something interests you find out as much as you can about it. Keep the radio dial on CBC in the mornings and on the CHFI-FM in Toronto in the afternoon. Read. Search out your past. Try to understand it. If a neighbour comes to the door ask her/him in and put on the kettle. Look your best. (In her world that would mean a perm, stockings, dresses, leather shoes and a handbag. That was the way things were then. My slacks and turtle necks would shock her but I do throw the odd string of fake pearls around my quilted vest just to meet her halfway.) Mind your manners. (She called her friends "Mrs. Harnden and Mrs. Inglis" until I talked her out of it.) And without words but with her actions and attitude she said this; keep your faith central to yourself but no need to exercise it in a maudlin or emotional way. And always know what you are doing.

As I record all of this I feel the often missing piece in our family jigsaw; my brother. The war cut a painful swath through family life in the form of absent fathers. It meant that babies born at the war's start never knew their fathers until they returned home years later. In the aftermath of war new babies were born and were added to the previous incarnation of family. By the time we took our trip to Florida Brian was already in his twenties and living in England. He was our reverse immigrant. Our grandparents came this way and he went that way. He once told me that he'd heard the sound of Big Ben's chimes every noon hour in his early childhood on the BBC radio news to which our grandparents listened. He wanted to hear them for himself and to discover new worlds. Off he went for the adventure that was meant to be for one year but instead became his future. There he met and married an American woman, my sister-in-law Gail. They developed a strong creative business and raised a good family. They introduced Jan and me to the glories of England when we were in our early twenties. They had two cats named Nowhere and Nuffink, named for the local dialect when they lived in Notting Hill. This was before that area became associated with the Hugh Grant movie and gentrification. We borrowed Gail's flowing skirts and ruffled blouses for evenings out. Such is family life. We spread out and enlarge upon our experiences but it doesn't mean that those who've moved away aren't loved and missed back at the ranch.

MONDAY, SEPTEMBER 5TH, 2017 ~ Witnessed a screaming, swearing match in the parking lot at the library this morning. Two young men, strangers, maybe university students, shouted at one another over the fact that one of them wasn't parked properly between the yellow lines. I wonder if there are more angry people of late? Maybe we've all been watching too much tv news. Sad to see that on a sunny morning, which I guess didn't feel sunny for either one of them. A parking situation cannot possibly engender that degree of anger so I assume they dragged along that toxic emotion with them to the parking lot. Now we have not only politicians going at one another but people in the parking lot at the library, of all places, following suit.

Mohamad came for coffee this morning. He has an interesting perspective and a first-class brain.

Got Spanish The Easy Way back down from the shelf where it has sat with unused intention for ten years. It was meant for me to learn daughter-in-law Ely's first language but I never got past the initial section of Work Unit Two. I'm still with:

"Es la lampara?"

"Si Senorita. Es la lampara."

Tomorrow will try new cello teacher with a one

hour lesson in late afternoon. He is a European trained professional. That fact strikes terror in my heart. He might see me as being not serious enough and may not want me. Or I might see him as being too serious and may not want him. Whatever, aging is freeing and I'll do what I want to.

I spoke on the phone with granddaughter Edwina tonight and she told me about her Kindergarten class and her Chinese lessons and said several words to me in Chinese. She said, "These words are about our feelings." If she gets twenty stickers she can choose a small Chinese doll as a prize.

"Si Senora. Es la lampara." ("Yes, Mister. This is a lamp.")

And that is all that I can come up with tonight with apologies to my brother and sister-in-law's family who are now citizens of Spain and would be appalled with me about this.

WEDNESDAY, SEPTEMBER 6TH, 2017 ~ Pond inlet, Baffin Island, had 20 cm of snow today.

We had fun this morning, RMB et moi. We go back to when we were twelve. Went to Europe together in our pre-husband days several times and thought we were being kidnapped in Casablanca as the taxi

driver drove for miles until he deposited us at his house in the countryside to have Moroccan mint tea with his friendly wife and five children. We spent fun weekends at Toronto theatres, restaurants, art galleries in our single years, had our babies together and walked them up and down RMB's neighbourhood in their carriages, have laughed and cried together. And now we're seventy.

This morning we celebrated our birthdays on her porch on her cool, leafy street. We ate sweet grapes and walnut loaf. RMB served tea from a flowered, antique teapot from a long defunct jewellery shop in the lakeside town in which we grew up. The elderly sisters who owned the shop were straight out of the pages of a Barbara Pym novel; print dresses and black oxfords, rotund and po-faced, the guardians of treasures galore. In fact I own their small mahogany sideboard which we bought at an antique store after we got married. I love thinking about those two sisters because they don't make those types any more. Or are my own sister and I just like them and we don't know it? Someone please inform. It was a perfect morning to celebrate being seventy. No need for fanfare when the joy and laughter in a well-worn friendship is what fills us up.

My new cello teacher is an interesting fellow. I like the way he thinks. He understands why I prefer to focus less on theory and more on a passionate response to music. This might work out well. I played a Bach Minuet and he yelled "Bravo!" I played some more and he hummed along; "Pum-pum-pum-pa-PUM!". He taught me several new ideas about practicing including this wisdom; "Like a math equation, each piece has an in-put, a middle and an out-come." Didn't have the heart to tell him how much I do not love math.

THURSDAY, SEPTEMBER 7TH, 2017 ~ Dear friend Lynn F is having a knee replacement as I type and I'm rooting for her. She is golden.

Had my walk early and showed a newly arrived Chinese man a heron sitting on the dead trees in the water. He was excited and got out his camera, all the while repeating "special bird", just as I told him. I like to imagine him going home and saying to his family, "Here's a picture of a special bird that a crazy lady showed me this morning on the bridge."

I must add that on the way back up the hill my leg muscles hurt so I kept whispering to Self "brain, heart, lungs, kidneys, liver, pancreas." Current

medical advice talks much about the benefits to our organs of a frequent strong walk. Perhaps this time next year the common wisdom will be for us not to walk as it might be concluded that it damages our hip/knee joints.

Or, the outcome of future research might be that walking damages "brain, heart, lungs, kidneys, liver, pancreas." Research seems to change daily.

FRIDAY SEPTEMBER 8TH, 2017 ~ John and I were excited to pick up Charlotte from her first day of Junior Kindergarten. Me, umbrella open, rain threatening, as I waited for her to come running out in her tiny navy uniform, throw her arms around me and scream "Grandma!"

Instead she stood frozen, like her favourite Disney girl, Elsa, in shock from her busy day. Not until we got home did she open up a tad. And that was to tell her mom that she had a new friend whom she has invited to her birthday party next March and to Lucia's birthday party next July.

Our Little Lucia is pulling herself up on her legs now. She loves her Granddad. I get why she loves him (I do too) but it's me that does all the little-kid work at our house and yet they gravitate to him like

lemmings to the sea. Does anyone know the answer to this conundrum?

Ely's mom and Aunt are coming on Wednesday for a long visit. Can I consume and memorize my Spanish language book in the next four days? Of course not.

SATURDAY, SEPTEMBER 9TH, 2018 ~ Glorious weather. 17 degrees. Sunshine. My imagination goes into overdrive when I see the thicket of gnarled sumac bushes at the bottom of the hill. In a fictional story I sold to a British women's magazine I called it "the Hansel and Gretel wood." Give it another few weeks and the leaves will turn scarlet and then it will look even more like a place for entrapment, with tongues of fire consuming it, a modern day Burning Bush. My heron was not there this morning. Nor my new Chinese friend.

Took the bus to the festival of the arts downtown this afternoon. John stayed home and pulled weeds. Car ownership has made me lazy but I enjoyed the bus. Many interesting types. My preconceived notions are challenged daily and that is a good thing. A man I see everywhere got on just after me, sat down and pulled latex gloves on his hands to protect himself from germs, from *my* germs perhaps. A woman in

her seventies, slim, blonde, curly and pretty in a novel-by-Joanna-Trollope sort of way got on carrying a glass jam jar of findings from her garden; pink cosmos and a purple flower that I did not know and some soft white and green wisps. She told the nosey woman across the aisle that she was taking them to a friend. Her mother was the sweetest tiny thing ever with a small face and round owlish glasses. She was another one straight out of a novel; this time Agatha Christie's Murder At The Vicarage. I mentally enlist people in the roles I think they should take from books. It's my free and wholesome entertainment.

The whole point of my going down there was to walk down to the place where Jock and a few friends had an art installation about the part of the city where they had all grown up. The intent of their interactive art was to showcase how their childhood neighbourhoods have changed from mono-cultural to multi-cultural. It was interesting and they are all smarter than me. There were a few thousand people down there. But home felt like a good place to be by the time I got back.

'In which novel would I like to make an appearance?', she asks Self.

SUNDAY, SEPTEMBER 10TH, 2017 ~ Our grandson Hamish turns four years old today. He's a bundle of sweetness if ever there was one. I spoke on the phone with him and he thanked us for the birthday gift and said that he will be eating cake that is both "white and chocolate."

A beautiful clear sunny day. Morning Prayer this morning and finally taught the Sunday School children the Queen Esther story. Lessons need application. I asked "What have you learned?"

HR, ten years old, said "Everyone is important."

Sat on back porch with King George and Queen Charlotte. I wonder if they are as taken with me as I with them? I am now on the last part, about his descent into madness. Recent medical findings indicate that he may not have had porphyria as previously thought, but instead perhaps a form of dementia.

After dinner we picked up approximately three million tiny white pills that John spilled all over the kitchen floor. "Who needs a gym membership," he commented, "when we can bow, bend and scrape doing this?"

MONDAY, SEPTEMBER 11TH 2017 ~ Lunch today at Easterbrook's with PW. Easterbrook's is a tiny old-world diner that claims to have served *"Canada's best hot-dogs, hamburgers, fries and real ice-cream since 1930."* It's a fun thing to do once a year. I had a genuine chocolate milkshake made with that real ice cream and milk. They say they have served over sixteen hundred miles of hotdogs. The thought of all those hotdogs sickens but one at a time with mustard and relish is as good as it gets.

I booked myself a discount flight to see our American grandchildren in December. It's pretty before Christmas with white twinkling lights shining throughout Old Town.

But in real time we are still in September and *"Todo el mundo esta muy occupado."* Everybody is busy.

TUESDAY, SEPTEMBER 12TH, 2017 ~ Ben Heppner is singing Let My Song Fill Your Heart and it makes me feel as if I could fly right out the window it's so lovely.

The latest issue of London Review of Books has arrived. In a back page there is a bolded ad declaring that *"Workshops are for jerks. What you need is an editor."* And that is probably a correct assumption.

Not that it is of interest to anyone but myself but

the same woman is still looking in the Personals for the man with a *"complicated mind"* and I can't help but wonder who she is and what she wants with him.

Another one hundred plus a few pages to go and I can wrap up the drama that was the joint reign of George The Third and Queen Charlotte. I wanted to read it because it's full of incidents concerning both Fanny Burney, who was Queen Charlotte's Dresser, and Mary Delany whose paper flowers I sat with in the British Museum. I did that at the behest of a woman with whom I ate breakfast at the New Cavendish Club in London in 2003. Her name was Ruth Hayden and she was descended from Fanny Burney. She wrote a book about Mrs. Delany who was a friend of the Court at that time. She told me to go to the Museum and ask to see the famous paper flowers, so I did. I entered the Sanctum Sanctorum, a man handed me the box of paper treasures, entreated me to put on the white gloves while handling them and left me to it. There I also bought Ruth's book on that topic. Ruth and I became pen-pals for a while. She has since died. I have kept Ruth's letters tucked in her book. I hope my children will preserve them.

Since that time a book on the same topic was written by Canadian writer Molly Peacock. It is called

The Paper Garden. I relished it, word by word. The salient piece about Mrs. Delany is that she didn't start her famous works until she was seventy-two.

The most effective line in today's reading was this, from Fanny Burney's diary, regarding the Queen's extreme distress with her husband's erratic behaviour: *"my poor royal mistress now droops."* (Hadlow, 2014.)

WEDNESDAY, SEPTEMBER 13TH, 2017 ~ *"...nothing can be done until Vicky reaches suitable age for Permanent Waving."* ('Delafield, 1947.)

Due to husband's eye problem have helped with his sermon typing today for Evensong this coming weekend. I learn much when I do that. For example, this interesting trivia about mustard seeds; when you plant them, as they were doing in Palestine two thousand years ago they grow into trees in no time at all, so large that birds can nest in their branches. So when Jesus was talking about the mustard seed and its relationship to the Kingdom of Heaven in Luke He was referring to the lightening-quick spread of the Gospel message and how it would push outwards until the known world was changed by it.

I've found and clipped a wintry recipe in The Globe And Mail from last week. It's a Lucy Waverman

recipe for Brisket; Dijon, soy sauce, onion, garlic, chicken stock, tomatoes. I am famous for clipping recipes, sticking them on the refrigerator door and never using them. This one I promise myself to use. Cold days ahead. Hearty recipes beckon.

Must do something with hair. But what? Flimsy. When I was a child my mother saw to it that every summer I had a perm. She'd send me across the street to Hannah's house. Hannah ran the neighbourhood salon in her basement. I was seven, eight, nine years old. Hannah sat me on a thick Eaton's catalogue so my head could reach the wash basin. Then the pain of screwing up my straight blonde hair into plastic rods followed by the stench of chemicals poured over my head and afterwards a while under the hot dryer until my desiccated hair set like jelly in a mould. I'd emerge with an enlarged head bobbing with curls as if I was off to the Coronation. Here I am at seventy still wondering how to keep it tidy.

THURSDAY, SEPTEMBER 14TH, 2017 ~ A hair cut this morning downtown. A walk along James Street afterwards and into Morgenstern's, that comforting department store where you can find any item that has gone missing from store shelves in the

last fifty years. I came across that arcane object known as a half-slip for just shy of twelve dollars. I bought it. I have been keeping an elderly version of a half slip for years for fear I would never find another. It looks like something out of Miss Havisham's wardrobe. But now I have this perfect new one trimmed in pristine white lace.

Morgenstern's smells like the Woolworths of my youth; homey, like wood and fabric. The floors creak and the floral aprons are folded in pristine rows (aprons, undershirts, longjohns, tablecloths!)

The South Americans have safely arrived. I hope I can remember how to say "Hola. Como estas?" followed by "El gusto es mio. Hasta luego."

FRIDAY SEPTEMBER 15TH, 2017 ~ Where is a rotary-dial phone when you need one? I am a Luddite and I want one. They always work. Our two mobile phones are not working and cannot be shut off. I have a cell phone for emergency use but cell phones are not the answer to the woes of the digital age. Things that work and don't cost the price of a sailboat are. Somebody help.

Synod weekend begins tomorrow so have been setting up tables, making arrangements, typing

reports. Will attend the meetings, help set the tables for the dinner.

SUNDAY EVENING SEPTEMBER 17th 2017 ~ A non-stop weekend of Synod meetings, report-giving, a renewal of friendships and an affirmation of many people in many ways.

TUESDAY MORNING, SEPTEMBER 19th, 2017 ~ Niece O's 38th birthday today. Not sure how that can be as I remember with clarity visiting her blonde newborn self at North York General Hospital.

I spent a shift at the Children's Hospital last night with our smallest family member. She slept soundly for two hours while I read. The nurses love her. So do I.

Four more pages and I can bid adieu to King George 3rd and Queen Charlotte. At this point in the book they have both gone on to their Maker, he with dementia and she with congestive heart failure, and I've now figured out the line of descendants from whence Queen Victoria sprang. I'll forget every bit of it soon, but I'll remember every detail of the houses they lived in, the numerous mistresses their sons kept, the rioting crowds. When the angry mob surrounded Queen Charlotte's carriage one day she said something

to the effect that she was seventy-two years old and had never had to put up with that sort of thing. After her admonition they reportedly left her alone. I must try that sometime; "Pardon me but I'm Seventy years old and I've never had to put up with this sort of thing."

It was eavesdropping I know but the other night when we were out having a hamburger the woman in the booth behind us said to her friend "So I told her how sorry I was for her loss but I also asked her how she could be so stupid."

I wondered how anyone could say such a cruel thing to a grieving person until I heard the rest of the story. Seems she had given a phone scammer too much info and she lost a large sum of money. So to that, were it my story to tell, I told John that I too might think she'd done something stupid.

And then to that John added "Let's just finish our hamburgers."

This afternoon, I had a quick visit with Consuelo and her sister Silene. Lovely women and fun to meet Silene and to see Consuelo again.

All I could say was "Como estas?" while any other little bits I had learned fell apart right on my tongue, little shards of language dropping at my feet and leaving me speechless as I stood in the kitchen.

WEDNESDAY, SEPTEMBER 20TH, 2017 ~ Am reading Laura Shapiro's book about the food that drove six famous women and the eras which sponsored their diet, (Shapiro, 2017, 210). She writes about Barbara Pym's take on bland British food like Chicken with White Sauce and Shapes, as they called things in moulds.

Barbara, in her sensible shoes and unadorned hair certainly wasn't a fusspot. I like this line; *"She loved her gastronomic era just as it was, a time when frozen fish fingers and Chablis were invited into the same kitchen."*

Barbara's food is the food I grew up with too, considering that I had two English Grandmothers. I can still find contentment embedded in roast potatoes and brisket. My Pollard grandmother taught me how to make good gravy ("scrape up the bits at that bottom of the pan") and my friend Betty gave me her best-of-all-possible-worlds recipe for Yorkshire pudding. My grandmother used to pour the batter in a ring around the roast. When the cold weather comes I must organize that sort of dinner. I did it on Sundays without fail when the children were young and for John's Dad who counted on being at our table every Sunday evening for years. I had candles and

music although was often asked that I "turn on the lights and turn down the music" by an unnamed member of the group.

It's the cost of beef now that means fewer people enjoy a Sunday roast, that and the trend towards eating less meat or none at all if you are in sympathy with our vegetarians, son Jock and daughter-in-law Ashley.

Always wanted to write about Edith Wharton's dining habits and her menus. Five years ago when we were visiting her home in Lenox, Massachusetts, The Mount, I was able to get a copy of the meat order from Kiley's Meat Market in Lenox on July 8th, 1911 which was allegedly the order that was made for Henry James' last visit there:

- 17 lbs of Roast Beef @ 25 cents a pound = $4.75
- 6 lbs of Lamb @ 25 cents a pound = $1.50
- 10 Broilers $1.50
- 8 Ham @ 22 cents a pound = $1.76
- Calf Liver 60 cents
- Total of $9.61

My thanks to The Mount and in turn to Ms. Mary Ellen Warkentin for making that information available.

Edith had a round dining table, bowls of flowers from her gardens in the centre and tall French windows which opened onto the terrace to the breeze of a summer's evening. She included places for her tiny dogs who were invited to sit upright, on dining chairs, at the table. I might not have gone for the dogs on the brocade idea but I would love to have been her dinner guest.

And I would also love to find roast beef that cost twenty-five cents a pound. I looked at a Brisket in the Kosher section of my grocer's on Saturday that was a special for Rosh Hashanah. It was a tiny piece and was marked fifty dollars and change. That put a swift end to my Brisket recipe idea from Lucy Waverman.

Autumn

FRIDAY, SEPTEMBER 22, 2017 ~ *From Ode To Autumn by John Keats "...to swell the gourd, and plump the hazel shells with sweet kernel;..."*

Barbara Pym wrote a concise and entertaining little novel about four loosely bound friendships in the Autumn of life. She called it Quartet In Autumn. It's a sad story but the last line redeems it with regards to aging: *"...life still held infinite possibilities for change."* (Pym, 1977, 218)

A glorious strong sun and a light breeze skims along the surface of the day. I've been reading on the porch again with Laura Shapiro and her menus, this time the chapter about Eleanor Roosevelt. She cared not a whit for cooking or menus and it reflected in the reputation of the White House at that time for its horrible food.

A friend told us this week that their walnut tree has produced a harvest like never before. "I'm sure I raked up three thousand of them," she said. And this morning when I stopped in at the bookshop I saw that the sidewalk in front was littered with acorns; a bumper crop. I love the smooth, brown roundness of acorns. In the past I have picked them up off the ground at the nearby park and put them in a dish on the Thanksgiving table but am afraid to do it now with the grandchildren. They could mistake them for edibles. I might scatter them in our back garden for the squirrels to enjoy.

Deepening twilight tonight by 7:17.

SATURDAY, SEPTEMBER 23RD, 2017 ~ Canadian singer/songwriter Bruce Cockburn, who is now seventy-two, has named his new album Bone On Bone. I thought how lyrical that title was until I read that he named it so because of his joint pain. That's a sane way to age; to write songs about the aches. Right now I could write my own song about bones. It's the damp, I think.

Spent the afternoon and evening here with Charlotte. The others went to Niagara Falls in this thirty-five degree heat. It would have been a long day for Charlotte so we had a happy time here instead, crayoning and making a fort with the cushions and the little table.

This morning I made scalloped potatoes, a big pan of meatloaf and topped and tailed the green beans for dinner tomorrow night when they all come. It's a "Mi casa es su casa" kind of a meal which might be a bit slap-dash considering the small dining space. But we will make do. Making do is a concept long forgotten nowadays but it's a concept well worth remembering.

MONDAY, SEPTEMBER 25TH, 2017 ~ Ely, Drew, Lucia, Charlotte, Consuelo, Silene came to dinner last night. Here I was with my scalloped potatoes that I consider a uniquely Canadian dish only to discover that they make them in Colombia all the time. What they notice most about Canada is the same thing every single person I have met from other places wants to know; "Where are all the people? Nobody is out on the streets."

This morning to the lakeside coffee shop and sat under a shade tree on the patio with LM and JS for two hours until the thirty-eight degree Celsius heat became insufferable. Slender yellow leaves of the Little Leaf Lindens made confetti of themselves on the patio. Very pretty with the lake beside us, blue sky over us, sweet sparrows at our feet hopping around pecking at the crumbs of our blueberry scones.

L and J are both remarkable women. L said "When you speak negative words you breathe life into them." Now there's something to remember.

A good afternoon to read some of Jane Gardam.

Am happy knowing that in the refrigerator are last night's leftovers.

TUESDAY, SEPTEMBER 26TH, 2017 ~ Another hot day. Over 30 degrees Celsius.

Household chores this morning. Must re-channel my Inner Housewife. Cleaning the tub on bended knee hurts more than it used to.

John at the English Second Language group tonight and me listening to Mendelssohn's Scottish Symphony. I turn the music up loud when he is out. It is powerful and brilliant. I first heard it at Holyrood House in Edinburgh where I was the sole tourist in the lime-green mossy Abbey courtyard with the earphones on that they hand out to tourists. Mendelssohn's beautiful music streamed into my ears and sifted throughout those decaying Abbey ruins where Kings and Queens were crowned. I stood alone in a soft rain with the ghosts of all that Royalty hovering in the haar and Mary Queen Of Scots upstairs in Holyrood behind me.

I have always connected music to place. If the memory was a good one the music stays within.

"Su hermana va a bailar y cantar en la fiesta." "Her sister sings and dances at the party." Lucia is now starting to dance with her upper body. She sways her tiny waist to that inborn Latin beat.

WEDNESDAY, SEPTEMBER 27TH, 2017 ~ In Jane Gardam's book, 'Old Filth', the character

Claire tells Filth that she keeps whiskey in the house to give to the window-cleaners and to the Police who come to prop her back up when she falls over.

I once heard the late Sir John Mortimer speak. He spoke about getting old and how he falls over when he puts his socks on. Everybody laughed. Now that I do a bit of a balancing act when I'm putting on my own socks I think about him.

Had the best cello lesson this afternoon. I told the teacher how much I hate practicing Humoresque ad infinitum and he said "Playing what you love is the whole point. What music do you like?" I gave him a small list including most everything that Itzhak Perlman plays on his violin. Au revoir Humoresque!

This heat wave will end tomorrow they say. And I shall dance.

THURSDAY, SEPTEMBER 28TH, 2017 ~ This morning spent some pleasant time with Consuelo and Silene. We had tea and blueberry muffins at the coffee shop. Who's ever heard of Colombians who don't like coffee? Imagine it?

Communication? We all did try with gestures, the odd Spanish non-sequitur flung into the air, scratched notes in half-English-half-Espanol on

paper napkins. Drove to the Basilica to please their faithful Catholicity, climbed up that huge Stairway to Heaven, tried to pry open the massive oaken doors with no luck. I found the Rectory. The person who answered the door said that there was too much weekday construction going on inside to allow people in. I told C and S "mucho trabajo", pleased with Self that I could choke out two words en espanol. We drove along the Lakeshore to see the casas grandes, then downtown, then home.

Tonight, driving along Main Street West, a license plate of the young woman in front of us had her birth date on it. I wondered how it would go over if I had mine on our license plates. People would stay out of my way. Just in case. Can you *picture* it?

Finished off the day with a quick drive down the hill to Princess Point. John's white goose waiting. A darkening sky and a golden sunset dancing on the tops of huge trees like candelabra lighting up the twilight.

FRIDAY, SEPTEMBER 29TH, 2017 ~ Skinny Chai Latte with MH this morning at the coffee shop. A table right at the window in the rain so a perfect spur of the moment thing to do. We talked about writing, about music lessons.

In the newspaper this morning a picture of women at a rally holding up signs that said "I am the boss of my own body." It brings back a poignant memory of my mom. In the midst of her confusion she often put her clothing on front to back. Dad one day said to her "You have your skirt on backwards" and she replied, "I want to be the boss of my own skirts."

Perhaps she'd been thinking that for years, that she wanted to be her own boss. Maybe when our minds travel to new places truths float out that have been tucked away. What's the difference between my Mom's declaration and Queen Charlotte's own words when she tells the rioting mobs surrounding her carriage that, at seventy-two, she should do what she pleases without any censure?

The idea about the last rose of summer being loveliest is true. We have a huge yellow rose the size of a newborn baby's head, two hot pink ones ditto, a mass of white cosmos that are so stunning John says he will try to save the seeds. And at last the blue Morning Glories have spread along the fence.

I've bought a turkey breast and butternut squash for dinner.

And a rotund orange pumpkin for the front steps.

SATURDAY, SEPTEMBER 30TH, 2017` ***"Quatro passi fra le nuvole" ("Four steps in the clouds", from 1942 Italian film by same name.)***

Walking the hill this morning was as serene as taking a few steps in the clouds considering my surroundings; glorious sky, chilly clear air, a peaceful hush in the deeply forested part, except that feet hurt on way back up so the romance of the idea fell apart a little. I see that I have marked only five hill walks on the September calendar where I keep track. In October must do better. But five is better than none. Chastising self is counter-productive to staying well and it was a wonderful morning to be outside. I stopped on the bridge to see what was floating past me. There on the half-sunken log sat the miserable old Cormorant all hunched over. Big changes underfoot. Thousands of pine needles, walnuts galore and pine cones; all have been cast off the trees and onto the ground for the coming winter. And no birdsong this morning. As quiet a walk as can be. Have they all packed their bags? Booked their flights?

SUNDAY, OCTOBER 1, 2017 ~ Harvest Home Sunday for Anglicans everywhere ~ Lovely phrases about the year being crowned with God's goodness.

And from The Old Testament Lesson (Isaiah 55.12, AKJV) *"...For ye shall go out with joy, and be led forth with peace: the mountains and the hills shall break forth before you into singing, and all the trees of the fields shall clap their hands."*

Pumpkins and carrots and gourds beneath the Altar table, deep purple mums in the Font encircled by long stems of ivy. Beautiful music. The perfect morning.

Charlotte spent some happy hours with us this afternoon. We coloured, she sang her Kindergarten songs, we baked Pillsbury cookies that have pumpkin faces on them and we phoned her cousins Edwina and Hamish.

A quick visit here with our newlywed friends and with C and S and D when they came in to pick up Charlotte.

TUESDAY, OCTOBER 3, 2017 ~ Lucia in hospital with another bug. Spent a peaceful evening last night at her crib side. I sang and sang and made up words to the tune she likes (This Little Light of Mine) or maybe it's me who likes that tune considering that the translation for Lucia is light. But when I rub her back and sing to her she calms. And I tell her that my love is pouring straight into her to make her all better. I noticed the little red heart-shaped logo on the computer monitor that charts her heart rate and saw that it had settled into a lower pattern after my aria.

I've made a casserole that should do us for three nights. I've peeled the Brussels Sprouts. John has both English Second Language conversation circle tonight and Vestry Council.

Fifty-nine people were shot to death in Las Vegas yesterday, at random. Guns; the ugliest symptom of brokenness.

WEDNESDAY, OCTOBER 4TH, 2017 ~ Charlotte came to play here with Uncle Jock last night. She got out the Fisher Price people that our kids had when they were small. She announced that her name would be "Princess Saliva". I can see why that name might sound pretty to a child. A bit lyrical.

Lucia is feeling better and will come home tonight.

The sky, the whole atmosphere, darkened this afternoon. The leaves blew and the thunder rumbled. I put on Mstislav Rostropovich cd playing Haydn's Cello Concertos One and Two. It suited the weather I thought. It was a dramatic lead-up to what I hoped

would become a crashing, banging kind of storm but it vanished and out came the sun. If it looks like it's going to storm then I want a dandy one. No more phoney beginnings please. We need a good downpour.

My music teacher shouted many "bravos!" again at me tonight but I overheard him yelling them out to the woman and her violin ahead of me too so it seems he gives them out to just anyone. I'm saving them in my back pocket to share with friends when they need one. In fact I emailed one to MH's daughter today for her labour and delivery efforts in the night for her baby boy!

Sent JB a bravo too. She is writing two papers towards her PHd. I miss her but she is working-working-working. When she has a break we'll have a good chat about it all. And I'll hear some of her sparkling new ideas.

MT too. Miss her. We have tried for so long to make a breakfast date. And soon she is off to Hong Kong and our breakfast will have to wait. Somebody keep the toast warm please.

THURSDAY, OCTOBER 5TH, 2017 ~ What happened to my eyelashes? Where have they gone and when did they leave? Or are they there but I can't see them?

FRIDAY OCTOBER 6TH, 2017 ~ I have been in conversations with English Second Language teaching friends regarding how long it takes for people to feel a comfortable part of the Western landscape. And what is the expectation that we place on newcomers? Blending in or retaining Self?

As an example, let's say we have a young girl whose name is Nguyễn My Linh. I don't know anyone by that name although there are bound to be many and we could use a name from another language group but this springs to mind. Let's say that she took the name Linda in school to please both her classmates and sadly maybe even her teacher who may have complained about her name being too difficult to pronounce. And if Linda marries Jack Simpson she might end up as Linda Simpson. Her birth name gets washed away and along with it her personal history. Has she been forced into conformity or has she chosen it?

Every woman has the right to take her husband's name. I did. But considering the huge renovations of ego that incoming families endure, isn't clinging to the vestiges of background a good idea? Losing one's family, home, language, physical goods is overwhelming. Add to that the devastation of losing one's place on the world map *plus* one's name. Our

names have their own histories. Names announce to the world from whence we sprang in terms of culture, country, who our great-grandparents were, what language we speak, how we think. Our whole lineage is wrapped up in our names. Keeping our names helps us to retain our selves.

On the other hand it can be seen as the miraculous nature of a multicultural society when we all blend so well that we can take on new names while retaining our own cultural practices. That is our right. It's a matter of personal choice. But when I hear people say "She should change it. It's too hard to pronounce," I reply "She's learned an entire language. We can learn her name."

The same argument could be used for keeping our maiden names when we marry. I incorporated my former surname between my first and married name in brackets. Now I see that as a kind of bracketing of myself as if my former name was only an afterthought when really, my former name is who I was and still am. And it was Philip Larkin's poem below that brought me to that conclusion a few years ago:

He wrote a poem called 'Maiden Name' which I have partially memorized:

"Marrying left your maiden name disused, Its five light sounds no longer mean your face." And later:

"Now it's a phrase applicable to no one, Lying just where you left it, scattered through Old lists, old programmes, a school prize or two..."

RMB was the only friend I had who kept her own name in the late 1970's. It was an idea that was only then starting to take shape.

About twenty years ago I removed the brackets off my maiden name and now it stands in the middle, a linking sentinel of my single self and my married self. Our names become who we are. Or we become our names. We each need to do it in the way we want to.

SATURDAY, OCTOBER 7TH, 2017 ~ Thanksgiving weekend ~ *"I think of the trees and of how simply they let go, let fall the riches of a season, how without grief (it seems) they can let go and go deep into their roots and sleep. Eliot's statement comes back to me these days: '...Teach us to sit still.'"* (Sarton, 1973, 34)

Most of the leaves haven't changed colour yet, let alone fallen to the ground waiting for rakes to come out of garages everywhere. In our back garden only the Cutleaf Sumac is yellow-orange and the Amora Maple is starting now into deep red. At Princess Point there is some colour and the big Maple tree at the corner house is blushing.

A band was playing American Woman at the street festival this afternoon and they were very good at it.

"That is my music," I said to John. And in a way it was because there was nobody else on the street. Empty.

Poet May Sarton and her Eliot quote; no line could be more important for good health than that one. Is sitting still becoming a lost art?

SUNDAY, OCTOBER 8TH, 2017 ~ Thanksgiving Sunday ~ Listened to the cd of St. Paul's Cathedral Choir before we left for Morning Prayer to inspire us into the *thanks* part of the *giving*. Come Down O Love Divine is my favourite (R. Vaughan Williams, 1906, Down Ampney). "O Comforter, draw near, Within my heart appear, And kindle it…"). It's the tune, the soft notes, and the dulcet tones of the Choristers that I love. Kindle is more warming a verb than light.

Sat on the porch this afternoon and read some old copies of The London Review of Books. In the July 13th edition there was a large ad for The Wigtown Book Festival in Southwest Scotland where Helen and Rob took me when I was staying with them in Moniaive. I loved that day. It was bucketing with rain, the books in all the little white cement shops were damp and piled on shelves right up to the ceilings and in heaps on the floors. Everywhere, books.

Another ad in the LRB took my fancy too. Someone is giving away "Musical instruments to a loving home". It includes a trombone, a flute and an oboe. I wonder in what venues they were played? And what music floated out of them? And who was giving them up and why? And who ended up taking them? I'm sure that most people who read The LRB read all of the articles and maybe one or two ads. I read a chosen few of the articles and all of the ads.

Thanksgiving dinner tonight at Drew and Ely's with Chinese food from The Dragon Court. It wasn't the week for heavy duty cooking (re the usual turkey, gravy, mashed potatoes, squash, stuffing.)

A phone conversation with E who was excited about her new school friend who is "Katherine with a K".

When we got home tonight a huge bundle in the door of freshly made Spring rolls from Mục Sư Anh and his kindly wife.

THANKSGIVING MONDAY, OCTOBER 9th, 2017 ~ A happy garden party lunch in Toronto at A and A's to celebrate T and T's fiftieth wedding anniversary. Old friends and much love in that pretty backyard. There were trays of Thảo's vegetarian rice paper rolls, Spring rolls, small bowls of Nước Mắm and bigger bowls of beautiful Vietnamese salads, shrimp on sugar cane skewers, every colour and shape of fruit imaginable. Fifty people there, many of them women from the same girl's school in Vietnam whom I haven't seen for years and who reconvened their lives in Toronto thirty-five years ago. All of them beam with gentility, intelligence, kindness.

It's friendships, old and new, that help make the world go 'round as it was meant to.

These riches are an integral part of the circle of our lives. The beginnings return to join hands with the loose ends. Things are as they should be. There is peace in that.

TUESDAY, OCTOBER 10TH, 2017 ~ The Dogwood Bush has decided to get on with it. This morning it is lit up in from within; in orange!

Tomorrow to southern California for the wedding of Tâm and Trung. We've known Tammy since before she was born. We took her parents on their first date since escorts were necessary to their culture. There will be tales to be told when we come home.

THURSDAY, OCTOBER 19TH, 2017 ~ *"California dreamin'..."* ~ It was a wonderful week. Do surfers ever work or do they just walk around all day in those tight rubber suits dripping into restaurants?

Huntington Beach left us with these thoughts: The Islamic women in the pool were having a happy splash in their burkinis. A burkini would make me braver about swanning around beside the other swimmers and their perfected, toned flesh.

Two small children and their mother were in the pool with their blind father, the little girl entreating her daddy to watch how she could swim. Antoine de Saint-Exupery in The Little Prince talked about how the most important sight comes from our hearts, not from our eyes.

We had our first taste of grilled Mahi-Mahi in Newport Beach.

The bulletin cover for the Hội Thánh Tin Lành in Fountain Valley says *"Leave uplifted".* We were invited to share a noon hour meal in the open-air courtyard in the company of fine people. We stayed on to chat so that D. could practice her choral music. And then we left uplifted.

T and T's wedding was outdoors in Capistrano. Perfect weather. Women floated through the piazza

like silk butterflies in brilliant Áo Dài of green, yellow, pink. Somebody asked me why I wasn't wearing mine. "Fits my left leg now", I replied.

John and I walked along the ocean pier and let the warm Pacific air blow us to pieces. I crossed the overpass bridge to the beach so I could get closer to the pounding surf, a fundamental sound, borne of the foundation of the deep.

Had a hạnh phúc (happiness) of an afternoon on Phú's boat with Lionel Ritchie singing in the background. ("Hello, is it me you're looking for?") And a BBQ with Hà and Phiên and Kim and Kimmy at Liên and Phú's house.

Dinner at Phán and Diệu's with Spring rolls and Phở Bò with more generous helpings of hạnh phúc. (See # 9).

A huggy-happy reunion with Nhân and Trang after a hiatus of twenty-five years. We joined them and their beautiful adult children for iced Vietnamese coffee and lunch. They asked us to tell their back-story to their children.

FRIDAY, OCTOBER 20TH, 2017 ~ Lucia in hospital so this morning to spend some time with her precious little Self. Humans are hard-wired for worry. It's the one thing that we all do that has no side benefits. "This little light of mine..."

SATURDAY, OCTOBER 21, 2017 ~ Lucia came home tonight. Happy us. Charlotte no longer goes to school due to germ control for her little sister; a wise decision.

An enjoyable morning playing in the orchestra, which is a fancy word we call ourselves, with upright bass, violin, banjo, piano, guitar, cello. This in aid of the Autumn start-up of The Women Of The Church.

Charlotte stayed with us this afternoon and evening. Uncle Jock and Aunt Ashley to the rescue: Eye Spy, Hide And Seek, colouring, a long speaker phone chat to cousins H and E while they discussed Hallowe'en costumes and how E can count to ten in Chinese and H and C can count in Spanish, (the way of the world for four year olds now), the alphabet card game, snacks, more colouring. Aunt Ashley read a beautiful children's story which John bought at Gordon Books on King Street beside Café Orange where we often stop for coffee/tea. The world needs more kind Aunties and Uncles to inspire children everywhere.

And to let the grandparents put up their feet.

SUNDAY OCTOBER 22, 2017 ~ Looked in the mirror this morning and saw my mom's face looking back at me; something about my mouth, my eyes. I look seventy. A new, serious look has set upon me.

I did the church lunch for fifty-five this morning and they ate it all up. We do this every Sunday, by turns. Social isolation is a blight in today's fast paced society. The old idea of breaking bread together brims with merit.

Lucia had a good sleep in her own cosy crib at home. E and H went to the garden centre this afternoon and Hayley sent photos of them sitting amid an array of huge orange pumpkins.

Already plans underway for the music for the two Advent Services on November nineteenth. How the time flows along.

By just after six p.m. the street lights went on. Lamps lit the windows up and down our street, small, squared vignettes glowing with domesticity. By seven it was black. A starless night with a promise of rain this week.

MONDAY, OCTOBER 23RD, 2017 ~ Overcast. The absence of strong sunlight today a relief. I

want it to start acting like October. Skinny Chai Latte at 2nd Cup with JB this morning. MH not able to join us as she was on Bubbe duty. JB glowing re her zest for her new academic work. It's geared for her. And she for it.

Listened to Brahms' Lieders this afternoon. Calming, peaceful music. Angelic voices. I told JB this morning that I'm sick of dystopian thought, chatter, books, movies. At some point surely we can celebrate those things which verge on the utopian. That is why I listen to this music, keep this journal, to remind myself that all is not lost as the vendors of distress would have us believe. I'll choose hopeful over hopeless any day.

Got halfway through listening to an online Jane Gardam interview on BBC Desert Island Discs interview but lost it at the halfway mark. This was sent to the Barbara Pym Reading Circle members by R.B. who is always on alert for these delicious bits of info which bring our discussions to life. Interviewees get to choose their favourite music to be played on Desert Island Discs (BBC radio). I was surprised that Gardam chose Oh What A Beautiful Morning from Oklahoma. She said it makes her happy as it brings back youthful memories of attending American musicals in London and being enthralled with the

joyfulness of them. When I was seventeen I thought that The Sound of Music at the Courthouse Theatre in my lakeside town was enchanting too. It wasn't until a few years later that I went to live productions (*Hair!*) on the London stage with my sister-in-law Gail and with sister Jan and later with Maureen and Belfast Dorothy. I spotted Robert Morley in the audience one night but mostly loved the fact that we could buy a box of chocolates to share during the performances.

TUESDAY, OCTOBER 24TH, 2017 ~ The early morning sky on our way to the eye clinic was grey shot through with shards of purest silver. A welcomed change in temperature; 14 Celsius.

A good eye appointment for John and a stop at Café Orange en route home for a Dutch Ginger Krinkle and a cup of English Breakfast tea.

I dashed into the library while John was having his flu shot, (I had mine yesterday), and I emerged with a gem in my hand; a book of the love letters between Elizabeth Barrett and Robert Browning. One day in 1845 she wrote to him that she felt the fault of a falling out was with herself, not with him. I can't imagine me writing this; "Dear Mr. Smith, The fault was clearly with me & not with you."

Note to Self: must try it sometime. I am sure there will be occasions.

To the dump moments ago. I love going to the dump; it's cleansing. We got rid of the patio umbrella that blew and smashed in the wind storm when we were away. It was cheap when purchased last Spring. My mom always said "You get what you pay for."

Getting rid of small items clears my mind. When we downsized eleven, maybe twelve, years ago from our bigger house to this two-bedroom cottage I thought it would mean a de-junked house for all time. Our basement, every drawer, the only two cupboards in the house are full of useless detritus again.

After our dump trip I removed the withering Coleus from the window boxes, swept out the garage, moved the one remaining good patio umbrella to the garage for the winter.

Spent some evening hours with Lucia at the children's hospital. Nothing else matters much when she's sick. The small things keep me going so I can deal with the big things, except that Lucia is our Small Thing and Our Big Thing at the moment.

WEDNESDAY, OCTOBER 25TH, 2017 ~ Chicken casserole, butternut squash and a vase of maroon Coleus leaves on JS's table today at noon, with V and L. We call ourselves The Four Amigas. We meet every few months for lunch to dissect the world and put it back together in the way we think it should go, like a giant puzzle where we all get turns at figuring out where the pieces should land. There's lots of laughter. We've known one another for forty years, raised our kids together and watched them move off together. And now we are growing old together and still enjoying the lovingly Saran-wrapped packets of Rocky Road chocolate that Joyce sends home with us. The Amigas are comforters.

So is the chocolate.

Sat at the hospital with Lucia this evening for a few hours. Those soft-spoken, baby-loving, Wonder Women nurses; I can't say enough.

THURSDAY, OCTOBER 26TH, 2017 ~ London Review Of Books Volume 39 Number 20, PERSONALS: *"Hunky chap seeks shy, petite woman..."* What kind of a man has the conceit to refer to himself as *"hunky"?*

Typed up Sunday Sermon for John on Psalm One and Psalm Fifteen, the theme being two paths; obedience/rebellion. Dear Reader, let that thesis annoy you if it will but I didn't write The Book nor did I set the world in motion. Cannot ever read John's writing nor can he. In fact it's brutal. I do my best.

John visiting our granddaughter now and I hope that when he returns he will tell me that she is feeling better. She did the sweetest thing I've ever seen last night. The nurse came in with the rolling blood pressure cart. Lucia recognized it and shot her wee tiny leg up high in the air so the nurse could put the pressure cuff on her leg. "She knows the routines," Nursey laughed.

An email from one of the children, now a young man, who was near and dear when the Hungarian Roma people were in Canada prior to the government sweep which deported them en masse back to Europe. Since my entire ESL class of nineteen adults was comprised of Hungarian Roma people I protested heartily with an article in the newspaper and with a letter to a Federal Cabinet Minister but it did no good. I had assumed we were way past the days when we punished the lot for the sins of a few members of a particular social group. The teachers at a local middle school loved K and his twin brother so much that they bought them suits and shoes for their grade eight graduation. K is back in Hungary and happy, with a good factory job, a

wife and two small children. He and his brother trailed sweetness behind them wherever they went.

Jock came tonight to carve a pumpkin with Charlotte; her first. We lit it up with dollar store lights inside. She was thrilled until we turned off the lights and she saw his wide, gap-toothed grin.

FRIDAY, OCTOBER 27TH, 2017 ~ John is out and about so enjoyed my tomato sandwich, yogurt and strawberries alone at noon listening to both Itzhak Perlman and Ben Heppner.

Elgar's Salut D'Amour and Dvorak's Songs My Mother Taught Me pour out of Itzhak's violin like honey but The Flight of The Bumble Bee and Humoresque irritate me so I put on Ben's CD and listened to him sing Let All My Life Be Music, Someday My Heart Will Awake, The World Is Waiting For The Sunrise. There must be a part of the brain that kicks into action and makes some people ecstatic over certain musical phrases that leave other people annoyed. How does that work, I wonder?

Housework awaits. Good women get at it I suppose. But as long as there are books and other things...

I need a servant. Or a cook. Or one of those people they used to call a Maid of All Works.

In Diana Athill's memoir 'Instead of A Letter' (1963, 33) she speaks about the time when her gentrified family lost their wealth and their servants along with it. Her despairing mother said to her *"The…thing about being poor is that if you leave something on the floor when you go out, you know it will still be there when you get back."*

Our little Lucia is feeling a bit better today.

SATURDAY, OCTOBER 28TH, 2017 ~ Woke up to see that it had rained in the night and was disappointed that I hadn't heard it. Night time rain is one of my favourite sounds. One dark night I heard an owl hooting in the woods across the way. On occasion the coyotes yip and the geese honk across the sky to the marsh. The sound of the early morning traffic racing along the 403 is calming white noise. It starts thrumming at 5 a.m. I stretch, curl up. I'm not on the highway, nor am I getting up for work. Such are the treats of being seventy. In the daytime it's the ringing of the bells at the Basilica that soothe; a sound from The Old World.

Went to the hospital to see our little girl. She smiled at me. She clapped when I sang to her and she tried to take my bracelet off so I know she is getting

back to herself. Met the paediatrician. He was warm, encouraging, interested in her.

I could nap now, but then what would become of a good night's sleep?

A phone chat with Hayley this afternoon. She loves her school, her students. E and H went to the neighbourhood Hallowe'en parade today, he as Batman, she as a Princess.

Will make Himself a turkey and cranberry sauce sandwich and put on my housecoat even though it's only just gone 6:30 p.m. Not hungry myself.

SUNDAY, OCTOBER 29TH, 2017 ~ The hymns at Morning Prayer (Book of Common Praise, University of Toronto Press, 1938, #'s 476, 618, 724) offered these small bits of loveliness:

- **from Spirit of God Descend Upon My Heart by George Croly, *"...thy love the flame"***
- **from Glorious Things of Thee are Spoken, Rev'd John Newton, *"See, the streams of living waters, Springing from eternal love..."***
- **from the children's hymn When He Cometh, by William O. Cushing, this small story; Mom told me that she used to sing it at Trinity**

Anglican in Galt in her childhood. She thought the words were "*Winnie cometh*". She wondered who Winnie was and when she was arriving. So, quietly, under my breath I always sing "*Winnie cometh.*" Just because.

Email from RSH, Great Granddaughter of Lady Harris, Alice Seeley, with a photo of Rebecca and her father Richard et al at the unveiling of the historic plaque dedicated to Lady Harris in Frome, Somerset, England. Am glad this has happened.

John to visit Lucia who was sleeping like a baby, as she would.

MONDAY, OCTOBER 30TH, 2017 ~ Wind howling when I awoke in the pitch dark at four this morning. John dreaming that we were in Cape Cod. Had to talk him awake as he was having quite a discussion with Somebody over Something in his sleep.

A true Autumnal day. Leaves blowing. We hired two women gardeners to put the garden to bed for the coming winter. Was kind of like having those two from the British tv show in our garden except that they didn't find any bodies buried under the

leaves. (Rosemary and Thyme is the name of that show.) The Cardinal Bush was cut back, the clump that had sprung up from the Russian Elms has been taken out, the small cedar tree in the green pot has been planted in the garden near the wooden fence. Annuals have been dug out, the yellow roses admired, the garden plot laid bare. She thinks that the Virginia Creeper I planted so that it would show itself crimson come every October has turned itself around where it thrives and turns scarlet on my neighbour's side of the fence. Wouldn't you know it?

A long visit with Lucia last night. A robot followed me down the hall at the hospital very late. Yes. It's programmed to deliver drugs to the various units. It zoomed along the floor, green lights flashing, scaring the wits out of me in the dimmed night time lighting. It was just the cleaning woman and me by the elevator doors. In a scene from Star Wars.

TUESDAY, OCTOBER 31ST, 2017 ~ All Hallows Eve ~ Boo! Our Lucia home from hospital today. The Happy Dance to follow. Charlotte came to Trick Or Treat in a Princess costume that would have made Walt Disney proud.

Lucia is one happy girl tonight by all reports. Me too.

Tomorrow John goes to Synod meeting and I shall go straight to Jan and Rob's in Kingston for a long overdue visit.

SATURDAY, NOVEMBER 4TH, 2017 ~ After three days in Kingston I left there for home at 5 a.m. after a night of on-and-off thinking about the long drive ahead and got back here by 9:30 a.m. I had Highway 407 all to myself for parts of the drive and could have held a barn dance on it.

A most perfect three days with Jan and Rob. Many noteworthy items. We took a waterfront walk along Lake Ontario and saw a bench there with an inscription of love in memory of an Aunt with a wonderful smile. Whoever she was she had a terrific name ("Auntie Boof") and must have been a thoroughly good woman to deserve that spirited memorial.

I had a short phone chat with Carol R. who was a good friend to me in high school years. We shared a Grade Eleven English class and a few reprimands from Mr. Ecclestone who one day flatly said to us "Shut up."

Sandbanks Provincial Park was adrift in yellow leaves as we drove right straight through it. "I love Ontario", I thought.

At an eastern grocer's I bought a roast of Sirloin for only thirteen dollars. John has just come in with some potatoes that I can roast with it tomorrow. Jan's kitchen pours out delicious food. We enjoyed ourselves in every way. And good things to greet me when I got home: John, the latest copy of The London Review, a second-hand book I had ordered called Being Seventy by an American woman, Elizabeth Gray Vining, from 1976. Raining now, cold, high winds, weather warnings for tonight.

Thankful to be back in our cosy nest.

SUNDAY, NOVEMBER 5TH, 2017 ~ *Remembrance Sunday at St. George's* ~

Rain, on and off. We held the Remembrance Day service outside at the city Cenotaph on the front lawn of the church after Morning Prayer. Someone commented that the weather is often like this at Remembrance. The sky weeps.

To our friend P's 50th birthday party to see his photography show. He has a keen eye that he has trained to capture minute details. His work proves the results of living with intent, with observancy; seeing, hearing, capturing. He has hit life's marrow.

MONDAY, NOVEMBER 6TH, 2017 ~ Needed my jacket and ski-band for my morning walk.

Took the Advent music to be enlarged at a local copy shop. It's music that I love and look forward to playing along with the others for the two Advent Services on November 19th including a piano/cello duet for myself and pianist JV in the morning service and MR in the evening.

Charlotte spent the afternoon here with us and her new colouring book. She asked John to help her colour but was upset that his colouring efforts weren't up to par. "I wanted this book to be nice," she said, her huge brown eyes pools of disappointment.

Roasted the beef and enjoyed a good dinner.

So tired I could drop and it's only just gone 6:45 p.m. Time change does that and so did the long drive home from Kingston at that outrageous hour. I enjoyed every mile of it. Driving can be freeing, under the right weather and traffic conditions.

TUESDAY, NOVEMBER 7TH, 2017 ~ A bright sort of a day with mild sunlight and a temperature of ten degrees.

An early morning appointment with the Dermatologist downtown who has replaced himself

temporarily with a movie-star sort of doctor-girl who looks eighteen. She was helpful; a mixture of beauty and brains that astounds me still.

Came home and set up the window boxes with fake cedar branches for winter. I swept off the back deck, covered over the pots with plastic and stacked the outdoor chairs, all this an effort against the snow that is sure to come before long.

Little bits of reading from Elizabeth Gray Vining's book ('Being Seventy, The Viking Press, 1978). No *wonder* she wrote it. She was the English tutor for the Crown Prince of Japan! How does a person get a job like that? What kind of CV must you have to apply? If it were me would this work?

"Dear Crown Prince I would like to apply to be your English tutor. I know my way around Gerunds and the Subjunctive. I put Panko crumbs on everything. I can say 'Watashi wa Judy desu'. I love Japanese woodblock prints. I hope you'll consider hiring me to read English novels to you while you make the tea. I'd be overjoyed to live in your palace. Any small space in the attic would be fine. Tatami mats I could learn to love. Best wishes. Sayonara, Your Friend..."

Once upon a long time ago I did take Japanese language lessons at The Japanese Cultural Centre

here. I like hearing it spoken and wish I had taken more time with it. Then maybe the Prince would have taken me on too.

Finished this lovely day with a pot of tea in my new red mug from Jan and some rye toast with Lynn and Andrew's strawberry jam. John at a meeting tonight so me in my housecoat at such an early hour I'd be ashamed to say just when lest people think me slovenly. I love the early darkness.

WEDNESDAY, NOVEMBER 8TH, 2017 ~ Gleanings of what other people, the famous ones, wrote in their diaries in the Novembers of their lives:

1. May Sarton, (Sarton, 1984, 184) wrote on Sunday, November 7th, 1984 in her book 'At Seventy', about a trip out west and how she had discovered Emily Carr's work through a friend; "*...the great trees, the cedars and the oaks, the firs, planted by Emily Carr, so I often felt myself seeing through her eyes and the reason I knew her was that Liz Hazlette sent me her remarkable journal years ago when we first began to correspond*".

Emily Carr; I admire the spirited brightness and depth of her work. Her oil paintings say much about her connectedness to Something Greater. I had once read that she had connected with the Theosophy movement that was *au courant* at the time, but see a quote in my book of her letters to CBC's Ira Dilworth that points to her feeling otherwise. She writes to Ira on November 6, 1942 about Lawren Harris, who encouraged her and gave her confidence in her work. She talks about a change in Lawren's work and comments that he went through a struggle during the hiatus.

I have also read about Emily's disenchantment with the Church of England and about how she and her family walked away from the Cathedral in Victoria, British Columbia and started the Church of Our Lord which affiliated with the Reformed Episcopal Church. She sang Breathe on Me Breath of God before she started each of her paintings. You can see the swirling movement in her skies as you can in Theosophist paintings. Perhaps that is why she was assumed to be a part of that Movement.

A few years ago John and I went to Victoria. As we looked around us we realized that we were standing right in front the house that had once belonged to her and was in fact the boarding house she ran. We recognized it by the name she had called it that still remains; The House of All Sorts. We assume she had named if from the line in The Book Of Common Prayer about *"all sorts and conditions of men."*

2. In Graham Greene's A Life in Letters (November 26, 1934), he wrote to Hugh Greene about how his trip to Africa had resulted in John Harris wanting him to be his successor as Parliamentary Secretary to the Anti-Slavery Association. This was of interest as John and I are attached to the same group in London. Lady Harris, Alice Seeley, and her husband were the first Joint-Secretaries of that organization due to their Congo work and their efforts to abolish slavery there. The Continental Hotel in Saigon, built during the French Colonial period, has marked off the room where Greene stayed when he wrote The Quiet American.

3. Barbara Pym, in her published journal A Very Private Eye (1984), wrote in her diary on November 7th, 1945 to the love of her life, Henry Harvey, that she was *"still in the WRNS and waiting to be demobilized,"* and further that she and her sister Hilary had *"taken a flat - in Pimlico, not a very good district, but perhaps we shall raise the tone."*

4. On November 7th, 1908, Edith Wharton wrote to her friend Tonni that *"there come turning-points*

in everyone's life when one has to go sharply round the corner without looking behind, and this was one."

Good advice I'd say. She wrote that quote while staying with Henry James and friends as she sought their friendship in coping with husband Teddy's increasing psychopathy. (Goldman-Price, 2012, 225.)

I cannot match any of those entries on this November day but I can say with surety that the Sugar Maple across the road from us has put on its Autumn clothes and as a result has become a scarlet and orange balloon. Its fallen leaves make a stunning carpet on the lawn and the sidewalk. I hope nobody rakes them up. Why do people insist on raking everything up? Nature will take care of them.

Charlotte and I opened her Piggy Bank today to count the money she has been saving for an orphanage. Forty-eight dollars and change. She insists it is "twenty fourteen" dollars when I ask her how much she has saved.

A refreshing cello lesson tonight practicing my timing for the Advent hymns. He told me to relax. And to slow down. And not to think about the difficult passages but focus on the timing. Worrying about switching finger positions is all in my mind, he says. If I slow down I'll stop worrying. Bravo!

One can only hope.

THURSDAY, NOVEMBER 9TH, 2017 ~ So chilly this morning that I wore my winter vest, my ski jacket and my headband down the hill. Not a deer in sight. The deer cull has decimated them from the nearby woods and trails. It has upset the balance. I didn't mind that they ate our pansies and our tulips last Spring. In fact, it's enchanting to live so close to nature and to imagine the deer strolling along our street when we are all asleep. Neighbours have seen them. The deer do what they have to do survive, just like the rest of us. And so they ate our pansies. I hope they enjoyed them.

To the plant nursery to find some more wintry things to further plump up the window boxes. Bought some red berries and stuck them in. Much improved. If you were to stand back far enough you might even think they were real. And if they *were* real the squirrels would eat them and ruin the effect.

A long and difficult music rehearsal today but we will practice again next week. I hope to find more confidence about a tricky cello/piano duet. It's a wonderful tune but oh my goodness. Full credit to both the pianists, neither of whom had heard it before. They did very well with it.

We are awaiting snow.

FRIDAY, NOVEMBER 10TH, 2017 ~ John is eighty-one today. As we age time moves more stealthily and fleetingly and to borrow from Carl Sandburg, it moves *"on little cat feet"*, although he wasn't talking about time, but fog.

I reminded John that we know too many people who did not have the privilege of aging. This is an important stage of our lives.

"We have to become more creative and find new things to do when the things we used to love doing are no longer viable," I tell him. We were remembering our frequent long road trip adventures. We miss them. It'll take some adjusting.

Lunch with several of John's friends from Teacher's College days. I enjoyed watching their interaction. Their friendships are solid, based on respect, shared histories, fun.

In Samuel Pepys' Diary on this very day in the year 1665 he found himself in a right snit with his wife. She came to dinner with him and they spent the evening together but it was not a happy evening for Mr. Pepys, the First Secretary of the British Admiralty, nor for his wife, Mrs. Pepys.

Some birthday cupcakes from the stellar bakery in this city called 'Bitten' arrived tonight from Jock and

Ashley. So good they should be outlawed (not J and A, but the cupcakes.)

The snow didn't amount to much. Just a light dusting.

SATURDAY, NOVEMBER, 11TH, 2017 ~ Remembrance Day ~ I joined MH and JB for Skinny Chai Latte at coffee shop this morning for a great long catching–up. Our lives have morphed and changed since we met and worked together; new retirement, new volunteer work, new babies in M's life, a new academic career in J's, four small new family members in my own life.

Chinese take-out from Dragon Court tonight at Drew and Ely's with Ashley and Jock for John's birthday. Charlotte and her cousin E on speaker phone together. Delighted to see Lucia climbing on and off the sofa and smiling over the Peppa Pig cartoon, her hair in three pigtails (one on top!)

Thinking of my Dad on Remembrance Day. He never spoke much about the War until he got very old although the camaraderie he shared with some members of The Highland Light Infantry (now the Highland Fusiliers) and with the Padre of his unit never waned. The war came back to him with full

force in his late eighties. He often told his stories, as if he didn't want them to go missing as had so many of his comrades.

"Go forward" was his motto, which I assume he was taught during the marches. It served him well all of his life in a never look back, set the goal sort of a way.

SUNDAY, NOVEMBER 12TH, 2017 ~ *"...whose service is perfect freedom..."* is my favourite line from The Book of Common Prayer, the Collect For Peace, pg 11.

A candle-lit evening meal at Beatrice and John's with E, M, J and P. A lovely old-fashioned Sunday dinner of pork roast, potatoes, squash and Beatrice's crusted fruit dessert.

Enjoyed the story telling at dinner. Small stories give context, an undercurrent to our lives. E spoke about the twelve-piece place setting of bone china an Aunt left and passed along to E and M in little pieces at a time. They use them at Christmas, chiefly because they are green. Would have been interesting to know who sat at that table in the cold Winnipeg winters of his Aunt's life. I wonder what kind of recipes landed on those green plates? I've had so much perfect food prepared by M over the years that I know what kind

of deliciousness landed on the green plates after she got hold of them.

Beatrice told of her family's past relationship with Canadian poet F.G.Scott (1861-1944), who was known as the Poet of The Laurentians. She remembers him coming to visit her father when she was a tiny girl in Quebec City. She also remembers how Scott's grandchildren taught her how to use a water gun. Beatrice is not the water gun type.

MONDAY, NOVEMBER 13TH, 2017 ~ Have a 2016 biography of Evelyn Waugh, (by Philip Eade, Henry Holt), from the library. And today I discovered a plate in the middle of the book on which is a photo of a young Elizabeth Harman, later to become Lady Elizabeth Longford, biographer of Queen Victoria. I once had the pleasure to chat with her at The National Liberal Club in London, Whitehall, at the AGM of The Society of Women Writers And Journalists. She was in her nineties by that time, in a wheelchair, and was with a Carer. She was wearing a black velvet jacket with a wide, white silk ruff around her neck. She looked as regal as could be. She was ninety something and died shortly thereafter. Happenstance. I was thrilled.

TUESDAY, NOVEMBER 14TH, 2017 ~ Who changed the colour of my egg yolks? Why are they glowing neon orange like the signage in Tokyo? And do I want to eat them?

The Chili I made yesterday was good last night with a ciabatta roll and will have a repeat tonight. I love repeats.

WEDNESDAY, NOVEMBER 15TH, 2017 ~ Spent thirty minutes on a conference call at noon with three young women in eleventh grade at an American high school. They had emailed me about their History project regarding Lady Harris and would I help? I told them how important their work is and that if they manage to change the world view of even a single person as to the oneness of the human family then they will have done something for the world. They were interested in the work of Anti-Slavery International. I told them that ASI is the vehicle by which Lady Harris's work continues to this day.

We drove through the city this afternoon. Saw all of this within fifteen minutes of our own house: a young woman was waiting on a street corner for a customer. She was jigging up and down to keep warm.

Two young boys in summer clothing came along on their way home from school. My guess is that neither of them has a warm jacket or long pants. On a corner the police had two teenaged boys on their faces on the cold ground, arms handcuffed behind their backs.

There's not enough love to go around. That's the bottom line.

THURSDAY, NOVEMBER 16TH, 2017 ~ It's true that when I get on a kick it takes me a while to get back out of it. Samuel Pepys and his famous Diary are keeping me much engaged. It is quoted every day in a newspaper. He was quite a ripe old guy.

Yesterday I had a lengthy chat with the American students about Imperialism and Colonialism, Colonialism being when outsiders move physically into your territory and set up shop and Imperialism being their political or economic control of an area.

In today's excerpt from Samuel Pepys he was talking about a time when his friends in London took him down to show him the contents in the hold of a ship that had returned from India. In that hold were bales of silk, copper, riches of many kinds.

Was it Imperial plunder that Mr. Pepys described on November 16th, 1665?

FRIDAY, NOVEMBER 17TH, 2017 ~ A lesson learned tonight about aging: went to the Horticultural Society meeting. They have instituted an annual award in John's name. He presented it tonight to a ninety-two year old gentleman who continues to change our local world with his botanical knowledge and his beautifications.

The speaker's topic was Conifers; Year Round Colour. It was well done by a brilliant fellow. He, the speaker, said that many of his trees take on human-like characteristics. He spoke of them with love and respect. It reminded us of a time when the Sand Cherry tree in our Sunning Hill house garden had a broken limb. Our friend Nguyễn Nam came and supported it with a pole and tied it with a rope in an interesting pattern around the other branch. He was careful, tender about it, as if he was helping a friend with a broken leg. That same ropey pattern is on many trees, like an art form, in the boulevards in Hà Nội.

I wanted to say Nam's name here. We loved him. John sat with him until the moment he died. By saying his name I'm keeping him.

I recently learned the most riveting information about Nam from his son, Thien, in regard to the

French novelist Marguerite Duras. I have read her novel 'The Lover' and will re-read it. Duras' mother left France during the Colonization in Vietnam to teach school in Sa Đéc. She took along her two sons and her young daughter, Marguerite, who grew up to become the famous writer. As it happens, Nam was a friend of the young man about whom Duras wrote. The young man in her book The Lover was Huỳnh Thủy Lê and his house still stands today for tourists. Further, Nam's grandfather was a tenant of *his* grandfather's who owned houses in Sa Đéc. The novel concerns the true story of a hopeless, sorrowful brand of young attachment that masquerades as love.

Nam, who was a wonderful tailor and once made me a suit, taught a nephew of the young man of the story how to sew. I wish he was still alive so I could hear the details from him, via translation. This is my new true favourite story. I will share it with Canadian writer Elizabeth McLean who writes beautiful novels about Vietnam and with whom I have had the odd email exchange. I thrive on stories. They oxygenate me. But this one is the best I've heard for some time. If only Nam were here!

SATURDAY, NOVEMBER 18TH, 2017 ~ A worthwhile morning studying the first section of James Chapter One at the women's meeting. Much tucked in there to keep us strong, alert, patient, wise and the most importantly perhaps, *still.* LM pointed out that unless we can sit still and be with ourselves we will never sort out what ails us.

Our discussion was followed by a two hour music practice for Advent Carols tomorrow.

Dinner with Ken and Rebecca tonight. When they landed in our lives due to our daughter's marriage we got an extra bonus in them.

SUNDAY, NOVEMBER 19TH, 2017 ~ Glorious hymns today at our two Advent Services. A joy to play them with Jane and Marlies on piano and Sara in the evening with her violin.

We played Tell Out My Soul this evening after the Processional with cello, piano, violin. It was written in 1962 by Timothy-Dudley Smith and later put to the Woodlands tune by Walter Greatorex. It stands as a paraphrase to The Magnificat so it is perfect Advent music. It is glorious.

My mom used to say that the message in a stained

glass window spoke volumes to her. I'd say the same about a wonderful piece of music.

A windy, dizzying flurry of snow this afternoon for twenty minutes but it didn't last. It was only pretending.

MONDAY, NOVEMBER 20TH, 2017 ~ Cold and clear and me with a few jolts in my hips due to sitting so long yesterday.

Have just made a casserole jumble with sliced potatoes, hamburger, onion, tomato soup, last night's leftover green beans. It's that kind of a comfortable take-it-easy day. It should do us for a few meals.

Tonight's sunset is hot pink. Beauteous.

TUESDAY, NOVEMBER 21ST, 2017 ~ RMB and I laughed our socks off over a bowl of steaming Phở Gà for two hours at Lạc Viên at noon. My Phương tells me that the name of the restaurant translates roughly to 'Happy Park' and it certainly is when RMB and I get there. We left no discussion of current news items unscathed. Much fun to age alongside someone who remembers me as I was at twelve and vice-versa.

The London Review has arrived. How does this sound? *"...bookshop for sale on Ireland's most*

beautiful coast...” And a huge article on the Brontes to which I look forward.

Charlotte came to visit this evening (Smith, not Bronte.). I promised her a Smartie for every basement stair she could climb without going up on her hands and knees as that set of stairs for her represents Everest. She has been trying to conquer them for months. She climbed six of them, so six Smarties, but no fool she climbed all eleven of them to show her dad later. I told her that we'd save the rest of the Smarties for another smart thing that I know she will do next visit.

WEDNESDAY, NOVEMBER 22ND, 2017 ~ To buy groceries. If four bags of groceries costs us one hundred Canadian dollars how do people feed their children?

Have just made a huge pot of Carrot, Sweet Potato, Sweet Onion, Curry soup for lunch tomorrow when our old friend Betty M. will come to have a good chat. Tasted it but a bit too much bite in it from the curry so have added a touch of honey. Looking forward to her visit. Will set a cosy table for us. Friendship is just the thing on a chilly day.

LB emailed to say that Marcus, our Grade eleven,

twelve and thirteen Latin teacher, has died. I never knew if Marcus was a moniker the boys gave him, when they weren't busy stuffing the keyhole of the classroom door with bubble gum so he couldn't open it, or if it was his birth name. Seems now that it was a moniker. He was a good teacher who loved his subject. I have silently thanked him when I've tried to explain the roots of English words to newcomer adult students who sometimes have backgrounds in Latin themselves.

When you are seventy years old it happens that you hear news of the deaths of childhood teachers. My kindergarten teacher died not too long ago. Miss Elizabeth Clare was a gem. Her obituary was gentle and outlined the good things she was, the kindnesses she bestowed, her small loves and hobbies, the cookies she made for her friends. It's those things we remember about people. She didn't grow up in the age of Facebook so had no LIKES to score, but she had the timeless things, the solid things that people acknowledged in her.

The obituaries in the Saturday edition in one of the major newspapers are interesting reading. Their life stories glow with bravado, with élan, courage, love, adventure.

THURSDAY, NOVEMBER 23RD, 2017 ~ Today my dad would be one-hundred and four years old. Stuns me the way the generations fly past. This means that my own grandparents, who seem as if they were just here yesterday, would now be classified as ancient.

John and I often think how lost our parents would be with the changes in the world. Ask them what a megabyte is and who knows what they'd come up with? Or Millennial. Hashtag. Brexit. Earworm. Selfie. Drone. Frenemy. Twitter. Avatar. Mansplaining. Bitcoin. Uber. Burkini. Emoji. Bromance. Chatroom. Fracking.

OK. Enough already.

Our friend Betty came to lunch. It was good to sit down with her after a long time. We had the soup I made yesterday, a sandwich, tabouleh, berries and lemon yogurt, coffee. I like mentioning menus. It fleshes out the scene, as well as fleshing out the bodies of the participants.

Am trying to find time to get through the Evelyn Waugh biography which is both good and awful. I'm sure the English masses must have despised the young aristocrats who played at life and threw opportunity to the wind.

Have taken down from the bookshelf Alan Bennett's latest book which I bought this past summer; Keeping On Keeping On, Faber And Faber, 2016.

Two years ago this month he wrote about overhearing two women in the village commenting on his plays. One reportedly said to the other *"I can't understand how he writes the plays he does when he had such two lovely parents."* (Bennett, 216, 372.)

FRIDAY, NOVEMBER 24TH, 2017 ~ Am about to type up John's Sunday sermon re Psalm 145. Am hoping that he will be able to read his own writing aloud to me as I type.

I told LB this morning how much I miss the old British tv mysteries. I want Miss Marple back in her tweeds with a cameo at her throat, a wicker basket over her arm and her neighbours clipping their David Austin Roses. The crime should occur in the sitting room without bloodshed, perhaps a brass candlestick to the Colonel's head followed by him falling down on a Turkish carpet. It would be the housemaid "who done it", not the butler, and then the unravelling of the housemaid's secret past. The new crime shows are too much about, well, crime. They are filmed with little to no lighting. There is no bucolic scenery. No picnics on the grass with people seated on tartan blankets. No lovely sitting rooms with pale yellow sofas.

I could make the world a better place if given half a chance.

SATURDAY, NOVEMBER 25TH, 2017 ~ This morning to the children's Advent party where I helped with both the music and with general noise control. When my Aunt Bessie was my age and was still helping with children's functions I used to wonder why she kept it up. Now I know the answer. It's fun. It keeps me in touch with the way kids think. The children at St. George's are nice to be with. They sang Advent music, they played terrifically rowdy games, ate a hearty pulled pork lunch, made Christmas ornaments in the Parish Hall which involved sparkles, tiny shiny bits and ribbons. This means that after the post-service lunch tomorrow the parishioners will go home with red metallic stars stuck all over their trousers and shirt sleeves.

SUNDAY, NOVEMBER 26TH, 2017 ~ A dullish day with a grey sky.

Taught the Feeding of the Five Thousand today. I

like that story. It showcases the importance of a small boy who willingly shared.

The children in that class have bright personalities and are full of intriguing ideas. One of them brought along a bucket full of woodchips that the beaver in the creek behind their house had gnawed. Where else could I see such delights?

A phone chat with Hayley. They spent American Thanksgiving visiting family to the south of them; a wonderful day together. Next Friday I'll fly down to see them for a few days. We miss them.

MONDAY, NOVEMBER 27TH, 2017 ~ One degree Celsius this morning but the sun is beaming.

I've already read Instead of A Letter by Diana Athill and now I have ordered Instead of A Book. I like her positive take on aging. She will be one hundred soon. When I last checked she was living in a retirement home in Highgate, London. I see that her nephew is the owner of the Museum of drawings across from the British Museum. He researched the book we have on William Strang, the artist who did the portraits of John's Great Aunt Jessie Smith and Great Uncle James Murray Smith. I discovered all of this a few moments ago after reading an ad in The LRB. And it's only 9:30 a.m. Who knows what new items I'll discover by dinner time?

At 10:00 we met R and J for coffee/tea at FINCH. They've kindly brought me a book bag from BRICK LANE books in London. It's the perfect size. I love it.

Afterwards we stopped at Holland Park nursery to pick up a small balsam tree for the front porch.

There is an upset Blue Jay in the back garden. He is telling somebody off in a raucous, scratching tone.

Off now outside to put out the Christmas lights. This will involve these things: unscrambling the several strings that I tied up so neatly last season and that will have twisted themselves into a ball of plastic wiring, finding which plug fits into which end unit, sorting out the coloured lights from the tiny white lights.

Or should I just stay indoors and read? Or phone Jan?

Later: stayed indoors and washed windows in the back room and vacuumed. Threw out a ton of papers that I no longer need. Brought out the Christmas CDs: Britten's A Ceremony of Carols, Handel's Messiah, J.S.Bach's Christmas Oratorio.

I promise Self that Christmas lights will go out in the morning.

TUESDAY, NOVEMBER 28TH, 2017 ~ The Christmas lights are up and shining. I've put them on the two small trees on the porch and threaded them through the pretend greenery in the window boxes. Forgot that last year we bought those blanket-like things that fit over the top of the bush and only need to be plugged in. Was happy to find them not in a scramble as I had imagined but hanging on their hooks in the garage as neatly as I had left them. So that is another thing off my list today.

Prince Harry and a young woman named Meghan are engaged to be married come Spring. General Hullabaloo to follow. I wish them much happiness.

WEDNESDAY, NOVEMBER 29TH, 2017 ~ Slender branches of the Dogwood are overreaching the fence in their winter garb of warm, cherry red. I miss the privacy the summer greenery offers. The barren landscape shows up our back windows at night time. They are open for public viewing seven nights a week with me in my ancient housecoat as scenery.

Wrote out Christmas cards and listened to the Bach Oratorio to establish my Christmas spirit as I penned them out.

On CFMX in the car en route to do some chores after lunch I heard a most glorious piece of music by David Foster (Sweet Remembrance of You) with pianist William Joseph and a cellist. Found it later on youtube. Must remember it.

Lynn F. here for berries and yogurt and tea this afternoon. We know how to laugh. We've been friends since our Sunning Hill Avenue days when our children were small. Friendship is good for the health. L is a gem in my box of life's treasures.

FRIDAY, NOVEMBER 30TH, 2017 ~ Gathering up the threads of tiny household things that need doing before I go to Hayley's tomorrow. Not all that far away but still, things to be done ahead.

A phone chat with BRD last night. We wondered why we don't love reading contemporary novels but fill ourselves up with our love of things past. We've enjoyed good book chats via phone for thirty-nine years. Those chats have no price.

THURSDAY, DECEMBER 7TH, 2017 ~ Waiting for me when I got home from Pearson Airport last night were small delicious things: the readings that MR did with the church women re Mary's role at Christmas, the newsletter Green Leaves from The Barbara Pym Society in Boston, the crossword from last Saturday's Globe and Mail and my book by Diana Athill.

Had a fun visit with our little family to the south of us. E sang me her Chinese songs complete with actions and H was his sweet self too. He loves his confreres at nursery school.

We took the children to the Botanic Garden on Saturday afternoon adjacent to the Capitol Building. The line-up for the tiny train was miles long with parents and overheated, wailing toddlers so we took them into the Tropical greenhouse instead and saw cocoa pods growing on trees, papaya, mango, bananas, vanilla beans, cinnamon. They could stamp their little passport cards as to what they had seen and that kept them busy and inky and forgetting that they weren't in that horrendous, cranky line-up for the little train. For that I silently mumbled humble thanks.

To Christ The King Anglican Church on Sunday. Glorious Advent music. The professional choir sang the traditional English Herefordshire Carol. I read the words as they sang and noted that it tells the entire story in five verses of four lines per verse. So in twenty lines you have the whole shebang; the power of good writing.

Sunday afternoon Hayley and I went to the Christmas women's tea in the afternoon while Isaac watched the children. Maybe there were one-hundred and fifty women. Delicious small treats and tea. I find Americans to be the kindliest, nicest of people so I'll forgive them for not making use of teapots like we do. In that splendiferous place I was dunking a tea bag up and down on its string in the cup as if I were jigging for Cod.

On Monday I had the fun of reading a book to E's Kindergarten class as The Mystery Guest. They were precious children, eager and wide-eyed. Three-quarters of the way through the book the fire alarm went so we all took to the outdoors and thus ended my story.

Two emails about Lady Harris, Alice Seeley, this week; one from a retired Clergyman in Somerset who wants information about her and another from CM who is writing another play to be put on at the summer festival in the English town where she lives. This time she is writing it from the perspective of King Leopold and his fear of Lady Harris's work.

Am thinking that if I were a playwright I'd set it in a metaphorical Garden of Eden, the jungle dripping with the colourful flowers of the liana vines, and then King Leopold's men enter and all turns vile as they extort the breath out of the Congolese for the sake of European greed. May be a stark way to demonstrate how goodness evaporates into evil in no time given a man's motives, just like the original Fall in the Garden with Leopold as the Serpent. Why not? John Milton did it.

A trip for groceries this morning allegedly to pick up one can of chicken noodle soup, Hot Cross Buns and rice for what would have been a total of $7.97. As life would have it I have just unpacked and put away much extraneous bounty from our expedition: margarine, olives, Halal minced hamburger, one giant cauliflower at the (now) good price of $3.49. While in the store the idea hit me that I could make Tuna Casserole that would last for three meals. So I threw in three tins of tuna on sale, one package of broad egg noodles, sour cream, celery, a small bag of onions, mushroom soup plus five other tins on sale at $.99 cents a piece.

Total = Too much. And so it goes.

I promised Self I'd leave politics out of this journal as am Sick Of It so won't rattle on but am worried again about the Middle East.

If we want peace somebody, some leader

somewhere, must locate a unique and selfless way through in spite of the fact that either side may feel they are losing too much. Sometimes in life we have to give more than we think we will get. Somebody must be prepared to do that. I can't see any other way. Forgiveness is all. There would not be a relationship left on earth if it were not for forgiveness.

FRIDAY, DECEMBER 8TH, 2017 ~ A long phone chat with Lynn B. this morning. Perfect to be able to reminisce because we knew one another when. A lovely way to start the day.

Am eschewing bread for now but this leaves me wanting a toasted Hot Cross bun and tea which I shall have anyway.

A few phone tips from LB who taught Kindergarten came in very helpful this afternoon with Charlotte who spent some time on a treasure hunt around the house for items that begin with the letter T. I had signs taped to the tub, the telephone, the tap. We phoned the Santa Claus number that Jan gave me. She heard his HO HO HO and then she froze.

Two high school contemporaries have died this week. Happens when you reach seventy. You switch up the Comics for the Obits.

Now here we sit on a freezing night hoping for something decent on tv.

SATURDAY, DECEMBER 9TH, 2017 ~ I typed John's sermon after he translated his handwriting for me, chatted on the phone with Jan, tried to finish my now overdue Waugh biography. And we had our favourite winter lunch; grilled cheese sandwiches and tomato soup.

St. George's Christmas Dinner tonight. Festive tables, turkey and stuffing, cranberries, friends and music. The Land of Plenty. For some. The best part was getting to hold our friend's new baby whose name is Quing. She's two months old. I pointed out that she has dimples and her mom was pleased as she didn't know the English word for those dear tiny dents at the corner of her wee mouth. (*"...but trailing clouds of glory do we come..."* from 'Intimations of Immortality', Wordsworth.)

SUNDAY, DECEMBER 10TH, 2017 ~ Advent Two, the Sunday for Peace.

Have set the table, made a tuna casserole, cooked some carrots for lunch tomorrow with guests from Toronto who are related to John.

Two crystalline poems from New Zealand emailed to me from Cherry this afternoon. She is a talented wordsmith. She's busy just now making sure the sheep get enough water and the roses too as the heat is insufferable.

Snowed here a bit last night.

Ready to put on housecoat and sit down with crossword.

MONDAY, DECEMBER 11TH, 2017 ~ *"These fragments have I stored against my ruin."* (T.S. Eliot, The Wasteland). I assume Eliot was thinking about life's small, touching scenarios to which he wanted to cling when he wrote this. Maybe that is why people keep journals. We want to hold onto small bits of beauty, like the two pots of white calendula I've put on the mantel for Christmas in Virginia's ancient blue and white urns.

Today, new friendships in JAH and her son who came for lunch. Since they live in Toronto it wasn't too far for them to visit. Good people, interesting, and we'd have enjoyed talking to them longer but snow threatened. We'll visit again.

Keeping the windows of our lives wide open is essential as we age so that new ideas can flow in.

It's a big, wide, wonderful world despite our human frailties. We need to dwell right inside the fray although having a porthole here and there from which to safely observe isn't a bad idea either.

A soft, calming snowfall. The street looks like Christmas, our small white lights shining in the darkness, waiting for the Advent of The Prince of Peace.

TUESDAY, DECEMBER 12TH, 2017 ~ Woke up to a silent blanket of wet snow. I shovelled it away once I got my music practice finished. The exercise and fresh air felt good.

Christmas cards arrive daily. I've wondered if there would soon be an end to that practice given the expense of stamps (a dollar plus each) and the ease of online well-wishing. The cards are all lined up on the walnut hutch, little tokens of friendships greeting us as we pass by. My grandparents used to hang their cards up with butcher's string across the sitting room ceiling where they blew in the drafts from the coal-fuelled furnace grate like a flock of colourful winter birds.

A warm and welcomed email this morning from our friend on the northern edge of Baffin Island.

John has a historic and happy connection to the Inuit community where he held many friendships including Davidee who died this past summer. One of his most enjoyable friendships was with the Povungnituk (now Povurnituk, after the re-namings) artist Joe Talirunili. It was Joe who did the famous carving called The Migration which I went to see when I was in my early twenties. It was at the Toronto-Dominion Centre in Toronto at the time. Never did I think I'd meet him. John took me to Povurnituk the summer we got married.

"Old Joe," as he was called, sat in his carving shed, soapstone dust covering his white hair and his face, a single light bulb dangling from the ceiling. He opened a tin box and handed me twenty dollars.

"For your trip," he said when he gave it to me. It would have been rude to refuse.

We told him that the Air Canada jet we had taken as far as Timmins, before getting on Austin Airways for the Arctic, had vinyl wall coverings printed with his famous images on it. He had no idea nor did he care. He wasn't concerned with the secular; he cared only for the things that don't have a monetary value. The choir from St. Matthew's Anglican Church used to go to his small house and sing to him when he could no longer go to them. He died in 1976, shortly after we were there. He had been born in 1899, the same year as John's father. Old Joe was a man of peace.

Winter is here. There is a bright sun and a strong wind. This morning we bought a calendar for the coming year and we picked up a white Cyclamen on the way home for the dining room table. I've put it in the blue and white soup tureen. Blue and white china suits flowers of all colours. I'd never serve soup in that tureen. It's too fragile. But for potted flowers it's *"just the ticket"* as my mom would say.

A friend is researching an aspect of Hamilton history and was here today to interview John. The researcher bemoans the lack of primary archival material (letters, notes, old programs). His frustration showcases the importance of keeping good journals, letters, small related items. John was able to add information and hard-copy material to his data base.

This afternoon I filled out the new calendar for 2018; birthdays, meetings, dentist appointments. One more thing off my list.

Left-over Tuna Casserole tonight with a scoop of sour cream and the remainder of the Tabouleh. Easy-peasy.

WEDNESDAY, DECEMBER 13TH, 2017 ~ *"The rosy face of the British immigrant is regarded as no beauty here. The Canadian women, like their neighbours the Americans, have small regular features but are mostly pale, or their faces are only slightly suffused with a faint flush. During the season of youth this delicate tinting is very beautiful, but a few years deprive them of it, and leave a sickly, sallow pallor in its place. The loss of their teeth, too, is a great drawback to their personal charms..."*. (Moodie, 1989, pg 61.)'

Bitterly cold. I put the hood back onto my down jacket, added a scarf, the knitted hat a woman made for me in Povurnituk years ago, mittens, an extra down vest, boots. I set off at 10:00 for an icy walk, a one-woman Polar expedition. The cold bit into my sinuses, attached itself to my back molars. I came home after two blocks. In spite of the biting cold I still didn't get the rosy cheeks for which I have always longed. But according to Susanna Moodie's observancy above there is scant hope for Canadian womanhood anyway.

I think that Baby Boomers feel guilty about everything. We live with so many rules and regulations about our bodies, as if we are in complete charge of our

shelf-lives. To a degree we are, but DNA and nature will do its own deciding. Should I have pushed myself harder and determined to get to the bottom of the hill despite the severe cold? I read a short article in the newspaper today at breakfast saying that a short walk is better than no walk and that a dish of berries every morning is a good thing. The berries and the walks are at least one thing I get right. I think we're too used to being in control. Now's the time of life to chillax (a new word comprised of both chill and relax) and to laugh our socks off like RMB and MA and I do. Happiness is vital to health, surely?

Lugged the fake but realistic Christmas tree out and up from the basement. I left the lights on last year so all I had to do was to plug them in. I can bring up the decorations later. This involved pulling an armchair into the back room to make place for the tree in the front. Realized this task was more difficult this year, the tree heavier, the chair more cumbersome. I have always been strong and would love to have stayed that way. I used to push the piano with my hands, my knees as leverage, across the room in our other house, and never feel a twinge. And now? Twinge City.

Charlotte was here this evening. We talked about five words that begin with the letter C. And then

we had some fun, including making play dough hospital beds for the ancient Fisher Price people as her patients. She made a play dough stethoscope out of a lump which she tucked under her chin and bent over the Fisher Price woman to see if that little plastic person had a strong *"heart beep."*

Glad of a warm cosy bed. Must be so awful if not.

THURSDAY, DECEMBER 14TH, 2017 ~ The temperature in The Spectator today says it's seven degrees Celsius below zero.

A few Christmas things to pick up; some items from Denninger's. Maybe one of their tourtieres.

May Sarton said in the December of her seventieth year *"I feel as if I have been climbing the Christmas mountain for weeks..."* (Sarton, 1984, 211.)

The Christmas mountain is the one thing I trust to bring hope to a complex, confounding world. It's not the climb, but the summit that matters, although without the climb we'll never attain the top.

And this morning I'm off to practice more music for Nine Lessons And Carols. A dear high school friend, LGE, emailed yesterday to comment on what I had mistakenly written on her Christmas card. I had referred to the Service of "Wine Lessons And Carols".

Back home again and never did get to Denninger's. Tomorrow. Made an enlargement of the music for Of The Father's Love Begotten and left the original that belongs in my music binder at the copy-shop. Called them and asked them not to throw it out. Too bothersome to go back to get it now. I'll do it tomorrow. After Denninger's.

We know someone who has no electricity so no warmth, no stovetop, no lights. When I came home and turned the furnace up the thought of it preyed on me. It's freezing out there tonight.

FRIDAY, DECEMBER 15TH, 2017 ~ Who said they could go ahead and change The Globe And Mail (font/shape/size/format) without my consent? The hard-copy Globe, I can see, is on its way to extinction due to online readership. Should I tell the Editor that I like my newspaper at the table with my tea and toast? The Globe has been a constant throughout my life. My mom and dad took The Globe when I was a kid.

A great email this morning from New Zealand, from C.H. We are becoming fast friends, the two of us. She is another of John's family members who have disseminated themselves over Mother Earth. She might not mind me using her real name which

is the lyrical Cherry Hill. I told her that my favourite walk at the Botanical Gardens here is at a place called Cherry Hill Gate.

A beautiful winter's day, the kind that Christmas card illustrators love; soft snow spinning slowly and all that sort of alliteration. It created in me a lovely mood when we were at Denninger's this morning buying treats for our adult progeny and their spouses. I love that store in any season but it's exciting at Christmastime with all the European food on the shelves. I've packed up three bags of small items (Baxter's Squash soup, German Egg Noodles, Cheese biscuits, Typhoo Tea, tins of British Ambrosia), for them, including the winner which is Walker's shortbreads packed in tins modelled on British taxi cabs.

Speaking of food, Paul C's Christmas cake is just the thing! This one is a couple of years old he says. He has doused it liberally with brandy more than once. I had some before I went to bed the other night and dreamed that I was in an opium den and couldn't get out. Huge, brilliantly coloured tilapia fish, much bigger than me, were guarding the doors. It was so awful that it woke me. I phoned Paul to tell him how potent his cake is. He said "Don't eat that cake before bed."

I've been re-reading some of this journal and see

that I've made myself look like A Beacon Of Light And Goodness. Not so. I can be an Old Cranky Clogs when I'm up for it.

That's the trouble with journals. They make the writer sound perfect, unless you happened to have been the Late Evelyn Waugh. His biographer ploughed through Waugh's personal papers, letters, journals. You can sense its truth. We all of us have feet of clay. I'll finish reading it tonight.

What a gorgeous winter's day this has been with light snow and so graceful in the way in which it came down. Reminds me of the winters of my childhood.

SATURDAY, DECEMBER 16TH, 2017 ~ Good news. H has passed the National Boards exam. Nobody deserves it more.

The winter world has started to melt and the air smells like March today.

Horrific traffic. Too many people with last minute chores.

Have ripped out five crosswords from the Saturday papers. They'll amuse me in the evenings when the tv presenters are droning on. The Globe Saturday crossword looks to be back to normal this week. More interesting again.

An endearing conversation with Charlotte tonight regarding the Doulton Easter Rabbits she espied in the hutch.

C: ***Grandma could we look at them?***

Me: ***Sure. But we have to be careful with them.***

C: ***Can we put them on the sofa and make them talk?***

Me: ***Sure. But we can't let them bump into each other or they'll break. Granddad bought them for our Easter table and he'd be sad about that.***

C: ***Did he pay Twenty-Forty for them?***

Me: ***Yes, I think he did.***

(Twenty-forty is her favourite number.)

She especially liked the smallest one, a rabbity woman in a blue dress and an apron with a cake in her paws. So she continued her play making the ornaments talk.

C: (speaking as the rabbit with the cake in her paws to the Mother Rabbit in the white mob cap): ***Look Mommy Rabbit! I made you a strawberry cake for your birthday."***

This chatter went on for a time. Then: ***Grandma, do you think I could borrow this little rabbit with the cake? I could take her home for a while.***

Me: ***I think we should leave her here with the other***

rabbits. We can play with it when you come to our house. But when you are a very big girl I could give it to you.

C: (running to stretch herself upwards beside the door frame) ***But I am very big! Look at how big I am! Grandma I'm four!***

SUNDAY, DECEMBER 17TH, 2017 ~ All of my favourite readings today at Nine Lessons And Carols, especially the one from the Gospel of John (1: verse 5, AKJV); ***"And the light shineth in darkness…"*** **I played the service this morning but just prior to the evening service the D string snapped. I sat with John and enjoyed listening instead.**

Jan has sent me an article from The New York Times. She knows that I'm interested in how others see us as we age; for example, the forty-five-ish woman who insisted in vain that she carry my potted plant from Holland Park nursery to the car for me last summer. She acted as if it was a fully grown oak tree that would crumple me under its burden. I'm hefty enough. She shouldn't have worried but she saw my white hair and made an assumption of weakness. She meant well. In the end it's not my pride that counts but her goodness at offering.

My first published article years ago was about taking John's dad to see doctors, banks, etc. when he was ninety and blind. I was stunned at how dismissive people were of his ability. The woman at the bank directed all the questions to me until I told her that it was his money not mine and that she should be asking him. We went to order flowers for his sick friend. The woman asked me "What does he have in mind?" I sassed her back with "It's his mind. Ask him."

And now Jan's New York Times article about eighty-two year old Nancy Root who says she remembered the very moment when she knew she had "vanished" to the people around her. Root had a stellar career, a daughter, a successful marriage, friends, a full and happy life. She wonders if people shrink from direct contact with her now that she's elderly and in a wheelchair because she brings out their fear about their own futures. The writer of that article, Frank Bruni, says that others edit the aging or disabled "out of the frame."

World-wide seasonal music on CBC Radio 2 today; Denmark, Austria, Germany, Finland, Estonia, Sweden, Canada (Montreal.) Peaceful and uplifting.

RMB and I were remembering how we played CLUE every Christmas at her parent's house at the kitchen table when we were kids. Oh the laughs we had with Colonel Mustard, Miss Scarlett and Professor Plum!

Maybe that's why I love the characters in Agatha Christie's novels.

MONDAY, DECEMBER 18TH, 2017 ~ Strange how things pile up all at once. Broken D string last night, this morning a flat tire, email still not working, my new vacuum cleaner semi-functioning.

"All of them First World problems," Jan declares.

I love getting mail. Someday there will be no door-to-door mail delivery as has already happened in many spots. But we still have the mailperson come and stuff things into the box under the porch light.

Today's mailbox treasures include the William Dam Seed catalogue, the place about which I wrote in The Hamilton Literary Arts magazine. The Dam Seed Catalogue is full of ravishing plants; spiky Delphiniums in blue and purple, Flowering Kale and ditto for Cabbage, a rainbow of Zinnias, Four O'Clocks, Foxgloves, Lupins, Hollyhocks.

Hollyhocks are the stuff of my youth. Jan and I used to remove the blooms, turn them upside down and hold ballroom dances with the twirling ladies in their skirts of pink, maroon, white. At our Sunning

Hill Avenue house we had a garden dedicated to them. I used to put the garden chair in the middle of them and read. They were so tall that I was well hidden. *("Have you seen mom?")*

The London Review was also in the mail so a lucky day if you forget flat tire, the water in the tire-well the automobile club man found, the broken D string, the broken vacuum.

A romantic message in The Personals in the LRB. Two people on the London Underground have been eyeing one another atop their copies of the LRB during their daily commute. He wants to know who she is and will she come forth when she sees his ad and chat instead of all this to-ing and fro-ing?

Also, this issue includes an article about letters from The Bastille. And I do love old letters.

Years ago I found a small cache of post-war letters from John's Aunt Gertie that were sent to their family home on Bayle Street (now Rue Baille after the Francophonization of street names) in Montreal. One of them was from a beau. She hadn't answered the door when he called. He wrote her a cryptic note; *"Your mother told me that you were washing your hair. That wasn't a good reason not to see me"*. Must take another look at the letters. See what else lurks in those tortured, scribbled, love lines.

TUESDAY, DECEMBER 19TH, 2017 ~ In 'The Book of Stillmeadow' (1948, reissue 1984, 59) Gladys Taber, the late American writer, wrote these Christmas words in 1948: *"We must do everything we can to defeat cruelty in our own country. I must think of these matters, and as we let the candlelight shine over new-fallen snow in our small spot of earth, I must remember the long centuries which have passed since this birth. I think of all the great and good men who have walked the earth, giving their strength and their lives for humanity. There have been enough of them to counter-balance the others...."*

Today we would add the peaceful contributions of women to that equation. How little politics and humanity has changed.

She closes her December chapter (pg 60) with *"I wish we could all say on Christmas night: "God rest you merry, Gentlemen, Let nothing you dismay."*

Never before have I noticed where that comma is. I have thought of *"merry"* as the adjective to describe the gentlemen. But what it says is *"God rest you merry"*, or in other words *"God keep you joyful"*.

Modern versions have put that comma in the wrong spot but the original form has it after *"merry"*.

A good thought to carry along with me as I am discouraged this evening. Husband reminds me that there is Divine Purpose. Am thankful for him and for that.

WEDNESDAY, DECEMBER 20TH, 2017 ~ Today was as Dull as Ditchwater; a grey sky, cold air, the car up at Honda getting things fixed. So that precludes my planned grocery shopping trip. The city will be busy tomorrow with the holiday rush. A snow storm predicted for Friday.

Spent this entire day doing nothing at all. As lazy as can be.

Reading Diana Athill's book of letters to her poet friend. A slow start but getting better. Some aspects of it too confessional for my taste; keep some things to yourself Diana.

Car fixed $$$ later. It's always something.

Winter

THURSDAY, DECEMBER 21ST, 2017 ~ Winter solstice. My dad said every December 21st "The days will begin to lengthen now."

Up early to get groceries done before the madding crowds. Success. Was in the store by 8:15 and out an hour later. And then to a neighbourhood coffee house with John and some tiny errands (i.e., gas in car as snow expected, bank, post office.) Such is the daily round.

The street where the shops are looks pretty; small white lights on the trees everywhere. Twice this past week we saw a wagon and a horse pulling people along the street, a man in a top hat at the reins.

In the coffee house the regular crowd; the man who tells us his fabulist stories, the fellow who asks after the friend we have in common, the server who is bouncy and friendly, the other server who knows to make my tea clear and weak in a mug and does it when he sees me walk in the door. It's as it should be; a homey and cosy spot.

MR popped in this snowy evening with a warm hug and some of her Christmas baking. We spent many wonderful Christmas Eves with M and E and their girls when our children were all small.

Wanted to keep awake tonight to see the crazy Bells of St. Trinian's movie on Vision tv. Love those

old black and white British films but was fighting sleep in no time.

I left the porch Christmas lights on all night as I wanted passers by to be cheered. I decided to keep the blind open in the bedroom so that we could watch the snow drift onto the little potted balsam tree and the fairy lights but I soon realized that the newspaper people who come at unearthly hours could look right in on us. It was bright, like trying to sleep in Piccadilly Circus. By the time I related this concern to the Mister he was deep into REM mode so I shut the blind and moved to the back bedroom where it's dark. So much for Romantic Idealism. He could sleep through A Major Anything.

FRIDAY, DECEMBER 22, 2017 ~ *"Snow had fallen, Snow on snow, snow on snow..."* That describes the scene when we looked out of our windows this morning.

Christina Rossetti wrote those words to In The Bleak Midwinter in 1872. I love it as much as I could ever love any Christmas music, both the tune and the words. It speaks beautifully to all those of us who are poor in pocket or poor in spirit; *"Yet what can I give him - Give him my heart."*

We ought to try to simplify our lives. Can't say I

want to live in Little House On The Prairie but we are overcomplicating most everything.

I spoke for a while on the phone yesterday to a close friend who has a strong Vietnamese Buddhist outlook. We need to get rid of the gadgets that rule us, she says. We need peace. Technology detracts us from the world around us. I'm sure she's right. I know we need some of it but I think it's another one of those false, misguided principles by which we have been convinced to live.

Shovelling this morning was calming. Snow brings people together. It's the one time in winter when I see the neighbours. We share light hearted banter and talk about how cold it is but I suspect that secretly there is something about it that we love. Seems to me it's Canadian to mock the snow but deep inside of us, snow is what we know and winter is who we are.

My concern at this time of year is that our little family from the U.S. gets here safely and back home again the following week and I wish for all travellers the same. And for that good reason I want the skies to empty themselves today and then take a breather.

SATURDAY, DECEMBER 23, 2017 ~ It was a beautiful day. Snow fell until 2:00 p.m. I shovelled twice. Have made scalloped potatoes, turnip casserole, prepped the beans, carrots, Brussel Sprouts. Hate to even record this as there are hungry people in our own city.

Today's fun came in the form of the newspaper's Christmas Crossword which is famous amongst crossword lovers from Charlottetown to Yellowknife. Sat for a few minutes with it but it's addictive and I had to force myself to get back into the kitchen and tie on an that apron. And all the time listened to gorgeous Christmas music on CFMX-FM.

A joy today was Phú's phone call from California with Christmas greetings. We spoke to Phán a few days ago. We love the week before Christmas when friends drop by with their good wishes. Who can say that there is enough of that in the world? And so they come. Tonight it was Nhơn and Hao and their Paul and Rebecca and later on Mục Sư Nguyễn and his wife. I spoke with Thảo yesterday. Nobody will ever know what this community means to us or how much respect and love we have for them. We shared a crucial time in world history. How thankful I am to them. They re-made me. I needed lessons about real life and they gently pulled me along with them, even when my lack of their language was a barrier.

We shared their sorrows, their joys and their new beginnings and they've shared our own.

An email from Mary in New Zealand. If Louise B. hadn't gone to all her meticulous research these great people would have remained unknown to us. The work those women do down there to help keep things going makes me question my own daily round. Doing the crossword and making the dinner pales beside baling hay and cutting grass and keeping the little lambs watered in the extreme heat. New Zealand men ought to be thankful in the extreme that they didn't marry me. ("Judy! Put down the book! Grab your shears! Get the four wheel drive gassed up!")

SUNDAY, DECEMBER 24TH, 2017 ~ Hayley, Isaac and the children here this afternoon and Jock and Ashley popped in with Lola, their smiling chihuahua who was wearing a red dress. Yes. True. The kids were thrilled. Lola shook with nervous glee. Don't blame her. That little dog has a perpetual smile on her tiny face.

Sunshine today. On the deck, a scene from a Beatrix Potter story unravelled in the form of a small black squirrel, his tail fluffed, his paws together.

Snowing all afternoon. Have shovelled tonight and won't think about it again until tomorrow.

The Collect in the Book of Common Prayer this morning, this: *"...put upon us the armour of light."* I can think of worse things to put on.

Christmas Eve. I cooked the ham to carve for tomorrow. John and I watched tv news. Phone chats and well-wishing with cousins Donna and Joanne with whom we shared every childhood Christmas. We spent those 1950's December 25th afternoons playing Old Maid, Snap, Monopoly, only stopping when it was time for feasting upon those little squares with cherries in them and pink icing that our moms used to make. We had crumpled up the Old Maid card so we'd all avoid picking it. And today how archaic and insulting the concept of the old maid seems. That notion and insult to women has thankfully been replaced by one of the many intelligentsia forms of womanhood; educated, independent, single professionals who often make society better in a myriad of ways.

MONDAY, DECEMBER 25TH, 2017 ~ Christmas Day, and a Redeemer. Sunshine spilling over blinding new-fallen snow.

John and I to Morning Prayer. Hot cider and biscuits afterwards.

We have a wooden box with Mother of Pearl inlay on the lid and a small silver plaque declaring that it was given to "Mrs. Quinn, December 25th, 1881" (John's maternal Great Grandmother who lived on Cathcart Street in Montreal.) So her lovely Christmas gift from her husband Edward Quinn sits on our bookshelves one-hundred and thirty-six years later. Inside, a treasure trove; old letters, programs, billet doux. The most fitting item I found in it for today is the Christmas Day Service bulletin for Matins and Holy Communion during World War One from the Church of St. James The Apostle in Montreal on St. Catherine Street. In it the famous Rev'd Alan P. Shatford commented that the war "has fallen heavily upon our poorer brethren. We will require much personal self-sacrifice in order to meet all the pressing claims upon us." Further, he wanted his "dear people" to do two things: to "seek the peace which passeth all understanding" and to make not a token contribution to a needy person but "to be responsible for a definite case during this coming winter."

In the midst of world terrors and the cruel Quebec winter he reminded his flock to take care of the poor.

A lengthy phone chat this afternoon with O.V. He will visit tomorrow.

A perfect Christmas dinner at Drew and Ely's with Charlotte and Lucia. Such good cooks they are; a coconut rice recipe from South America and other delights.

Ely's decorations for the girls made their place look like Santa's village. A lovely, quiet evening.

"I could get used to this civility" I thought to Self.

TUESDAY, DECEMBER 26TH, 2017 ~ Boxing Day ~ When I was small I thought that Boxing Day had something to do with people having ring-side seats for fights, as in *boxing.*

Got up early enough to do a myriad of cooking tasks.

O.V. came over this morning and we had a lengthy chat. He told us that on his first night here when he was eleven years old he laid in his bed and cried because it was so cold (it was May) compared to the heat in the refugee camp from which he had come. Then he added this bit of light; "but by winter I was out playing hockey with my new Canadian friends."

We talked briefly about the French Colonial period in Indochina and the French Priest, Father Alexandre de Rhodes, who Romanized the Chinese symbols into Roman script. It made it possible for outsiders to learn the language, ergo pushing Vietnam into the wider world re trade routes, circa 1651. A young man in Vietnam told me that they didn't resent their French Colonizers but recognized that they brought them into a wider world of agricultural possibilities, including coffee crops. At least that was his opinion. Others may feel quite differently and he was perhaps working for the government.

Wild and woolly here today with Hayley and Isaac and the kids and Jock and Ashley but fun to see them all and to spend time together. Jock as Entertainer did flashlight shadows which kept them amused for some time.

In spite of my belief in The Peace that was born at Christmas a part of me always ends up cranky by the time the work is piled on. My better self goes straight out the window. "What happened to that "armour of Light?" I ask myself. But I love it all and wouldn't want to forgo it. So I morph into an amalgam of cranky-happy; but a cranky-happy woman who is over-ridingly thankful.

WEDNESDAY, DECEMBER 27, 2017 ~ Seems that Mrs. Pepys and I have something in common after all these years. On December 27th,

1665 she was annoyed with Mr. Pepys (and he with her) because she wanted him to let her have a 'mayde' (maid). Samuel didn't want one as the bubonic plague was waving its death mask above the London fog and he thought a new maid might bring the disease into their house.. *"...by coach to London, there home to my wife, and angry about her desiring a mayde yet, before the plague is quite over."*

Poor Mrs. Pepys. Poor London. But good for Mr. Pepys for not inviting strangers in while the plague was having its way with the city.

Hayley's old school friend D. J. for tea here this morning. She still lights up the room with her stories, with her whole being.

John and Hayley to the coffee shop this afternoon while I napped. Had an overwhelming need to close my eyes. Slept for an hour. Children at the Botanic Gardens with the other grandparents to see the toy train.

On Boxing Day in 1941 Emily Carr's best friend Ira Dilworth of the CBC radio wrote this in his letter to her: *"Your heart and hand have done great things for Canada: they have felt deeply into the life of things and have created sanctuaries for bewildered men and women to rest in..."* (Morra, 2006, 80.) His comments were

important to her. The establishment didn't recognize her worth until it was too late for her to know it.

A bright, cold moon tonight hovering above the garden. Emily would have taken it all in.

THURSDAY, DECEMBER 28TH, 2017 ~ On this day in 1941 Emily Carr wrote back to Ira Dilworth (Morra, 2006, 81) and told him about having gone into what she called her *"dear woods."*

"Such vivid patches of unrivalled green moss that couldn't have throbbed one bit more green into its greenness..."

I love how she describes colour as *throbs.*

That word is connected to pulse, to her life blood, to the excitement of rich swirls of colour rushing through her veins.

A super afternoon with grandchildren Hamish and Edwina here. E was interested in every little thing in the house and wanted to know how we got things and who gave them to us and about my mom's antique candlesticks. She was able to point out the beehive pattern in them. She loved the old wooden box of letters and entreated me to find *"a mystery"* within them. Fortunately H found the missing part of his new Batman thingamajig. Made him happy.

I love that Charles Ritchie spent this very day, December 28th, in 1941 writing about his stay with the famous and peculiar Sitwells at their home in Weston, England. (Ritchie, 2008, 146.)

"...my favourite house – fire in the bedroom with a view of a piece of lawn with conifer-shaped shrubs. White frost on Christmas day. We sang carols in the family pew in the stone, stone cold of the little church... There is magic in the place..."

Shrimp Toast and celery soup for dinner. Perfection.

FRIDAY, DECEMBER 29TH, 2017 ~ The advert in the mail from The Mayo Clinic Health Letter tells me that John Glenn returned to space at age seventy-seven, that Frank Lloyd Wright was still working at age ninety-one, that Christopher Plummer performed at age eighty-eight and that the Mayo clinic itself was founded by the then seventy year old Dr. William Worrell Mayo. All this is meant to make me say *nil desperandum* to Self and to focus upon the wondrous things yet to be accomplished as I age. But mostly it's meant to persuade us to buy their monthly Health newsletter.

A busy, noisy afternoon with the children. Drew,

Jock and Ashley dropped in to say au revoir to Hayley, Isaac and children and to eat pizza.

Grandson H and his sweet round face asked me for scissors.

"Why?" I asked him.

"Because I want to cut something," was his reply.

I helped him cut a picture out of a tiger that he wanted but he thought I didn't do a proper job of it and was disappointed with me.

Tomorrow will seem too quiet. Always a let down after holidays as they drive off into their own lives. But that is how you raise kids, to be able to lead their own lives.

SATURDAY, DECEMBER 30TH, 2017 ~ This morning Hayley, Isaac and the children left for their long drive back home. We were glad when they phoned tonight to say "We're here!"

Still cold but more amenable for going outside for chores. Went out to the hardware store, the drug store. It was colder in our city than the North Pole one day this week, The Spectator reported. It was twenty-two degrees Celsius below zero.

I napped on the sofa with CFMX-Fm playing

beauteous music and woke up two hours later, bathed in both sunlight and the music.

After dinner I read aloud The Globe And Mail Obituaries to John. They are riveting, like a compressed novella about somebody's life.

Dark as can be outside at 6:04 p.m. as I write this. In spite of the solstice on the 21st the night still drops early, a heavy black curtain like a scrim at the theatre.

SUNDAY, DECEMBER 31ST, 2017 ~ New Year's Eve ~ We sat teary-eyed through the video that a friend sent us this morning about a charity event on the border between Cambodia and Vietnam with many beautiful children, most of them orphaned and several from families with a single, ill parent. We had lunch with N and her lovely Dad in Đà Nẵng. If I were younger I'd like to think I'd be over there helping her with this; not that she needs me. They have many youthful volunteers who speak the language. That is the shocking part about aging. You have to put some things out of your mind that you otherwise might have considered. But then I have to remember John Glenn, Christopher Plummer, *et al* (see entry of December 29th).

Morning Prayer. John to bed with a head cold. I

helped AB with the post-service lunch and taught Sunday School about finding lost items. Jesus used that reference so often; the Lost Coin, the Lost Sheep, the Lost Son. He knew his audience and drew His stories from the parts of society that they understood; fishermen, farmers, the poor, the wealthy, children, squabbling families, greed. And all of them pointed to how happy He is and we all are when we find our lost.

A stunning walk this afternoon to the bottom of the hill for thirty minutes. Poet Robert Frost was my partner on the way down, in the silent woods to the left of me. Not a sound; filigreed branches interwoven over the snow beneath.

On the frozen surface of the marsh a dozen boys were playing shinny hockey, just like in my childhood and just like a bucolic Rockwell painting. Dad used to flood the back yard for Brian's hockey when we were little. In fact this entire winter brings back memories of being seven, eight, nine years old with the squeak of hard-packed snow underfoot. I used to help Brian deliver his newspapers, The Galt Reporter, in this kind of squeaky snow after dinner when I was maybe eight. The nights were as black as pitch, the kitchen windows up and down Vine Street lit up in small vignettes of family life in our comfortable town.

My last walk of 2017 was perfection.

Chinese food from The Dragon Court for dinner. Happy New Year.

JANUARY 1ST, 2018 ~ New Year's Day ~ A walk to the bottom of the hill on this first morning of 2018. Not a soul in sight, neither beast nor fowl with the exception of two black squirrels who chased one another's tails through the woods. Minus thirteen Celsius so not as biting as last week.

Was thinking as I crunched along the snow how much I enjoyed reading Peter Rabbit's Christmas to Charlotte and hearing Edwina read the first page aloud to me. The tiny book was a birthday gift to John when he was eight years old and remains in perfect condition. I want our grandchildren to understand how lovely Peter Rabbit's world is. There is a hole in the trunk of a tree on the hill which I have shown them and have told them that Peter Rabbit lives in it. I suppose they'll soon catch me out in that trite little bit of make-believe.

Last night I read some Wordsworth. We do live in Dove Cottage after all, just as he did, albeit the differing size and romance of location. I can think of less civilized ways to spend New Year's Eve. John was

in bed early with his head cold and by the time he got up, feeling a bit more chipper, I was too tired to do much ringing in.

We had a quick drive downtown this afternoon with the express purpose of getting out of the house. A simple supper. You can only do so much with sausages and a can of green beans. I boiled two onions to help his cold. I had one too. It was delicious.

Tonight some tv and more Wordsworth and some unexpected wildlife.

At 9: 24 p.m. John called to me to come to the front window. A fresh snowfall and dancing down the street in front of the house were three beautiful deer, all Does, enjoying a good gallop. Girl's Night Out; a wonderful sight to start the New Year.

TUESDAY, JANUARY 2ND, 2018 ~ Downtown for a haircut. Bitterly cold. In spite of it, three sweet and tiny Juncos on the back porch late this afternoon. How do they keep warm? John threw them some bread but it fell into the deep snow and they'll never find it. They need seed. Must get some tomorrow.

Several emails today from members of the Barbara Pym Reading Circle who hope to continue meeting for the remainder of Jane Gardam's novels. The Librarian was helpful and has booked us a room for the evening in Spring for a discussion of The Man In The Wooden Hat. Read it years ago but forget everything about it.

RH, who lives in East Sussex, has sent me a magazine from Somerset called The Mendip Times. On page forty-two is an article about the plaque dedicated to his Grandmother, Lady Harris, Alice Seeley, and the story of her life along with coloured pictures of the unveiling. Am pleased to have this. Richard lives in Kipling Cottage in Rottingdean which was close to where Neil and Sylvia Pentland (dad's cousins) lived in Brighton. They drove Jan and me past Kipling Cottage when I was twenty-one and Jan was nineteen. Never then did I think that when was in my late sixties I'd become friends with the man who has since lived there.

Life spins in circles.

WEDNESDAY, JANUARY 3RD, 2017 ~ To the library to get the Wordsworth biography. May not read it all but leafing through it will be interesting.

Took myself down to the harbour to walk in the icy breeze for a refresher. Bitter wind. Invigorating. Loved it.

We phoned our niece Susan (John's niece by birth but mine by 'adoption') in Ottawa to wish her a Happy Birthday today. They are on their way to Florida tomorrow until the end of March.

And to E, this letter today. Being a long-distance Grandmother calls for some creativity. Now that she can read and since we had such a good snoop looking at the old box of letters to see if we could find a mystery, I sent her this slightly abridged rendition:

"Dear E, It was fun when you and H were here. We miss you. This morning I got out the old box of letters again. This is what I found. In the Christmas Day church service 1914 in Montreal the Minister asked everyone to be kind to poor people. And a small note to your Great-Great Aunt Gertrude from her music teacher saying that she couldn't teach her piano lesson that day. The last thing I found was a picture of a beautiful young woman sitting in an open window. She is wearing an old-fashioned dress with a white collar. I'll show it to you when you next come to Canada. I think we have found our mystery! Who was she? What was she thinking about? Why was she sitting in the window? Much love, Grandma Smith x"

Tried to read some of the Wordsworth book. It is riveting but so tortuous and sorrowful that I don't

think I can do it. Those poor Wordsworth children. No wonder William connected so to the landscape. Perhaps he connected to that as a replacement for his lost childhood home.

Two perfect things to close off today: the three Deer came back at 9 p.m. and stayed on the neighbour's lawn, then left. Tomorrow we'll buy them apples.

But sweetest of all was that Drew put the phone to Lucia's ear and I spoke to her and he told me that she smiled.

THURSDAY, JANUARY 4TH, 2018 ~ My paternal grandmother's photograph sits on the table near my reading chair. She looks about twenty-three, has already immigrated to Canada from London, has met and married my granddad and has given birth to her two sons. My aunt was born after they returned to Canada. Her wavy hair is pulled back into a chignon at the nape of her neck, a style she wore until she died at age eighty-three in 1975, the year before I met and married John.

I was as close to her as any grandchild could be to her grandmother. I think of her every day. Her name was Catherine Ada Gatehouse, then Pollard after marrying my Granddad who was himself an immigrant (Fenny Stratford, Buckinghamshire.) They returned to England when my dad was three months old and didn't come back to Canada until Dad was eleven. Until we moved away when I was ten we lived two doors from them and spent a part of every day with them. Brian and mom lived with them during the War for the five years when Dad was overseas.

This past summer I happened to see in the LRB the cover of a new book of the edited letters of Augustus John's beleaguered wife, Ida (nee Nettleship) John. The photo of Ida on the cover of the book and the photo of my grandmother are remarkably similar and I knew I had to own the book. I gobbled up every page of the letters of this woman who was coerced into living in a menage a trois to both please her husband, (British portrait artist), and to have household help with her numerous pregnancies, the resultant babies, her overwhelming workload, loneliness for Augustus's attentions, money shortages, housing woes. In one instance her husband painted his mistress Dorelia and Ida side by side in the same portrait but eventually he painted Ida out of it. It pained me to read the distress that caused Ida. Easy to declare her as a fool but if you had no money, nothing, what would you do? My grandmother and Ida had the same bowed lips, the same hair, the same forehead, the same face shape, the same nose, the same slightly overwhelmed, homesick visage. So now when I look at Grandma's photo I'm happy that she wasn't married to Augustus John but to my dear, fun Granddad who fastened his black tin lunch bucket onto the handlebars, clamped his trouser leg with a bicycle clip every morning and rode off to his factory job, whistling. (Rebecca John and Michael Holroyd, 2017.)

A wonderful short but brisk walk at the harbour this morning. The wind bit into my face and blew snow across the ice. It lets me know I'm alive. It energizes me.

Should add this so future generations will know that I did do the odd bit of housework. Spent fifteen minutes after lunch with a toothbrush and Vim getting the kitchen sink to shine. Have put this item in here to make Self Look Good.

Hayley and children have a Snow Day in Virginia schools today as they have a light dusting on their deck.

K-and-L-next-door sent us a generous share of their ham and so tonight we dined as if it were Sunday with the ham, potatoes, creamed corn and carrots. K-and-L are kind to us in many ways. They call us "The John and Judy Show" for reasons unbeknownst to us.

John bought apples home from the grocery store for the deer. The three of them came at 10 p.m. We knelt on the sofa and looked down at them and they were three feet away from us. Am brave when there is plate glass between myself and Mother Nature. It was thrilling but the mother deer ate four of the six apples and didn't share with her children which upset me no end. In fact, she was batting one of them on the head to keep her away from the apple. I'll check in the morning to see if the other two apples are gone.

I can see now why Sir David Attenborough loves his job.

FRIDAY, JANUARY 5TH, 2018 ~ There is a picture in The Spectator this morning of our three deer. I'll mail the picture to H. He loves animals.

What better thing to do in seventeen degrees below zero than to root again through John's Great-Grandmother's box of papers? It is full of things from John's mother's family and her sister's letters. Among this morning's discoveries:

1. a letter to Gertrude dated May 7th, 1918 from a fellow in "C Company, 3rd Divisonal Wing, Canadian Forces. He tells her that he hopes her friend has recovered from the gas poisoning as the effects last for

six months. He has been stationed in France, ergo has missed the births of his baby nieces and nephews but when he gets back to Canada he will "sing to them in my Basso Profundo voice". The French village where he lives has a church that "looks as if it was built in the time of Noah" with rabbits leaping everywhere on this land that belonged to a Count. They are not allowed to kill the rabbits for "a little extra meat" although the French themselves "keep a few tame rabbits not for pets but for pot pies on special occasions."

His small comments paint a vivid picture of the harshness of wartime; missing out on the births of family members back home, hunger, the effects on the health of young men, his hopes and desires. In the midst or terrors he was dreaming about cradling the newborns, singing to them.

Also in the box I found: several ancient coupons for Magic Baking Powder (war rationing), a scribbled, unsent note written in Gertrude's penmanship saying that they had been "to Toronto by motor car," and a white calling card with the name Miss Laura Huyler engraved on it, and a dental bill from March 15th 1917 for five dollars from Dr. F. Chris Nicol at 883 Ste Catherine Street.

This one startled me, from the Protestant Board

Of School Commissioners, Berthelet Street School in Montreal, 1908, declaring that "Children suffering from loathsome or infectious disease, or living in houses or tenements where infectious disease prevails, must, under the requirements of the law, be kept at home by their parents..."

The world still had another twenty years to go before Alexander Fleming would discover penicillin so that regulation made sense for the time frame.

On other fronts, the books I ordered from Amazon came. When the delightful twelve year old Annie returns to China in March she will take along Anne of Green Gables and Little House On The Prairie. She has learned to speak and read English well in these short months and is learning French. She loves her friends here but I'm sure that her grandparents are waiting for her return to her home across the waves.

Outside for only twenty minutes today. It involved running from car to drugstore and back to dodge the icicle-laden wind. This is cold, the kind we haven't had for years. I'd forgotten what it felt like to have hands that were so cold they ached.

Our feet used to be frozen numb as Jan and I stumped through knee high snow in the ditch along the Highway in Guelph on our way to SS #1, that wicked little scholar-killer of a two-room schoolhouse, she in grade three, me in grade six. Brian was already at The Ontario Agricultural College by that time so he was spared the horrors of that Dickensian outpost.

Our feet took ages to regain their warmth. Jan's class-room job was to clean up the mess if a child was sick. My elderly teacher regularly beat children across their heads with her meaty hands. She never touched me but by noon every day I faked illness so I could go home. Fortunately that torture lasted only one year until we moved to a lovely town on Lake Ontario where we lived amid bucolic acres of grass and trees, a swing and a small bridge that crossed over a stream.

Memories like the one of that awful school remind me of the powerlessness of childhood. Parents didn't complain in those days. Teachers, doctors, dentists were imbued with a sort of majesty. In the Canadian class system, which we pretend we've never had, they were at the top of the heap.

After Heartbeat was over tonight we dashed to the window to catch the deer for their 10 p.m. visit but they had arrived early and were just leaving K-and-L's front lawn to head back down the hill.

SATURDAY, JANUARY 6TH, 2018 ~ Ontario has temps today between thirty-eight and forty below zero with the Wind Chill factor added in.

I see that the apples in the front garden have been tossed like soccer balls by the deer. John says they were too frozen to eat. Hate to think of the deer alone and cold, hungry and afraid in the dark woods. I'm transferring my own fears to them.

E turned six years old today. Her small house party with three friends and her brother was a happy success. They made Fairy Houses. And when Jock married Ashley we got another Epiphany Girl so we have two happy birthday wishes today.

Today I stayed in the house and read a few articles from The Toronto Star, The Globe And Mail, The Spectator, The Post and did two crosswords. It was wonderful. It was a tea-drinking day. Heaven.

We put out more apples tonight, this time Green Delicious. But alas. Nada. Nil. Not a deer in sight. Except then who/what ate the apples? Only one left.

SUNDAY, JANUARY 7TH, 2018 ~ Every Sunday at the close of Service we sing God Be in My Head from the Sarum Primer (Book Of Common Praise,

567). It was written in 1558. I must train myself to focus on those incredible, poetic ideas every day.

A quiet afternoon. I made cauliflower/ham/potato soup which we had for dinner. Lots left for tomorrow. If I have a favourite food in this world it's called "leftovers."

Elizabeth Gray Vining was an American. In her journal, (Vining, 1978, 83), she wrote this small tense phrase in January, 1978: "When I think of what we are doing in Vietnam…".

That harsh legacy must have shaken her Quaker sensibilities to the core. I like that woman and wish she was alive so I could contact her.

A crossword and some CFMX music tonight.

The deer came early and we almost missed them. I happened to walk into the darkened living room after dinner and noticed six pert ears sticking up above the sill. And then they bounced over to K-and-L-next-door. We hadn't had the chance to put out their apples. And before we went to bed I went to pull the blind down in the front room and they were there again. Wonder if they stayed, like lawn ornaments, all night?

We saw three episodes of Victoria on Masterpiece Theatre last night. I was taken with Prince Albert and his strong support for The Anti-Slavery Society which is dear to my heart, re Sir John and Lady Harris.

JANUARY 8TH, 2018 ~ Took self over to Burlington this morning in this mucky, spewing weather to get cello restrung. Decided to replace all four strings and the fellow did it right there for me so I didn't have to return. Forced Self to take Highway 403 home as I have developed an irrational loathing of that Highway, but maybe it is *rational,* considering the backups at rush hour and the number of accidents. Not counting the messy, blinding spray from the trucks it wasn't bad.

I emailed The Canadian War Museum in Ottawa this past weekend to ask about a painting that John and I had seen there a few years ago when some items from The Mountain Fund To Help The Boat People were featured in the Peace Exhibit.

Had a full response this morning. The painting I asked after is titled The Pink Frock. It stood out in my mind until this day because of its shock value. Without words it tells the full story of the heartbreak and loneliness of war.

The story is this. The war artist Harold Beament (Royal Canadian Navy) was on a Sunday morning walking along a street that had suffered a severe bombing raid the previous night in London, England. The rooming houses had been blasted open and gaping, the front walls gone.

And in the artist's words, which were provided to me by the Canadian War Museum, this; *"On the first floor, in what had been a tiny bedroom the one thing that moved idly in the gentle breeze was a pink dress swinging on a hanger. It almost seemed to do a sad little dance of mourning for its owner – now dead. I found myself reflecting on the reaction that would arise in the feelings of a young soldier on shore leave after a lengthy tour of duty at sea, bursting with love and high hopes for his reunion with his sweetheart – the girl who owned the 'pink frock' - and now this."* (This information came from a 1983 letter from the artist to a Joan Murray.)

The artist captured on canvas exactly that; the bombed out shell of the house with the pink dress floating on the hanger on the top floor. The only other thing in the room is a white iron bedstead. You can find it online at Canadian Art In The Twentieth Century and then search a bit.

When I think of the huge story behind that dress and how innocent young people on every side of every conflict get sucked up into history...

I shovelled twice today and put out some sliced apples and carrots for our night visitors.

TUESDAY, JANUARY 9TH, 2018 ~ I see that last night's carrots and the apples are gone.

When O.V. visited us at Christmas he brought with him a beautiful orchid (*Lan Phương.*) Vietnamese women are often named after flowers as was the little girl to whom my year's worth of words are dedicated. I counted nineteen blooms today and the four buds. It lives on in its purple and white glory in the back room. I'm surprised at its health, considering that I'm not a star with house plants. He also brought us a Christmas cactus which I keep in a green pot in the kitchen window. We'll see how that does.

Plants do warm up the room, especially when they were given by a friend. The two white calendula on the mantelpiece I have let wither beyond salvation. They've found their way to the recycling bin. The white cyclamen remains alive and *in situ* on the dining table.

When the snow is fresh, white and sparkling winter is at its best. When, like right now, the snow turns into filthy piles of soot at the roadside and the sky is grey and overhung with damp, winter is at its worst.

John to ESL and Vestry meeting after dinner. I stayed home with the intent to read but it didn't happen because I spent every twenty minutes jumping up to see if the deer had arrived at the front window. All else is on the backburner while we indulge our nightly thrill. It's like a daily re-run of Marlin Perkins' Wild Kingdom. The deer arrived at about 9:45 to find their apples halved and their carrots in generous-sized chunks at the foot of the steps. Seems that only the mother is allowed to eat. I saw her bat the little one on the head when he/she tried to get a bite of apple the other night. Lynn B. wonders if she's nursing. I wonder if she's pregnant. Great-Niece Devon thinks she may be trying to teach her little ones to forage on their own. Could be any of the three.

This a wonderful thrill on winter evenings. It's the free things...

WEDNESDAY, JANUARY 10TH, 2018 ~ More circles. John delighted to get a joint-email from two women with whom he worked during his sojourn at Queen's Park in Toronto forty years ago. The two had been visiting one another and were talking about old times and googled him to see if he was "still around," as they put it. We have emailed them his thanks and an invitation to drop over for lunch. So, the circles continue.

The day was a grey one. Unspecified mist coming down; not slush, not rain, not snow but the off-putting wetness that mid-Winter drips. I'm calling this 'mid-Winter' but is it? Please say "Yes."

Bought a bouquet of orange tulips this morning and have put them in the clay jug on the mantelpiece. They're just the thing. The perfect antidote for this dull damp.

Jan and Rob arrived. They've suggested that the four of us go to Niagara Falls tomorrow to see the ice formations. Brilliant. Would never have thought of it in a million years but those two think of everything.

We finished the day with an Indian dinner at Shenai and later with Rob shocking the stars out of us coming out of the bedroom dressed in his Santa suit which is so good he could be playing that role at Macy's.

We all four sat in the dark waiting for Santa's deer to come for their apples and carrots. But a no-show. They probably saw Rob through the window in the red suit.

THURSDAY, JANUARY 11TH, 2018 ~ *"Elizabeth came to see me in the morning and brought me a cyclamen."* (Ritchie, 2008, 149).

Charles Ritchie wrote the above note on this very day, January 11th, 1942. I was glad to read that

Anglo-Irish novelist Elizabeth Bowen bought him a cyclamen like ours. Am glad she can't see what unsufferable damage I did to our own plant. Our cyclamen looked dandy until today. Shrivelled and drooping. Have reminded Self that watering is essential so must remember to give it.

A perfect day with Jan and Rob in Niagara Falls. The main thoroughfare is the tackiest streetscape in North America; Madame Tussaud's, The House of Horrors, Fortune tellers, cheap motels, but the power and the beauty of the Falls remains and the rushing of those frightening rapids with drifting chunks of ice are as startling now as they were the first time I saw them.

A stop in Niagara-On-The-Lake for a late lunch. It was like Spring. The snow melted, the temperature rose to several degrees C above zero. People coatless, chatting with the passers-by on the doorsteps of their shops, some riding bicycles, nobody hurrying.

And then the weather alert came on to say that there would be a "flash freeze" on the highway so Jan and Rob headed for home at 6 p.m.

Last night's dinner for the deer is still on the driveway if they want it.

It's warmer now and maybe they had a better day for foraging.

FRIDAY, JANUARY 12TH, 2018 ~ Samuel Pepys, on January 12, 1665, stated something to the effect that his wife had been working like a horse all day sewing huge hangings for their bedroom, which I assume were the curtains they used to draw around the bed to keep the warmth in.

A few other of his more salty writings have come to my attention this past week. Had I been Mrs. Pepys I might have told Mr. Pepys to make his own hangings and his own supper.

An iota of the melting snow remained this morning but I learned something about the bread that John threw out for the birds on January 2nd. The bread is still there, a soggy mess splayed across the wooden boards of the porch. What ingredient do you suppose is in that bread that made it last for ten days through a deep freeze, eight inches of snow, buckets of rain?

Started reading The Art of Rivalry today in hopes of getting to The Art Gallery book club later in the month.

Snowed this afternoon. Not much, just a dusting but the weatherman says it heralds more cold to come.

SATURDAY, JANUARY 13TH, 2018 ~ Tempted to say when I cleaned off the car this morning that I'd had enough of winter, but I don't want to get into that negative frame of mind. I reminded Self that I am a weatherproof Canadian as I shivered and scraped. But really, the mess, the ice that needed chipping off the windshield, off the front steps, the putting on of snow boots, parka, mittens.

Then the sun came out and the world looked brilliant.

A cosy morning with a steaming cup of tea at the women's meeting studying the wisdom that is the book of James. It provides a strong reminder to act, to be not only a hearer but a do-er.

Charlotte with us this afternoon and a pizza party for dinner. She worked on her new workbook from Aunt Hayley and traced alphabet letters for a long while. Bless you Aunt Hayley. Then we switched to play dough and made a series of hospital beds in which the plastic Fisher Price people were ill, complete with sneezing sound effects from Charlotte. They were so ill in fact that the animal finger puppets were sent in to be their doctors. When the elephant, the tiger and the monkey puppets succumbed there was no choice other than to appoint Charlotte and Self as Joint Chiefs of Medicine.

The crossword, my worn old housecoat, and Escape To The Country, the British Real Estate show, beckons.

SUNDAY, JANUARY 14TH, 2018 ~ Bright sun. John preached this morning on Ephesians Two which features God's Grace as the agency for change. His sermons are more like Homilies; short and to the point. Depending where one sits on the Theological spectrum this can be seen as either a good thing or not. It is his idea that people want the main event. "What's this all about?" people ask, ergo are entitled to the most expedient, well-explained route. Every sermon model is a good one if it works.

John saddened, reflective, after a call last night from Montreal to say that his cousin has died. They spent many happy hours together in their young summers in the Lower Laurentians.

In the online obituary messages in The Montreal Gazette someone has commented that the *"sweet notes"* of Ross's saxophone will be missed.

The trouble with dying is that it renders people inaccessible. Our future questions to them go unanswered. Messages that we meant to pass along go unsent. Words of encouragement go unspoken. Must get things right while we have the chance.

K-and-L-next-door say that the deer are back so apples out tonight, quartered.

MONDAY, JANUARY 15TH, 2018 ~ My orchid is still blooming; twenty-one blooms today and a bud. I think of little Lan Phương when it greets me in the morning. I promise never to forget her place in her family's, and in our own, wider story. Lan Phương; 'Beautiful Orchard'. A friend from Vietnam brought us this orchid at Christmas. I didn't tell him that it meant more to me than he assumed.

Hoof prints on the lawn and the apples gone save for one small slice. I checked for them at 10:45 last night and thought "Well then, come whenever you want to but I'm off to bed."

Made a casserole of hamburger, potatoes, onion. It's a sort of cheesy 1950's recipe. Winter comfort food.

Making decent headway reading new book, The Art Of Rivalry. Got through the section on Francis Bacon and Lucien Freud. Almost done with Degas and Manet. I'll never remember who said what to whom and when but am marking the book per usual. I am the Queen of Marginalia.

And because life is full of coincidences, The LRB arrived today with a huge article about Degas including a photo of the portrait that I have just been reading about that caused him enormous stress. The painting is called The Bellelli Family. It's gorgeous. I can't understand whey the public overlooked it. The blue is stunning.

I've booked tickets for the 2Cellos concert in April with MH. The tickets were already on my computer by the time I got off the phone.

Just before bedtime (our's, not their's) Jock and Ashley and their little dog Lola popped in. She wiggled out of her blanket as she hasn't much fur to keep her warm and ran about the house as if she owns it. She's a dear little thing.

Apple slices and leftover corn niblets out for the deer.

TUESDAY, JANUARY 16TH, 2018 ~ An email full of joyful thinking from LM this morning that provided a *"best of all possible worlds"* moment to start the day. (That great quote courtesy of Gottfried Leibniz, the founder of Optimism. The quote found its way into Voltaire's novel Candide, published in 1759. Must re-read.) The contents of LM's email will remain private but it was energizing. She is originally from an African country and she would know why I say that. What I really mean by declaring it is that it follows through with the spirit and the title of this Journal; The More The

Merrier. What would we do without one another in this whole wide world? She brought along the riches of her background which she shares with a heart wide-open. She has the richest laughter in Canada. She brought the sunshine in her suitcase with her.

RMB and a steaming bowl of Phở Gà on a freezing cold day are one of life's best combinations. We remarked that current affairs seem dire to both of us. But if I were to draw a picture frame around the table where we sat you would see would this; RMB, me across from her, two bowls of hot delicious soup, light pouring in from the window. That's it. That's all you'd see if that scenario were to be framed and no contaminates let in. So maybe what we should focus on are the small vignettes in life that showcase the things which can't be improved. All else is beyond our control.

Came home from our soup and walked to the bridge and shovelled a bit. Snow was light, fluffy; the day mild, calm.

Deer's food is on the driveway. K-and-L-next-door say that they came at midnight last night. The two babies slept on their lawn as the doe fed. Endearing. Pardon pun.

John to volunteer with English Second Language conversation group. Me with my book.

WEDNESDAY, JANUARY 17TH, 2018 ~ Freezing but sunshine. A trip out for some groceries this morning. A catalogue arrived with bathing suits in it. Are you kidding me?

Our smallest member spent the afternoon at the children's hospital with her mom and dad making waves in Medical Science. Won't talk about it in here but truly, she did make waves. This was all due to the determined efforts of her dedicated mom and dad to get the best for her. She came here later and was up on her feet and cruising. This was new for us to observe as we haven't gone near her since after Christmas when John was sick. Our precious little girl is on her way.

THURSDAY, JANUARY 18TH, 2018 ~ Dinner here tonight with ER and MR. As always, good conversation in this old, sturdy friendship. MR reading a bio of Wordsworth and loving it. ER planning their week in New York. We ate by candlelight and I plugged in the tiny white lights on the trees on the porch. Winter needs these kind of extras, or as they say in Denmark "hygge"; cosy, charming, special. Our evening together provided another opportunity for my new picture framing theory. (See entry of January 16th.)

Some tv news and a few pages of my book before bed. Have finished reading about the relationships between Manet and Degas, Matisse and Picasso, Lucien Freud and Francis Bacon and now into the last part of the book re Willem de Kooning and Jackson Pollock. Tension-filled friendships; tension and competition. Seems that love/hate, honesty/dishonesty were all of a heap with those guys.

FRIDAY, JANUARY 19TH, 2018 ~ Wonderful visit here this morning with friends bearing gifts of pistachio-filled Gaz from Isfahan and a disc of Saffron that will turn my rice into the softest shade of yellow. Everyone is ok. The uproar on the news has died down for now at least. A complicated world. We feel rich in people.

Why don't Household Items Work? An accident with my beauteous, lime green, enamel, whistling kettle this morning. Am not naming the perp. So this afternoon to buy a new kettle, a new element and a bowl for it to sit in. Why doesn't the element fit the bowl? Now must return it.

Indian dinner at Shenai with K and R tonight. Delicious small bites of butter chicken, aloo gobi, naan, lamb curry. We spoke about many things including Old Testament genealogy, John's DNA findings, R's music program at the hospital, the progress of K's book, the possibility of the three of us trying to play a tango again and the much-loved grandchildren whom we share.

I read that the British Government has recently made a Cabinet Portfolio called The Ministry of Loneliness to address the growing isolation of elderly people, some of whom are reported not to see another person for ten days in a row. Positive interaction, laughter, new information is life-giving.

Granddaughter E is collecting money for the American Heart Association by jumping rope. We are pleased.

SATURDAY, JANUARY 20TH, 2018 ~ This morning to return the stovetop element to the hardware store and pick up one that fits. While there we noted that on the counter for sale were Salt Licks for deer. It mentions that sheep might be attracted to it too but it also says that sheep can get ill from it so if they come we must take it away. No sheep around here. But must tell Ted, Mary, Cherry in NZ. With our luck our postage-stamp of a front lawn will look like the cover of a Gerald Durrell novel. We bought one for

K-and-L-next-door too. Perhaps the whole herd will show up. Come Spring there will be another deer cull I'm sure. At least we will have given this small trio a decent last few months of life.

The Bolshevik is pleased that the new element fits the stovetop. Our pretty green kettle has been replaced by a white plastic pedestrian model that does not have even half the cachet of the lime green whistling one!

Found my CD, The Essential Yo-Yo Ma, that has Libertango on it. Played that side over and over while I was reading this afternoon. Had forgotten how lovely it is. At the end he plays I Could Have Danced All Night. I'm a sucker for that piece but don't like the way they've rearranged it. Why do some musicians ruin the melody lines that made songs famous in the first place?

Cabbage Rolls for dinner.

Couldn't decide if we'd rather watch the Peggy Guggenheim Documentary on TVO (have seen it before but it fits the spirit of the book I'm reading) or the Inspector Lynley episode on WNED so switched back and forth between the two and therefore enjoyed neither.

SUNDAY, JANUARY 21ST, 2018 ~ *"We spent a most perfect week there and went away with this sort of "nunc dimittis" feeling of entire satisfaction that is so rare."* (Irene Goldman-Price, 2012, 91.)

Taught the Sunday School lesson about Zacchaeus and how important he was to Jesus although not remotely important to the rest of the society which spawned and spurned him. Given that he was a tax collector, albeit a tax collector who overcharged and kept the change, he was well-despised. The Pharisees were sure that Jesus would have nothing to do with Zacchaeus given his uncommonly small stature and his lack of social credibility. The very person to whom Jesus paid tribute in that huge gathering *was* Zacchaeus, which is telling about both the mission of the Godhead and the aim of Christianity, which in itself gets badly damaged at times due to the off-course humans who pretend to represent it. Zacchaeus apologized and said he'd give back what he owed and Jesus said something to the effect of *"Gotcha covered."*

AW and I, over lunch in the Parish Hall, spent time trying to sort out the clues regarding a mystery that is untangling its horrifying web in the papers. With the two of us on the case I believe it might get

some advancement. Together we could come up with one of those huge white boards with pictures and intersecting arrows linking the suspects like the ex-Coppers on New Tricks.

Evensong tonight for one hour and only a handful there. No pianist so we sang *a cappella* and it was fine, just like being in the Hebrides in the old days. The Nunc Dimittis sounded well with only the human voice as accompaniment.

Edith Wharton was bang on when she talked about the elemental satisfaction of it.

MONDAY, JANUARY 22, 2018 ~ *"Ni vous sans moi, ni moi sans vous."* (from 'Iseult' via Joseph Bedier's 1909 retelling and then Hermione Lee kicked in with it in her biography of Edith Wharton (Hermione Lee, 2007, 345). She made an oblique reference to Edith and Morton Fullerton's love affair. I thought theirs was the most tragic affair, in the way in which he turned against Edith. I digress. But it's a lovely quote. *"Ni vous san moi, ni moi sans vous. Neither you without me nor me without you..."*

Monday, and rain.

Looked in the mirror this morning and instead of seeing my mom looking back at me (see entry for

Sunday, October 22nd) there was Andy Warhol! Yes! Too much white hair. Should I try streaks again? What?

An impossibly sore thumb joint. Why?

Remembered later today why sore thumb. I carried those heavy Salt Licks and stood in line at the counter for ages to cash them out with them weighing down on my thumbs, wrists. The things we do for wildlife, the exception being any kind of wild life of our own.

RMB popped in with some herbed salt for meat, salads, vegetables and two frozen chicken breasts about which she has been telling me. Generosity has always been her stock in trade; that and her rollicking sense of humour.

After lunch to snuggle up with John LeCarre's novel. Before I could say "Bob's your Uncle", I was off to the Land of Nod on the old sofa for ninety minutes. The perfect day for that kind of inactivity; dark, foggy, soft rain, the haar as they say in Scotland. We need more days like it. I'll propose that the Government give us one reading/snoozing day per month.

The bread that has been on our deck since January 2nd is still out there. It's soggy; looks like a scoop of mashed potatoes. What is sticking it together?

Supper simple tonight; a salmon sandwich and a bowl of strawberries while we watched the CBC news.

TUESDAY, JANUARY 23RD, 2018 ~ Spring in the air today. It's only a ploy, a bit of a jest to make us remember how lovely it is without snowboots on our feet.

To John's eye appointment this morning with Opthamologist. Disappointing results. A follow-up on Friday. Downhearted.

But then to the coffee shop and the music they were playing was a great new rendition of the old war song, Pack Up Your Troubles In An Old Kit Bag, which altered our mood. Came home and found it on youtube under Eliza Doolittle Pack Up. Have played it over and over. Must be pumped up as loudly as possible to get the true sentiment of it.

Charlotte spent the evening with us and outlined the plans she is devising for her birthday party to come in late March. Amusing. "We're going to have mashed potatoes and Chinese food and donuts and..." She held Jock hostage on speaker phone for twelve minutes outlining the fun we'll have with the Pinata.

If a journal is to be truthful then I should add that I was annoyed with Himself today who is the usual suspect in my moments of frustration. The beauty of forgiveness is that it must all be explained away and expunged before bedtime. My grandmother's favourite

mantra was the Biblical injunction about not going to bed when you are angry, with your "wrath" intact.

Now there's a dandy word; wrath. The letters themselves in that particular order form an angry sound. Wrath couldn't possibly mean anything but what it does.

Resolved. And so to sleep.

WEDNESDAY, JANUARY 24TH, 2018 ~ A cello practice this morning. Badly out of it (practice, I mean, although some might concur that *I'm* also badly out of it.) Have noticed how much more difficult it is to play recently, given the weight of the cello, the use of shoulder, neck, wrist, back muscles. Haven't had a lesson since before Christmas and now time to practice the Lenten music. Tried to play Libertango as Rebecca brought the music over yesterday. I find the timing confounding. Have to clap it out, over and over, and still, it doesn't take. But am not giving up as I'm remembering John Glenn, Christopher Plummer et al. (See entry re December 29th).

Our regular Porch Party this afternoon (indoors in the winter) at JB's with MH. Hot apple cider and treats. Many topics. A good afternoon in every regard. Reaffirms the value of togetherness.

En route home dropped John Le Carre off at library. We didn't get on together. I stopped at drug store to pick up some eye drops for John. Noticed that the cream I've been admiring on Helen Mirren's rosy face on the tv ads was half-price. A rosy face is something have always admired in others. This cream guarantees it. I know that is a pile of rot but bought it anyway. Mid-winter will do that sort of thing to me. Am guaranteed a pink face within four weeks.

Tonight a chicken pie and zucchini sautéed in Parmesan Cheese and toasted Panko crumbs.

The bread on the back deck has dissipated as of today. It lasted for twenty-two days outside.

THURSDAY, JANUARY 25TH, 2018 ~ A visit this morning with friends BC and PC. They look out over a forested ravine. They see a herd of deer, a fox, hawks, coyotes. The deer have carved out a path to Princess Point so I assume that three of their herd are the ones who visit us. They seem to have forgotten about us in this January Thaw. We thought the Salt Lick would be a huge hit. Just as well now that they can find their own food with the snow cover gone. Maybe we've kept them alive for a bit.

The most wonderful book club tonight at the Art

Gallery and a lengthy discussion of the four sections of the book regarding all of those previously mentioned artists. Only eight there plus the librarian. My one comment was this: thinking of Bacon, Freud, Pollock, de Kooning what part of their fame was true genius? What part was the alcohol and drugs talking? What part was due to having great publicity agents? Next discussions will be held the two nights of Compline and promised I'd play music so will miss them both.

TV news at night abhorrent. What is the point of watching sex abuse trials, dysfunctional politicians, news clips about abuses in nursing homes, ads aimed at Baby Boomers regarding chair lifts, buzzers that are worn around the neck to press when in difficulty although the elderly gentleman in the ad who falls down appears not to have the strength to push it, piles of drugs that have even more piles of side effects?

Dear Reader, how's a girl supposed to get a good night's sleep after being submerged in all that dystopia?

FRIDAY, JANUARY 26TH, 2018 ~ *January, 1963;(Ritchie, 2008, 456.) "How strange it is always to be seeing one's country from abroad as I do. One becomes very conscious, perhaps over-conscious,*

of the showing that Canada makes in the eyes of others. Perhaps one begins to think too much about what others think. Also, one builds up a sort of ideal Canada in one's own mind which may have increasingly little to do with reality. What depresses me is the thick coating of self-congratulation which covers every Canadian official statement."

That statement was written this very month in 1963. Nothing has changed. Canada remains self-congratulatory. We do have lots on which to congratulate Selves but we carry our own disgraces.

Ritchie (above quote) threw around the pronoun "one" as if he were Her Majesty The Queen. I like it because it takes the intended message one step further away from the personal, but it sounds pompous.

The Dogwood is glowing scarlet. It changes with the season. Was softer red before Christmas and now it's screaming in crimson.

John's Opthamologist's appntmnt went well. Her needle to his eyeball a few days ago worked wonders. He can drive again. Himself happy. Me too.

A soft afternoon with reading the LRB and some of Diana Athill and listening to CFMX's beautiful, tender music including a Bach Sarabande with Yo-Yo Ma.

SATURDAY, JANUARY 27TH, 2018 ~ To the theatre to see the PT Barnum movie (Hugh Jackman, Zac Efron, Michelle Williams.) It was a sad story. It did subliminally showcase race issues, the need for accepting others as they are, how money can turn people's heads. Some saw him as a humanitarian for giving people jobs and a sort of belonging. Others, like me, for instance, saw him as a businessman who got wealthy on the medical situations of others. It was, I felt, altogether soppy.

Thrilled to see in The National Post today a full page article on Edith Wharton's book The Decoration of Houses that she co-wrote with Ogden Codman in 1897. The front page of Post Homes has the famous picture of Edith at her desk at The Mount. I'm mailing the entire section to The Mount.

Raining and overcast. Puddles everywhere.

SUNDAY, JANUARY 28TH, 2018 ~ Sunday School lesson today re moneychangers in the temple. I see more and more how these ancient texts reflect 'everyman' and every era. Switch around a few names to contemporary ones and it's the same story.

A visit here with Jock and Ashley this afternoon. Jock got out the old photo albums and will scan some of the pictures for us; the kids posing in Hallowe'en costumes, blowing out the candles on birthday cakes, photos of our dogs.

M.H's annual Potluck And Paperbacks last night. A sterling group of women. Discovered a book about Vietnam titled The Beauty of The Humanity Movement. Will read it! And great chickpea/curry/bacon soup. Will make it! Was suggested that we bring toiletries for a homeless women's shelter which made the evening even more worthwhile. I like the way these women operate; straightforward, no malice, pragmatic.

Home to watch Masterpiece Theatre's Victoria with Himself. A good look at the history of the era, of the woman who wore the crown, of the intrigue between Britain and Louis Phillipe of France, of the fact that the Belgium King was not in fact Albert's father as he had always believed but he was instead fathered by his Uncle Leopold. It threw him for a loop, as it would. *"Rather."*

MONDAY, JANUARY 29TH, 2018 ~ (Goldman-Price, 2012, 165.) My new word for today is straight out of Edith Wharton's letters to Anna Bahlmann. *"Unberufen"*. It's the German word for

"May no evil befall us." It's the sort of word you can love.

Winter is back. A thick blanket of snow. Lower temps. Shovelled after dinner in the twilight. The tiny white lights on our porch which I've switched back on helped the hygge factor and made for a beauteous evening.

Made soup first thing this morning from a bag of frozen asparagus I spotted at the bottom of the freezer. Carmelized an onion in butter in the bottom of the pot. Threw in a chopped cauliflower, water, sea salt, pepper. All of this inspired by M.H.'s great soup last night. But then forgot to watch it and the water boiled out of it. Caught it just in time. Had no broth so added a can of mushroom soup and a can of milk at which point it became fake homemade soup. We had it for supper tonight with a grilled cheese sandwich. Apple slices for Himself, a mandarin orange pour moi.

Phở Bình Minh for lunch with John today as went to check out exact location for my lunch later this week with EKD. Grilled lemongrass chicken and Cà Phê Sữa Đá. Cold sweet iced coffee a strange thing for a January day but the it went down well.

Volume 40 Number 2 for London Review of Books came today. This sounds fine; *"Mentored writing*

retreats…; quiet rooms, inspiring surroundings, good food, professional mentoring…"

Does sound nice but I like being home too. I'm comforted by this small house.

"Snow on snow". **We are right back to where we were in December with Christina Rossetti. Sifting down. It's endless.**

Should not have had that Vietnamese coffee at noon as I'm higher than Annapurna at the moment and it's twenty-five minutes after ten, or, as my grandmother would have said "It's five and twenty past the hour."

TUESDAY, JANUARY 30TH, 2018 ~ Today there are twenty-four blossoms on our orchid, all of them with purple splotches and a yellow-rimmed cup in each centre. All it asks of me is one-quarter cup of cold water every Saturday. It flourishes in the west-facing sunroom window. I keep it on the pine table beside a stack of CD's: Haydn's Cello Concertos, Ben Heppner's My Secret Heart, Johannes Brahms' Lieders, The Essential Yo-Yo Ma, Faure's Requiem, Mendelssohn. I am no expert in music but the music that uplifts me I keep nearby. Maybe it's that same music that also encourages our orchid along.

To Cambridge this afternoon to visit our friend but the sign on the residence door said "No admittance." A virus. I left her a phone message when we got home to say this; "We know exactly where you are now." Learned this from friends who have had to change places in the wider world. They told me that the power of people knowing your exact location lends comfort and security.

Our trip along Highway 8 to see J and J was a beautiful drive on a winter's day. Fields of blinding sheets of snow. The number of times our various cars have travelled that route, back and forth, when mom and dad were alive and happy and then when they were ill, countless. And priceless.

John to the ESL program tonight. Me to sit with a book, music, maybe WNED.

The moon a huge silver disc. Unberufen.

WEDNESDAY, JANUARY 31ST, 2018 ~ *(Rebecca John, Michael Holroyd, 2017, 208).* Am not sure why those British Bohemian writers and artists fascinate me so. They lived in total disarray. Maybe that is why, because it's the opposite of my own array.

I re-read the following small quote this morning from out of the mouth of Ida John, wife of portrait

artist Augustus John. Ida took second place to his mistress Dorelia and it was Dorelia to whom she wrote these words;

"...you are the one outside who calls the man to apparent freedom and wild rocks and wind and air - and I am the one inside who says come to dinner and whom to live with is apparent slavery."

I love the way she wrote about the wild rocks and the air but I've always felt sorry for Ida. She had swarms of his children and made no complaints and even accepted Dorelia as his sort of second wife. Maybe it was because she needed the help with the housework and Augustus' children. I keep looking at her sweet youthful face on the cover of my book and I say to Self "What were you thinking, girl?"

Typed up John's sermon for February. He went off to Kingston early this morning with PL to visit RS.

Self to lunch at Phở Bình Minh with EKD. We were roommates during a year in a mid-Ontario town in our first jobs when we were twenty-one and here we are at seventy still laughing over past inanities. By the early 1970s we had both relocated to different spots in this region. We rode our bikes on bucolic summer evenings along the Niagara Escarpment, spent a weekend up north learning to cross country

ski with a Norwegian instructor, took ballet lessons, wore miniskirts to a Pierre Trudeau rally. E bought a red sports car and I a navy Fiat. We had a corn roast one night and visited back and forth at our cute apartments for dinner. In the 1980s I took cooking lessons with EKD. She taught me how to make Pesto Sauce. We married, bought houses and gave life to our sweet babies. Now here we are in 2018 talking about politics, books for our grandchildren and which exercises are best for cardio; all of this over steamed rice and snow pea stir fry.

John satisfied with their wonderful visit with RS. And me satisfied with mine.

THURSDAY, FEBRUARY 1ST, 2018 ~ Seems that every time I ask what day it is the answer comes back Thursday. And now it's not only Thursday but it's February.

The most fun we've had yet on our coffee shop mornings with JB and RB, this time at a spot we have neglected for a while. It was cosy and almost nobody else in there save for two young businessmen in yarmulkes who probably heard every word we said in those tight quarters but kept at their laptops and were too polite to scream "Enough! Off with your

heads!" We chatted about eye surgery and sciatica, London, books and annoying changes to things that we loved doing and places where we loved going and lamented about how nothing stays the same and ergo, how we must get more creative. I told them my idea about asking the Government to make July 1st 2018 into National Forgiveness Day rather than a day when they plan to celebrate Canada Day by legalizing marijuana. National Forgiveness Day would encourage all cultures within these borders, all conditions of humankind, to embrace one another and forgive past wrongs. Forgiveness is the most basic of concepts. It has been forgotten and shoved aside in favour of committees who are paid mightily to sort things out and never do. Forgiveness is the only way anyone can ever start again. So enough pot-talk. Let's get down to the business of getting along.

This afternoon to James Street. Trouble finding parking downtown so walked a few blocks which was good for the cardio that EKD and I were discussing yesterday.

En route back to parking spot got up the nerve to go into the fancy chocolate shop. Have avoided it because wondered if I'd have to buy a whole pound which would not be a good thing. The Heavens shone on me; it's possible to buy small bites. I bought three tiny Peanut Butter Smoothies with every intention of sharing with Himself when I got home but remembered that I was annoyed with him earlier so decided to eat them myself. Learned that trick from our five year old granddaughter who declared when she was three at her daycare *"I'm not sharing today!"* They were gone by the time I got back to the car and I loved every bite. Later wondered how I could be so childish. (And *I'm* the one who has the nerve to propose a National Forgiveness Day?) I told him when I got home. He chuckled. If it's the calories you're thinking about Dear Reader, forget it. I'm seventy and if I want chocolate I'll have it. But I do regret the not sharing part.

A hearty letter and a poetry book arrived from Helen and Rob. The book consists of poems written in homage to Scottish artist James Paterson (1854-1932) who lived in Moniaive, Dumfriesshire and painted the local scenery. Much of his later work featured Edinburgh as seen from Arthur's Seat, etc.

In May 2002 I spent a stellar afternoon with H and R's friend, Ann Paterson Wallace, who was the granddaughter of James Paterson and is an artist in her own right. She and I sat for a cosy few hours in her tiny whitewashed cottage in Moniaive as she told me about her life and her grandfather. I loved her cottage. It was tiny, efficient and comforting. She had tartan blankets on the backs of the sofa and chairs. She took me into the cottage garden that her Grandfather was said to have patterned after his friend Monet's garden at Giverny. She has turned the cottage into a small museum in his memory.

Note to offspring: There are photos in the garden of Ann and myself that I stuck into the front cover of the book I bought from her (The Dictionary of Scottish Painters – 1600 to the Present, Paul Harris and Julian Halsby.) Also there is some correspondence between us there. Keep it.

FRIDAY, FEBRUARY 2, 2018 ~ A brisk walk this morning to the bottom of the hill. Always much fun whizzing down but much less fun coming back up. Loved the cold air (eleven degrees below zero). Nothing vivant except for one black squirrel who was working his way up the dried, grey trunk of an enormous pine tree and one male jogger who was wearing spandex shorts and a thin hoodie. Shiver me timbers.

MR has kindly emailed me a list of great music for

us to play for upcoming Compline services in Lent. I spent a pleasant and fruitful hour this afternoon sorting the music into piles. Pleased to see that there is nothing to photocopy and enlarge so I'm ready to rock and roll.

Except that rocking and rolling is not the point in this case.

SATURDAY, FEBRUARY 3RD, 2018 ~ Spent one hour this morning with my cello while Himself was at the grocery store. Most of the time spent on Compline music and that went well. Some time spent on the Piazzolla's Libertango and that is coming along. Some time spent on trying to play things I learned two years ago and that was not ok. Note to Self: must work harder.

Made soup this afternoon from the recipe that Marg gave me; curry, bacon, chickpeas, vegetable broth. Pureed. Making soup on a snowy day is as enjoyable an activity as I could imagine. I took it to Drew and Ely's along with a wheel of sourdough bread so that they don't have to think about making dinner tonight. And no I didn't make the bread. That would be some other woman you're thinking of.

But I did play with the two little girls. Lucia was

feeling her oats today and was much fun. She took my hands and we walked around the room. She laughed when I turned her upside down on my knee and wanted more. I left there with real joy to see the fun they have. Charlotte and Lucia are loving companions.

The usual evening. Some tv. Chit-chat. Just the way we like it.

SUNDAY, FEBRUARY 4TH, 2018 ~ Lynn B's birthday today so an early morning call to wish her well. Not sure how she could be seventy-one with me fast on her heels, but aren't we lucky? Seems not long ago we were watching the Diana Ross concert (Stop! In The Name of Love!) at Winter Carnival in the Auditorium at school or sitting at The Dairy Queen in her old maroon car planning out our futures. And one summer's eve a long time ago there was a drive to Rice Lake in two MGs which I will not mention in this Journal, nor will I mention the names of the drivers.

Snow overnight. Shovelled, put the garbage out, got the car cleaned off before Morning Prayer.

Have been thinking a lot of late about sisters, not necessarily the Catherine Parr Traill and Susannah Moodie famous types of sisters, but the ordinary ones like Jan and me, and the sisters of my childhood

who ran the fine china shop. I can think of a whole list I could make right here. Try the March sisters; Mary, Jo, Beth and Amy of Little Women fame. What makes the relationship between sisters special? Or not? Independent or co-dependent? Both? There was the set of Biblical sisters named Mary and Martha both of whom did different tasks. The question which arises about those two sisters is this; who did the more important job? Martha, who got the dinner ready? Or Mary, who sat and listened to the guest ? (the guest being Jesus and no matter what you're thinking about all of this He'd have been an interesting fellow with whom to chat.) If you'd asked me to guess I'd have voted for the one who got the dinner on the table but it seems that Martha asked Jesus to give Mary a nudge to help with the serving but He took Mary's side instead. I suppose this is a lesson in being a good listener and in paying attention to people rather than the extraneous issues. Except that how and when would they have eaten?

This morning before leaping out of bed onto the cold floor I remembered two elderly sisters when I was a teenager. They wore wire-framed glasses and had innocent old-world faces that you could put on greeting cards to make sick people feel better.

Whenever one of them coughed she'd raise both arms straight up in the air. I found it alarming until one of them told me that it was a good way to push the air into the lungs. Their names were even sweeter than their faces; Clara and Susie. I'll forever hear those coughing spates that were inevitably followed by the ensuing drama, spindly arms in the air as if at being held up at gunpoint.

We've all heard stories of sisters who surrendered their own dreams by staying at home to help elderly parents. I see it as a kind of noble, Victorian concept. Oftentimes they remained loyal to their elders until they themselves expired in heaps amid their black boots and swishing skirts.

Belinda and Harriet Bede feature in both Barbara Pym's novel Some Tame Gazelle and in An Unsuitable Attachment. Pym had her sister in real life in the person of Hilary.

There is often, both in literature and in life, a sister who has been held down by the dominant one, or one who is toxic and one who remains meek, in a kind of sisterly balancing act.

Nicole W. reminds me that Edith Wharton's novel, The Bunner Sisters, features sisters Ann Eliza and Evelina. Must look at that novel.

Queen Elizabeth and Princess Margaret? Now *that* had to be complicated. What if I got to be Queen and Jan hadn't? I'd be the sister who got to wear all that heavy jewellery. And she'd have to do what I said. And she wouldn't.

Email today from cousin NR in Winnipeg who has retired from the University and is setting out to do some research on family matters. I have some photocopies to send him including the sorrowful letter from the archivist of The Mother House of St. Joseph's here declaring the dates that my maternal grandmother had no choice but to drop all of her children off at the orphanage. She found herself a widow with six small people, my mom included who was very tiny at the time. Must have broken my Grandmother apart. How did she get back to Galt on the bus/tram/streetcar on that day on April 16th in 1916 and go home alone? What kind of heartbreak is that anyway? I so wish I had known her better. I know that she got the children back five years later after she remarried. My mom spoke lovingly of her.

MONDAY, FEBRUARY 5TH, 2018 ~ My Word-A-Day message says that a snollygoster is a *"shrewd, unprincipled person."*

So there's yet another word that suits its meaning. "Take that you old snollygoster!"

Sat down over lunch at JS's with Joyce and Linneth and the best bowl of chicken soup I've ever had. A bowl of soup with friends is worth more than any money can buy. And some people, many people it now seems, get neither the soup nor the friend to sup it with. In the best of all possible worlds aging means that you have more time for one another and appreciate more fully the journeys you're sharing. But in the real world too many people don't have that opportunity.

Thought I was clever with recipe-making. Dipped semi-boiled Cauliflower clusters in egg, then into a mix of Panko Crumbs and Parmesan. Then baked in oven until crispy and golden. It should have been delicious. But not. And why not?

TUESDAY, FEBRUARY 6TH, 2018 ~ A quiet day. JB and RB gave me their copies of The Times Literary Supplement some of which I skimmed today. Behold! An article about how people have forgotten Walter De La Mare, the same WDLM who has been on my mind of late. The article listed other writers who were subject to having been forgotten and were later resurrected, including Barbara Pym. This article should have been compiled by...let's see now. By *me!*

I recently bought copies of Walter De La Mare's Peacock Pie for E and H and for the dear little boys who belong to L and L in Ottawa. I remember his lilting verse from my own childhood. We were weaned on books, some, but not all of them, from England. There were colourful plates which drew us right into the vivid vortex of the worlds of Toby Tyler, The Wind And The Willows, Uncle Wiggly, Black Beauty, Little Women, Heidi, The Little Prince (a most gorgeous blue and gilt edition sent to Brian from Belgium when dad was still overseas) and the fat, hard-covered Girl's Own books via Britain that Aunt Gladys gave us. One of our favourites was The House at Pooh Corner. Jan had chewed off a bit of the yellow and red cover. I can still see her tiny teeth marks. Those bright worlds stayed close to my heart. I still have one which was given to me in the early 1950s by the leader of a children's group at my church. We met on Mondays after school. The book had a brown cover and is titled The Pig Brother. It had a frightening black and white plate of a highly-feathered angel with long braids and a jazzy, incongruous beaded get-up on her hair in the style of a 1920's flapper. At her feet sits a horde of

children all dressed up in pinafores and sailor suits. It was first published in 1881. Can you beat that?

John at Vestry meeting. Me with the evening to myself.

In closing off the day I must say this:

"I know a tiny cupboard,
With a teeny tiny key,
And there's a jar of Lollypops for me, me, me..."
(De La Mare, 1958, 34).

Thank you Mr. De La Mare. You've not been forgotten at our house.

WEDNESDAY, FEBRUARY 7TH, 2018 ~ (*Larkin, Philip, 2010, 385.)* On this very day, February 7th, in 1968, British poet Philip Larkin wrote to his beloved Monica, whom he called Bun, this:

"Dearest bun... I was amused to see the two pigeons that live on the roof opposite my bathroom sitting together, very cosily, the one nibbling on the other in an affectionate way; and thought of my poems on pigeons and how you told me about birds choosing their mates..."

The two pigeons that sit on K-and-L's roof next door have abandoned post. John says it's the weather. If I were a pigeon and had the skinny legs they have

I wouldn't want to be upon a roof with snow up my shins either. I'm not a pigeon fan as Larkin seems to have been but I am a fan of their Mourning Dove cousins. We like their soft chortlings on summer mornings to ease us into the day. We live, after all, in Dove Cottage.

Snowed again throughout the night. I plugged in the tiny white lights when I went out to shovel this morning. I like to think that passers-by will be cheered by them to and from work today.

A walk to the bottom of the hill. Even the Burdock looked pretty covered in small caps of white fluff. The sole footprints all the way down the hill were mine. I looked back at them, proud that to be the author of such valiant tracks. On the way up they conflated with those of a young man and his cherry red stroller, his baby zipped under the plastic hood, and those of two joggers. Silent. Peaceful.

A music practice for an hour. Was alright this time.

THURSDAY, FEBRUARY 8TH, 2017 ~ Friend JB had her eye surgery today and all was well.

Picked up Xiaolu Guo's Nine Continents from the library. It is sparse, clean writing that draws me in.

MH recommended it. It's a memoir so fits my current reading projects.

Baked a small heart-shaped cake for Charlotte to decorate this evening. She loved putting the sprinkles on it and the Smarties and popping them in her mouth. She talked all evening again about the party she's planning. Pinatas, shiny stickers and brightly frosted cakes are right up her street. She had a phone conversation with Jan and Rob and invited them to her birthday in March.

Snow storm expected overnight.

FRIDAY, FEBRUARY 9TH, 2018 ~ The overnight snowstorm didn't materialize. The sky was thick and white this morning with not one porthole of blue. But it snowed all day. I enjoyed my walk. Nobody to be seen neither uphill nor down.

Some ongoing problems with our Carbon Monoxide monitor. I took it back to the hardware store and the man heard my story about how I have reread the instruction booklet, moved it to a new location, changed batteries but still it beeps and screams. He advised me to maybe call the fire department who will send someone out to check it. John out when I got home so I called the non-emergency number to talk to the girl.

"Are you dizzy?" she queried.

"No."

"We'll send somebody right over."

"No. We're fine. The beeping noise has been going on and off for two weeks and the hardware store says it's not the batteries and I should call and ask your advice. Can't I just talk to somebody?"

"They will be there in 5 minutes."

A little man in a smallish car would have done nicely. Instead, the huge red truck came blazing down the street and out got three strapping youths. Was embarrassed. They checked everything. No problem to be found but suggested that I should buy a new monitor. Felt ridiculous.

Made a huge pot of chicken soup; leeks, carrots, onion, celery, chicken of course. Added pre-cooked Farfalle at last minute. Then lime juice to give it zest.

And after dinner shovelled snow which fell all day long without ceasing.

Armchair looked good. Watched BBC's New Tricks and was saddened to see what I thought was the demise of ex-cop Jerry Standing but seems it was a ruse to make the Connor Gang think he was a goner. Instead, he is living in New York City under the Witness Protection Act. I assume that this means that the guy who acts as Standing has retired from the show. Or worse. I don't like it when they remove my favourites. They've already bumped off the lovely Brian and Sandra and the other fellow who may have died in real life. Now a totally new group of actors.

SATURDAY, FEBRUARY 10TH, 2018 ~ John told me at 1 a.m. that the deer were outside. We opened the blind in the living room to get a better look. They heard it and ran off. Only two of them. What happened to number three? Perish the thought.

A busy day. Inclement weather so only a few showed up for the continuing study of the Book Of James. Today's focus was a strong reminder that churches, of all places, should not show bias towards wealthy parishioners nor against the impoverished, equality being the proper thing. My favourite part is at the end of Chapter Two where Rahab the harlot is favoured by Jesus for protecting the Israeli slaves from those who wanted to dispose of them. Always, always, always the poor in both money and spirit were His focus and tucked under His wing.

Stayed later to set up tables and sort out small items for Rev'd L's Ordination tomorrow. Expecting one hundred but forecast for freezing rain tomorrow so we might end up eating five tonnes of salmon, tuna, egg sandwiches ourselves.

Snowed. Shovelling my way through the days.

SUNDAY, FEBRUARY 11TH, 2018 ~ Several years ago I became interested in the concept of Grace. I wondered what it meant on a personal level and how it manifests itself in daily experience. I've been taught so much about Grace in the past three years that I could draw a physical diagram of how it works, with links to situations and arrows to people in our deep past involved. Someday I might try it to see what that would look like if it were on paper.

This morning there were one hundred and nine at Rev'd L's Ordination. I stayed to help clean up after the reception and came home with sore feet and great fulfilment, a funny combination if ever there was one.

My warm nightie and ancient housecoat went on at 3:00 p.m. on this freezing rain afternoon, along with the Voltaren on my shoulders.

Tonight another episode of Victoria. A hard life for Royals; total lack of freedom to live like the rest of us. But she did have several cooks and a few dozen maids, whereas I'd be fine with just one of each. Think I might try to find a copy of Lady Longford's biography of her.

MONDAY, FEBRUARY 12TH, 2018 ~ A welcomed email from our friend in Baffin Island. She received the letter we sent. I hope to meet her and her small son face-to-face someday.

Sidewalks were ice-covered but I chipped at it with the shovel until it cracked and then I could scoop it up. The sun on the iced branches covered each twig until they sparkled. Then they melted and dripped.

Spent the major portion of today baking sausages for St. George's Annual Pancake Lunch tomorrow.

Listened to a bit of Faure's Requiem tonight when John was at the hospital visiting an ailing friend. It puts me in a seasonal frame of mind. The vocalizations are some of the time so tender, at other times unsettling but altogether it is beautiful music. It was partially first performed in the winter of 1888 in the Madeleine Church in Paris. We've heard it sung twice, both times here in our own city. I love the musical phrasing, the way it builds, then lets go and softens into Faure's soothing melodies.

Margaret-Anne called and we had a good catching up.

TUESDAY, FEBRUARY 13TH, 2018 ~ Shrove Tuesday ~ When I was a child we called today

Pancake Day. I loved it. It felt like an occasion. So today I carried my one-hundred and fifty cooked sausages over to the Parish Hall along with everyone else's one-hundred and fifty cooked sausages so that we could feed them to the crowds after they breached the barriers, scaled the ramparts, took a battering ram to the doors at noon for the Annual Pancake Lunch. If I were to be honest my sausages reduced themselves by the two that got stuck in the pan and broke that I ate, the one that fell into the sink that I threw away, the two that John confessed to eating to make sure they were cooked before we fed them to the public. We fed ninety people and it was a good event. I love these things that mark out the year; a child at heart.

JNR invited us to go along with her to hear a political speech. Funny to be back in that situation again when it was once our whole life. Was impressed by this woman who was straight-forward and not self-obsessed. We need honesty, intelligence, kindness, strength of character in our politicians.

When we got home a skunk was waiting for us. Bold as brass he was. Is that why the apples we left for the deer were in little nibbles on the front porch this morning? In that case, enough already.

WEDNESDAY, FEBRUARY 14TH, 2018 ~ Ash Wednesday ~ In his 2016 book Keeping On Keeping On, (Bennett, 2016, 202), Alan Bennett says on February 14th, 2010, this; *"I am said in today's Independent on Sunday to be pushing eighty with a photo (taken at seventy) in corroboration."*

Am I, too, all of a sudden "pushing eighty"? Is that how it works? That fast? I'll show them. I'll insist they play Bob Dylan's Knock Knock Knocking On Heaven's Door when they're lowering me into my bath.

Valentine's Day today and Ash Wednesday. The year we got married we spent Valentine's Day overnight at the then new Prince Hotel in Toronto. We had a splendid dinner. Since that time our attempts at celebrating have decreased steadily if you consider whimpering babies, howling dogs, teenage rock bands practicing in our basement and General Duties. Our Valentine's Day hooplas have slid from a Perfect Ten to hovering around zero if you think of it in terms of the Hallmark factor.

So there you have it Ladies and Gentlemen. After forty-one years this marriage is strong enough to swing through the Season of Hearts and Flowers without either of them although a drop of chocolate would have been perfection until, that is, that I heard

the really perfect news today. Our smallest Valentine has just taken her first step without holding anybody's hand. And that is much better than an entire box of peanut butter smoothies.

A long, focused music practice this afternoon and feeling up to snuff now.

Charlotte phoned and chatted like a chipmunk. "Grandma Happy Valentine's Day. Daddy left a note on my table to say he loves me. I went to eat pancakes at the church with mommy last night. Grandma, Lulu is jumping on her knees on the bed. Grandma remember when we went for a walk? Can I come to your house?"

Today was four degrees above zero. Smelled like Spring.

Ash Wednesday Service tonight. Peaceful.

THURSDAY, FEBRUARY 15TH, 2018 ~ A good checkup for John at the clinic this morning. We topped it off by stopping to buy bagels at the Deli. He lost his footing as he was trying to get to the meter to put money in it and fell into a filthy, slushy snowbank. I had already taken his hand to help him so when he went down *"Jill came tumbling after…".* I went into the Deli to get a chair which gave him leverage. Up he

got. Told the woman he was "just fine" and off we went with our bagels. Were I the Mayor I might insist on better snow removal near meters in shopping areas. Me for Mayor; can you picture it?

I heard someone mention today the small red money envelopes called hong bao that are used in the Chinese New Year celebrations. And as it happens I have been using a hong bao as a bookmark. I had found it in the drawer when I was digging around for something to mark my page. It was left over from last year's Chinese New Year's party for the English Second Language group. So now I know the proper name for it.

FRIDAY, FEBRUARY 16TH, 2018 ~ *"As against having a beautiful workshop, studio, etc., one writes best in a cellar on a rainy day."* Van Wyck Brooks, writer, critic (Feb. 16 1886-1963; A.Word.A.Day.) Have often thought that quote must be true for serious writers. Am suspicious when I see pics of people in their glorious writing rooms. I wonder if they enjoy the actual work of writing or if they are enamoured with being thought of as a writer.

I'll make the exception for the brilliant Margaret Drabble. I once saw a photo of her work room. It's

beautiful, complete with splendid draperies after which I lust.

Edith Wharton, too, had a most regal place in which to write. Her small desk, a replica, I've heard, still sits in her library where she kept the books she treasured most including Walt Whitman's 'Leaves of Grass' which was gifted to her by one of her two great loves, Walter Berry. Nicole at The Mount reminded me recently that Edith also loved writing in bed. Inspiration wasn't hard to come by with her view of her gardens below and of the blue forever sky. The Berkshire Mountain air would be enough to oxygenate anyone's imaginings. A fine idea Edith, but my back would scream if I tried writing in bed.

Honore de Balzac's writing room was in his white-washed cottage in the Passy District of Paris. In his small room sunlight pours through the ruby stained-glass of the window onto his desk. When the Docent wasn't looking I patted the surface of the wood. It pooled there, that warm red blood-light, prodding Balzac to spill out his stories of the post-Napoleonic era.

I realize that I've now made three huge exceptions to the above quote which means I have to take back my original premise, about writers who sit at fancy

desks. But let's say that my theory might be true for wannabe writers.

A quick trip out to get some store-made soup (Lobster Bisque, Potato and Bacon, Butternut Squash) as requested by friends who are stuck at home these days due to a fractured ankle. Must try that soup. Looks degenerate, delicious.

A quick nip downtown to Cafe Orange, to Denninger's for cooked chicken breasts, potato salad. An easy dinner tonight.

Weather has changed. A cold wind sliced through my jacket. Glad to be home.

SATURDAY, FEBRUARY 17TH, 2018 ~ Forty years ago today along came our baby girl, silver haired and rosy cheeked. She is the world's best daughter. 'Nough said.

New Tricks did come on last night. I've recorded it so we'll see it another time.

Am still waiting for my face to turn rosy as the new cream promised. So far, nothing. (See entry of January 24th.)

On the kitchen countertop sits the following necessities of any well-run zoo; a bag of seeds, nuts, grains *"to attract Blue Jays, Cardinals, Goldfinches,*

Evening Grosbeaks" and a bag of peanuts to be fed each day to the squirrels in K-And-L-Next-Door's back garden while they are warming their bones in Palm Springs. Ditto for the bird seed and a big bag of apples for our deer.

A drive around the city today. Everything at its dimmest; dry grey streets covered in the detritus of late winter, piles of sooty snow gathered on corners and kerbs, a sodden iron sky, trees that looked beautiful covered in snow now with bare, outstretched branches begging for greenery. And a dampness that chills to the bone.

John napping. Me to read a bit from a book I found about China. The authour talks about learning English Grammar and how astounded she was to learn the ease with which Westerners use the First Person Singular. She mentions how in China there is no strong concept of the individual as *I* because life is about *we.* They are a part of the collective in Communism, not individual units.

Contentment equals armchair plus book.

SUNDAY, FEBRUARY 18TH, 2018 ~ Gladys Taber, in her 'Book of Stillmeadow', (Taber, 1948), talks about the joy she had when the seed catalogue arrived.

As well as the William Dam Seed catalogue that came a while ago we have now received the Spring Lindenberg Seed catalogue from Brandon, Manitoba. It is true in the way that Gladys Taber explains the joy those magazines bring. Leafing through the glossy pictures of flowers makes my heart tap dance.

This morning our back garden was a sea of drab. No sun, half-melted snow on the porch, dreary rooftops without their usual coating of frost to soften them. But the greening to come is worth the wait. The Dogwood Bush is the only dash of colour right now with its cherry-red warmth. Come Spring it will turn lime and other hues of green will surround it, providing bright contrast.

I'm sure the pictures of one of my favourite flowers, Sweet Peas, in the Lindenberg catalogue have been included to annoy me. K-and-L-Next-Door have them twisting up the fence at the side of their place so we get the benefit of them but for a reason known only to the secrets of the soil they will not grow for us. I'd like to try the one called Prince Edward of York or Prima Ballerina. Some have old world names like Mrs. Collier and my favourite, Flora Norton, which is clear blue. I think that Flora Norton would make an interesting name for a work of fiction. She must have

been a real person. With a name like Flora Norton she'd be a good listener, a decent friend.

Hollyhock and Larkspur. Now *those* two words could make winter get a move on.

Morning Prayer with the dulcet notes of Sara's violin floating through the rafters.

Evening Prayer and John's sermon combining the three Scripture Lessons: Moses striking the rock to make the water flow so the Israelites could survive in the dessert, David in his mental anguish post-adultery and post-murder as he begs God to *"Create in me a clean heart",* (Psalm 51:10 AKJV) and Judas who missed the entire point of his best friend's time on earth and betrayed him for thirty pieces of silver. All of them most modern stories and in all of them, including David's murder of Bathsheba's husband, the possibility of forgiveness and redemption.

Home to the next episode of Victoria where the Corn Laws are overthrown in favour of Free Trade.

MONDAY, FEBRUARY 19TH, 2018 ~ *Family Day Holiday* ~ It's a good idea, this Family Day holiday in February. It comes on the heels of a cold winter. The thought of the weary masses either

relaxing in their pj's or doing something special together today is heartening.

Practiced music for an hour this morning. Enjoyed myself.

John ordered a Mid-Winter Box Of Treats from The Dancing Deer to go to Hayley and Isaac's family. He thinks it's time for a pick-me-up and he loves sending surprises.

A lazy afternoon with my book about Degas and the ballet dancers. Historical Fiction isn't my favourite genre but yet, some new learning. This book concerns La Belle Epoque, a time in French history when the arts flourished Post WW1, including music, visual art, ballet. It was paralleled in America by The Gilded Age by Edith Wharton *et al.*

Charlotte phoned us this afternoon. She is a friendly little person and loves to tell us everything that is going on in her four year old life, including the kind of birthday cake she'd like; pink.

RMB sends humorous emails. I had told her about John and I falling in a heap on the snowbank. She said that we were originally *"meant to fall* for *each other, not* on top of *one another."*

Weather warnings about rain to come, just short of telling us to build ourselves an Ark. Has been quietly

dripping all day. The fog rolled in this evening, then cleared.

A visit here with Jock tonight. He has been nominated for The Prism Prize by a panel of cross Canada art jurors. He devised and directed the video a while back, forgot about it, never expected it to be looked at. He says that being nominated pleases him but he'll be fine with not winning. He has also been to a workshop about the demise of the middle class in Canada which is alarming but not surprising.

He left and we watched Fake or Fortune, our favourite new tv show about art collectors. Morpheus came calling and I fell asleep. When I woke up and said *"What happened?"* John told me that the painting that was thought to have been done by Sir Winston Churchill was in fact unproven. This means that the poor guy who thought he'd won big will have to partially sell off the property he's inherited from his Uncle in France. Oh dear. The machinations of it all.

TUESDAY, FEBRUARY 20TH, 2018 ~ Rained all night. All day too. 14 degrees above. Green shoots in the garden of the daffodils and muscari, their yellows and blues to unfold in due time.

Spent a bit of time reading my Paris book. Makes

me want more. Must google to see if there is a book written solely about La Belle Epoque. Can't get enough of this.

Often think I'd love to be re-educated. This time I'd focus my learning through a narrower lens because now I know what it is that I love. But I'm afraid I love most everything.

A trip to the postal outlet (more about that in a moment) to pick up a parcel and on the way home drove down the hill and saw our three deer, all of them soaking wet. They walked across the road in front of us without as much as a "How d'ya do?" Their gait was haughty. Did the Doe say to her Bambis when they saw our car, "There they are and never once did they think to ask us in."

Speaking of postal outlets as they are now called, their demise is a Canadian sorrow to me. When I was little, under ten years, our Uncle was the Post Master in our town. We loved to visit him at work with our cousins Joanne and Donna. We'd step up to the brass wicket and demand to *"see Uncle Ernie."* The clerk would check to make sure he was in and then he'd invite us to sit in his office. The place was hushed and smelled of stamps and mucilage. Mucilage! When was the last time you heard that word? The resounding of the granite floor gave our footsteps an air of gravitas. The Queen smiled down at us from her picture frame. Postal outlets now, no longer under the aegis of the Federal Government, are afterthoughts, stuck at the back of the drug mart between the potato chips and the cold remedies.

Everything changes, given time.

A most wonderful evening tonight with fifty-two people in the Parish Hall to celebrate Chinese New Years with our Visiting Scholars and ESL students. We had a sing-along including Bob Dylan and Elvis and one woman sang a Chinese New Year's song as did twelve year old Annie. Will feel sad when she goes back to Asia next month. She has been a vital part of us. Three cherubic Chinese babies there tonight. F and L's little boy, eighteen months, clapped and sang and danced. Another baby boy and a baby girl were there too. We missed M and A and baby Quing. N.B. pointed out that over the past five years we have had one hundred Chinese students pass through the ESL program. They keep in touch when they go back home but most salient is the fact that here they find a home away from home, friendship, NB's watermelon slices and hot tea.

WEDNESDAY, FEBRUARY 21, 2018 ~ Rained all night. A sound sleep with the soft drumming on the rooftop.

Met with my teenaged friend today at the mall at noon. A fruitful chat. A sweet person if ever there was one.

I cried in front of the tv tonight. Those beautiful kids from a highschool in Florida spoke with eloquence beyond their years and beyond what they should have ever had to witness at school, about how it felt to watch seventeen of their friends lose their futures to gunshots. Swore I'd not include this stuff in here but how not to?

I'd like to erase the above paragraph. It taints this Journal. It's the opposite of my intent with writing it. But the horror is real.

This is the media diet that tucks North America into bed every night.

THURSDAY, FEBRUARY 22, 2018 ~ Today Drew is thirty-eight years old. He's Sterling. Note the capital 'S'. He's the oldest of our two best sons.

Canada's Olympic Medal Count today in Pyeongchang, Korea is: nine Gold, five Silver, seven Bronze. We're good athletes. I'll dismiss myself from

that. *Factoid:* Am still using double knots to tie my shoelaces.

A bowl of chilli in the Parish Hall followed by a peaceful service of Compline this evening. Played music with M.R. Put me in an appropriate frame of mind. It energized me.

FRIDAY, FEBRUARY 23RD, 2018 ~ Didn't sleep well as have overnight developed a head cold. My sleep cycles change from time to time anyway. According to The Mayo Clinic Newsletter a change in sleep patterns is a common phenomenon of aging. Charming.

Glanced through Graham Greene's *'A Life In Letters' (Greene, 2007, 186),* again this morning. Noticed this from March, 1951 in a letter to his great friend Evelyn Waugh; *"I loved Indo-China and finding a new religion in which Victor Hugo is venerated as a saint."*

Although he didn't name the group, I know he was talking about the Vietnamese Cao Daists. Thirty-five years ago some Cao Daists from the temple near Toronto came to our house for help. They all wore white. They are a combination of world religions and they do worship Victor Hugo and Sun Yat Sen, whose great desire was to move China towards modernization through westernization. We have lost touch with the Cao Daists. What I remember most about them is their white garb and their high manners.

John went to his Teacher's College Reunion lunch while I spent the afternoon with my stuffy nose, my kleenex and my book. Have ordered a book about a period in French history known as La Belle Epoque written by an American scholar.

RMB asked me today if people still get dressed up for Easter Sunday. John said "yes" and I said "no". She was talking about how when she was small she'd have new shoes for Easter Sunday and a bonnet and off she'd go to the Presbyterian Church. It was the done thing. When we were very small our Great Aunt Mabel worked in the Savage Shoe factory and she'd buy us what were called "seconds" every Easter. They were black patent and had a sewing error in them which meant they couldn't be sold in stores. For years I thought that "seconds" meant they had belonged to other girls first. I marvelled at how nicely they'd kept them, all shiny with unscuffed toes and soles.

In the book I'm reading a young man is about to meet the Guillotine in Paris. I just asked John what he'd request for his own last dinner. He thought for a bit and answered "scallops". I've lived with Himself for forty-one years and never knew that he loved scallops that much. I said that I'd go for brisket and Yorkshire pudding.

John saw a Junco on the back porch today. I heard something trilling and it might have been him. I mean the Junco, not John.

SATURDAY, FEBRUARY 24TH, 2018 ~ More birdsong this morning. A sound we haven't heard for months; a happy chirruping that comes with the demise of winter greyness and the return of feathers flashing against a bowl of blue sky.

There are wonderful words to describe bird groups; a Clattering of Jackdaws, a Gaggle of Geese, a Murder of Crows, an Ostentation of Peacocks, a Parliament of Owls but my favourite two are a Charm of Goldfinches, an Exaltation of Larks.

What do we say about Juncos?

SUNDAY, FEBRUARY 25TH, 2018 ~ Sunny, bright and gusty. (Not me. I mean the weather.) We watched the closing ceremony of the Olympics in Pyeongchang early this morning.

In Lent we sing the *Benedicite, Omnia Opera* every Sunday as we did this morning. It ought to be the theme song of Environmentalists everywhere. This old Canticle includes thankfulness for the Waters, the Firmament, the Sun and the Moon, the Stars of Heaven, the Showers and Dew, Winds, Fire and Heat, Winter and Summer, Dew and Frosts and Cold, Ice and Snow, Nights and Days, Light and Darkness, Lightnings and Cloud, Mountains and Hills, All Green Things upon the earth, Wells, Seasons, Floods, Whales and things that move in the Waters, Fowls of the air, Beasts and Cattle. Who wouldn't want to take care of the natural world after singing about those marvels?

This afternoon I finished reading The Painted Girls by Cathy Marie Buchanan. To my delight discovered in her notes at the back that Degas' original statue of The Little Dancer Aged Fourteen lives at The National Gallery in Washington. Hope to see it with Hayley et al sometime. The authour's strong archival sources breathe life into every page. It concerns the true story of the van Goethem sisters. The middle one posed for Degas and for the famous statue. It has re-stirred my love of Paris. I may try to find Emile Zola's L'Assommoir.

The evening chilled quickly but remained light until 6:20 p.m.

Come Spring we'll plant some raspberry canes so our grandchildren can have the fun of picking their own bowl for breakfast just as our children did with Grandpa Smith's raspberry canes. We lived three doors from him. They still talk about the joy of summer mornings in childhood when they'd take their bowls over to his place and set to it.

MONDAY, FEBRUARY 26TH, 2018 ~ I had the best email this morning from friends north of Toronto who asked me to help think up a name for their family's new restaurant. The food and style is based on their home in Shanxi Province. The Chef throws the noodles around in the air in huge long thick ribbons. They sent pictures to show how it's done. I've suggested "The Dancing Noodle" as it is self explanatory for both native Chinese speakers and English speakers. It was fun to be asked.

The beefy junk removal men came today and for a hefty price carried away the old sofa and armchair. John's parents bought it when John was twelve. It lived in St. John New Brunswick first, then Ottawa, then Hamilton. It looked lovely until the fabric we reupholstered it with wore off. Everything has a shelf-life and this sofa expired long ago so no tears from me.

Vacuumed today, moved heavy things around, threw things out, did the groceries, made a substantial dinner of pork chops, baked potatoes, broccoli. Fell into bed shortly after 9 p.m.

WEDNESDAY, FEBRUARY 27TH, 2018 ~ It's eleven degrees above zero today. Spring jacket weather. Went downtown to get my hair cut.

Home and made a big pot of chili for friends tomorrow. Added some pink tulips to the orange ones on the mantel and in the blue and white jug on the table. I set a table to welcome Spring with my new turquoise plastic bowls (four dollars each.) I hope they don't melt when I pour the hot chili in them. Even if I were wealthy and had a maid I'd set the table myself. I love setting the table. So did my mom. We'll have chilli and rolls. And there will be chocolate.

Society has regressed although some might see it as progress. I picked up a free copy of the local University newspaper as I often do to see what young people are thinking. This month's issue is full of advice and anecdotes about frisky, risky activities and I'm not talking about bungee jumping. Seems this lifestyle is commonplace, something now taken as lightly as table-tennis and with many and various partners, but with potential for dire emotional consequences if you're asking me. And large coloured pics to boot. The innocent publication that came out of my school in the late sixties was called The Cord. The articles discussed academic freedom, who is the best History Professor and why and would we prefer to invite Peter Paul And Mary to perform at Winter Carnival or Gordon Lightfoot? So I've put this paper deep into the depths of the recycling bin under the weight of the dailies so that if the wind blows them all over the street the one with the colourful high-jinx in pictorials will stay put. And we won't have to move.

THURSDAY, FEBRUARY 28TH, 2018 ~ An interesting day for both of us. John to the church for 8 a.m. for the free coffee morning for the university students and passers-by. Even the bus driver pulled over to get a cuppa. They asked him if he'd like a stir stick for the milk in his coffee and he said "It's ok. The potholes will take care of the mixing." They served forty-five cups and thirty-six chocolate chip cookies, had wonderful chats with neighbours, students, people from all over the world and a mom with two small children. They had a tent outside with Christmas lights on it and a good time.

A fun lunch with The Amigas (JS, LJ, VM). We talked about politics, grandchildren, the creative initiatives downtown to address poverty including the wonderful 541 Restaurant. We talked non-stop for three hours. And we still had more to cover.

Picked up the two books which have arrived at the library; The Beauty Of The Humanity Movement and The Man In The Wooden Hat.

The last thing I did today was to replace the calendar on the refrigerator so it says March. As always I wondered how it got to be March when only yesterday I was fixing up the window boxes for winter. Soon will be time to put out the pansies.

THURSDAY, MARCH 1ST, 2018 ~ A Cardinal sang me awake this morning with his long clear whistle and the throaty chortling of a Mourning Dove followed. It was a good way to begin the month of March. Hayley emailed a picture of their first Daffodil.

A windy overcast day so I stayed in and blew my nose and tried to nap but couldn't. Tired and cranky.

John went alone to the Compline Service as I

couldn't imagine playing the cello while blowing my nose.

A storm expected overnight with twenty centimetres and upwards of snow.

Our grandchildren make us laugh. Charlotte has registered for Senior Kindergarten next year. Lucia is tall and slim and is making progress every day and is getting ready for Something Great. She has two pigtails, sometimes three (one on top!), and I could gobble her up. E lost the Kindergarten Spelling Bee on purpose when she realized that the kids who made errors were given lollipops and told to sit down to eat them. H has constructed an amazing paper stoplight with the right colours in the circles. He hung it on string between the kitchen doorframe and made a road underneath it with a trail of toilet paper across the kitchen floor like the DC Beltway.

FRIDAY, MARCH 2ND, 2018 ~ Everything was flocked in white this morning from an overnight snowfall. Looked pretty, melting and dripping off the branches of the tallest pines, icicles crashing down from the eaves onto the back porch.

An email from Cherry in New Zealand this morning full of her lively stories of life on their sheep

farm in the "wop wops" which is the local slang for countryside.

Have been looking over the multitude of things in our china cupboard and am thinking that it's all a bit of much. What to do with all these tiny items to which I have attached significance? In the cabinet are many things, the smallest of which I list here: a bright blue antique Japanese cup and saucer with a white stork flying across it that my mom gave me when I was expecting our first baby, a dainty pair of floral china egg cups from the Katherine Cornell home in our lakeside town that were given to mom by her friend who bought the house and some of the contents including the egg cups, a china Buddha that belonged to John's uncle John. It is unmarked so not valuable but interesting in that it belonged to JRS who loved all things Asian, (including people, art, furniture, literature), and a miniature clay Creche from Dr. Maria, of Recife, Brazil. She attended the English classes at St. George's when she was at the university hospital for a year and gave us all one. Edwina and Charlotte love to hold it and make Mary and Joseph talk to each other.

The children want some of them but "not right now". They have no more room than do we; less, in fact.

John had a successful appointment at the Opthamologist's today so he can keep driving. I prefer that he drives so that I can look out the car window into other people's living rooms at night to see the cosy vignettes within. Yes. Shameful I know. But true. Other people's windows: that's where the stories live.

SATURDAY, MARCH 3RD, 2018 ~ A visit from N and H and children this afternoon. They want to go with us to York University to see the archives of The Mountain Fund to Help the Boat People. They hope to find some of Nhơn's letters he sent from the camp to John thirty-five years ago. It's interesting to watch the younger generation question what it was like for their parents. They've heard their stories but know nothing of their parents sacrifice to get here and to forge new lives. According to the York University Centre For Refugee Studies website our donated materials have been digitized but I could not find them online.

Himself and I to a different coffee shop late this afternoon. The scones were stale, crumbling and tasteless. And those nasty little blighters plus one tea and one coffee cost...way too much. All in all, *"tạm tạm". So so.*

SUNDAY, MARCH 4TH, 2018 ~ We said farewell to 12 year old Annie and her mom this morning as they head back to Chongqing. We'll miss them. Annie has been an enthusiastic player of the children's games and learned to sing, to speak and to read in English. She will return to her school of four thousand children which she considers small. She gave me a card this morning on which she had written a sweet message of friendship.

This afternoon at 3:00 to Choral Evensong at Central Presbyterian Church. Their Sunday afternoon concerts are a part of their Lenten series. The Soprano voice was as lovely, as uplifting as any voice could ever be. The stained glass windows are enormous and the acoustics stunning. John closed his eyes. Highly-pitched voices are hard on him. But I loved it. Next week I hope to get to their concert that will celebrate some of Bach, Telemann, Vivaldi although I could forgo the Vivaldi. It scrapes at me in the same way that some high notes get to John. Funny about how music works on each of us.

Drove down Locke Street afterwards to view the harm that came about from a group of thirty people dressed in black masks who took to anarchy last night. They pitched rocks through windows in the

beautiful shops. That included a clothing shop, new restaurants, cars, whatever got in their way. They were protesting gentrification. Confounding and sad to come outside after the beauty of the comfortable words at Evensong and witness the devastation that this angry mob perpetrated on the hardworking shopkeepers.

And on to Sagarmatha on King William Street for curry.

This entry, among others, is all about privilege or lack of it as it turns out. It's a divided world; the haves and the have nots. And I'll bet that it was the have nots who threw the rocks. But no excuses for the destruction.

We're missing the middle ground now. Forty years ago it was possible to have a solid factory job, buy a decent small home, earn a fair wage with a pension at the end of it. Not now.

MONDAY, MARCH 5TH, 2018 ~ Spent the majority of the morning organizing music and clipping it into proper bundles.

I promised Self that I'd make an entry in here for every day this year. Because of that I must say that the only thing that we did today was to go to Home

Hardware to buy some WD40 oil for the squeaky hinge on the bathroom door. And afterwards we drove down the hill and saw that John's white goose has wintered well and was back on his exact spot on the grass by the water. His exact spot mind you. We were glad to see him (her?)

TUESDAY, MARCH 6TH, 2018 ~ Our orchid still blooms; twenty-four blossoms today and as beauteous as they were in December. It has brightened up the sunroom all winter.

Last night we lost a friend in D. His stories of early Toronto were amusing and a bit historic by now. He was a wonderful musician and a spirited conversationalist. We leave our uniqueness in a trail behind us. We'll miss his friendship and our chats. We'll miss bumping into him everywhere we go. The servers at the coffee shop will miss him and his chair at the library will sit empty. We'll miss seeing him at the piano at Evensong. Again, on another shore.

Spent the morning chopping vegetables, (carrots, celery, leeks, onion, red pepper and two cans of corn), so that I'm one step ahead of myself for making the soup for Compline. I'll do the rest tomorrow. And then John and I discussed the Scripture Lessons for his next sermon which appear to be about the redemptive cycle.

Had I not over-planned my life this week I would be in Ottawa right now with N and her sweet son from Baffin Island. Maybe next time.

RMB's emails set my brain in gear. There are so many things to talk about, including the anarchy that unfolded nearby her own leafy neighbourhood and those quiet streets where we used to walk with our babies.

I love the way Himself knows which towel is my favourite and hangs it on my towel hook for me so it's ready for the morning. It's the small things...

A long music practice tonight.

WEDNESDAY, MARCH 7TH, 2018 ~ In March of 1996 Alan Bennett wrote this in his journal Untold Stories, (Bennett, 2005, 184.)

"I read the Sunday papers first thing, otherwise they hang about all day like an unmade bed. I find less and less in them to read and feel like somebody standing against a wall while a parade goes by."

I expressed that same sentiment to RMB yesterday, the feeling that the world has taken a peculiar turn, is marching on without me and leaving me speechless.

This time it's not about aging. It's about the fact that there is too much crazy-thinking and there are too many untethered reactions.

Note to Offspring: Tucked inside Bennett's book Untold Stories is a postcard from him. I had sent him a note about his helpful recollections when he took his mom (his "mam") to a nursing home. Don't toss it.

Found chicken on sale which I cooked this morning and added to the vegetables stewed in broth. I boiled the pasta which I'll add just before serving tomorrow night, enough to feed fifteen. I had to fiddle with it after I added the lime juice. Needed some sugar and sea salt to balance the flavour. It's in the refrigerator where the flavours can settle into themselves overnight.

THURSDAY, MARCH 8TH, 2018 ~ In March of 1940 (war) Charles Ritchie wrote this beautiful love note (Ritchie, 2008, 56); *"She has gone. There is nothing to show that she has been here except the toothbrush glass of faded violets and some talcum powder on top of the dressing-table...My heart hurts. I should like to have it removed and taken away on a silver salver."* Imagine!

Twelve people for Soup night; the warmth of the

friendships a panacea for a chilly evening. Yawning and ready for sleep.

FRIDAY, MARCH 9TH, 2018 ~ When HK/RK left their Ottawa posting to return to Britain in 2001 they gave us a wonderful book entitled Between Silk and Cyanide, A Codemaker's War, 1941-1945, by Leo Marks, Touchstone, 1988.

In the front piece Marks shares the poem he wrote in 1943 for Violet Szabo to use as a code. It's lovely and the first line is this;

"The life that I have Is all that I have And the life that I have Is yours."

He solved his first code at 84 Charing Cross Road, about which Helen Hanff wrote her novel of the correspondence between herself and the bookshop owned by Marks And Company at that same London address. It put her career over the top after she had declared herself a literary failure. She knew the value of saving old letters, even something as seemingly unworthy as letters back and forth about her book orders. Must find another copy of that gem of a book she wrote.

Was smack inside a Barbara Pym novel at a friend's funeral this morning; Surplus-and-Cassock clad Clergy, the singing of Abide With Me, the white satin Pall, a reading of Psalm twenty-three. M was ninety-seven. A small gathering of friends came to celebrate her good life.

June emailed to say that one of our favourite coffee shops has closed its doors. Where will we find another place with a wooden patio that overhangs the CPR tracks where we sit in Autumn sunshine, enjoying our hot drinks, our chairs shaking as the train whistles past? That spot was full of our city's messed-up romance that falls somewhere between funky and badly-in-need-of-repair. We'll miss the rocking clickety-clack rhythm of the tracks. Coffee mornings with JB & RB will never have the same cachet.

SATURDAY, MARCH 10TH, 2018 ~ A most beautiful sunset tonight. Dark gray, then a layer of orange-pink backlit with silver.

Went to the toy shop this afternoon to pick up a colouring book for Charlotte and two sticker books (dinosaurs) for our little friend on Baffin Island. I've wrapped them up in a big brown envelope with a pack of crayons. Must be difficult to find crayons at the top of the world and they'd be ten times the cost.

An entertaining tv night watching the political provincial leadership race. A boondoggle. Political life was once our own. Strange even now to be sitting on the other side watching that particular parade. We had fun together being armchair spectators tonight. Brought back old memories of times that were very good. Hayley emailed and said "I wish I was with Dad right now."

Time change tonight. It will mess around with my inner clock and I'll be nodding off at odd hours again. Spring Forward. Fall Backward.

Sunday, March 11th, 2018 ~ This is what it says in my Dad's copy of 'Pilgrim's Progress' (Bunyan, John, The R.T.S.,London, 320) which he received on this very day, March 11th, in 1923; *"Presented to George Pollard on leaving the Spurgeon Memorial Baptist Sunday School, Bletchley (England), for a new school in Canada. March 11, 1923."*

I've become the guardian of this treasure. It's in perfect condition. He was eleven years old when they returned to Canada. He was born here and they went back to Fenny Stratford, Buckinghamshire, when he was three months old. I'm glad they came back or he wouldn't have met my mom and I wouldn't be here to record these notes. Life is funny, isn't it? My paternal

grandparent's immigrated from England at different times and met here. My maternal grandmother, Mary Ellen Trotman from Woodstock, Oxfordshire, met my grandfather from Cork, married him in London and they arrived here. Our daughter's family has immigrated south and one of our daughter-in-laws has immigrated here from South America. We've coalesced from all corners to form a bunch of coconuts called "us".

Our two little Smith girls here for a visit. Fun to see Lucia cruising around the house, making new discoveries. It's all new to her now that she is grabbing the table edges and holding on. She no longer sees the world from the floor.

Brother-in-law has accidentally glued his index-finger and thumb together with Gorilla Glue, the major problem being that inside the 'O' shape of his glued fingers is the Drone he bought to play with last week. Rob! What would we do without him?

Public television has a most wonderful program of Sephardic music on just now from the Portuguese Synagogue in Amsterdam. It's brilliant. A young Orthodox man singing, his voice pouring out like honey.

MONDAY, MARCH 12TH, 2018 ~ A while ago I was talking in this Journal about sisters and about how they operate as individuals and sometimes as co-dependents. Found this nasty but well-written passage by Charles Ritchie (Ritchie, 2008, 23) this morning from 1938: *"The last of the three old Miss Odells is dead - foolish, ugly, innocent ladies coming down the aisle after Holy Communion, their silks creaking, their gold bangles tinkling..."*

The rest of the passage is too long to quote but it's worth buying the book just to read those two pages. A wonder he didn't devote his lifetime to writing rather than to life as a Diplomat. His is the old-world kind of writing; a bit precious I guess but descriptive, observant, flowing.

A snowfall all day today. It won't last.

This is the school's March Break week. Late this afternoon to the Frog Show at The Royal Botanical Gardens with Charlotte and Drew. She loved it. I had no idea that frogs came in such fascinating packages, not only camouflaged but some of them huge enough to eat small mammals. The tiniest ones in garish colours (black and orange) are poisonous enough to kill up to ten people. Oh dear. She enjoyed the frogs and the Spring bulbs in the Mediterranean Garden

but mostly she loved running around in circles in the empty puppet show pit at the bottom of the steps.

A reading marathon most of the day (one of those nod-off-then-jerk-my-head-awake kind of marathons) in order to finish Jane Gardam's book for the Reading Circle at the library. There are so few copies that it seemed fair to finish it asap. I should have made notes. How will I remember the nuances in May?

TUESDAY, MARCH 13TH, 2018 ~ More snow overnight and most of the day. It fell in big white chunks; everything covered, but not deep.

An email from LM in Stockbridge, Massachusetts this morning regarding news about her writing coupe. Am happy for her over this. She excels as a wordsmith. Her writing voice is clear, lyrical, intelligent. It pulls you along and encourages you to keep reading.

Friends in this morning for tea while they planned a Memorial Service with John for their dad who was full of intriguing stories and new ideas.

Charlotte came. She stood on a chair at the kitchen sink chatting away as she watched me make squash/carrot/onion/curry soup to help cure Granddad's cold.

WEDNESDAY, MARCH 14TH, 2018 ~ It's a grey day. John has a head cold and feels as miserable as the weather.

This morning to one of those walk-in hair places to have my hair trimmed in a straight line. I'm intimidated by hairdressers. What powers they wield over womanhood! In their hands are both sharp scissors and razors. Who's going to argue?

At noon a bowl of the soup I made yesterday and later a bit of reading. Our new sofa for the back room has not yet arrived so nowhere to rest my head when I feel the need which descends on me whenever I pick up a book. My eyes cross, my head feels too heavy.

There is something about taking a nap on the actual bed in mid-day that goes against Max Weber's Protestant Work Ethic. *Unberufen!*

THURSDAY, MARCH 15TH, 2018 ~ *"Et tu Brute?"* The Ides of March today. Friend Brock phoned to tell us to beware of men in togas who carry knives.

Another grey day and John in bed with his head cold. Staying in bed while ill goes against my theory that improvement only comes with acting as if you aren't sick at all. Unless you have malaria. Himself takes the opposite view. My method of acting as if

you aren't sick involves getting up at the regular time, taking a shower, getting dressed, eating regular meals and generally appearing normal. There is *man sick* and there is *woman sick*. Or so I've heard.

In preparation for Lenten Service this evening took cello to church this morning for a quick run-through. As was the case a few months ago, the G string offered up only a series of flat twangs. Refused to tune. How and why does happen? I brought it home. No point keeping it there hoping for a musical miracle. Disappointed as love to play with MR but feeling loyalty to sick husband as well as a return of my own cough. So no Soup And Compline tonight for us.

FRIDAY, MARCH 16TH, 2018 ~ (Nguyễn Ngọc Bích, Burton Raffel And W.S. Merwin, 1975, 26).

I have three books of Vietnamese poetry. Included in the above book is the work of poet Trần Nhân-Tông from the 13th Century who wrote these words in his poem called 'Climbing On Mount Bảo–Đại': *"Leaning on the balustrade I play my flute. Moonlight floods my heart, my coat."*

Bảo Đại was the last emperor of Vietnam. His real name was Nguyễn Phúc Vĩnh Thụy and he died twenty-one years ago. I'm not sure why the Mountain

in the poem was named Bảo Đại so long before this more recent Bảo Đại lived but the name must have significance.

John and I and Phán and Diệu went into one of the summer palaces owned by Bào Đại in Dalat, Central Highlands. It is Art Deco. I'm a nosey type so I loved it. The original furnishings were *in situ.* He had an escape hatch in his bathroom which led to an underground tunnel and then to a church in case he needed Sanctuary. His wife had her own Moon Watching Balcony in her bedroom. It was semi-lunar in shape and hung over a garden with mimosa trees below. I watched a fat red spider spinning away on that balcony and wondered if she had any idea as to the historical real estate on which she had chosen to weave her web. So when I read that sweet line today from Trần Nhân-Tông I thought about that balcony and imagined someone playing the flute there. Vietnamese culture attaches strong significance to the moon and to the natural world. Their poetry is full of beautiful and life-giving imagery. But the most recent Bảo Đại was a law unto himself I'm told so I don't envy his wife or his mistresses but a Moon Watching Balcony we could all use.

AB popped in with some of her Pea Soup from last

night. A treat indeed. And I picked up a few items at the grocery store towards Sunday lunch as AB and I are sharing the task this week. Stopped off to set up Parish Hall with mugs, cups, plates, napkins, bowls, trays so it's done.

Began to read my new book, The Dawn of La Belle Epoque. Love it.

I've painted my nails pink with some old polish I found in the bathroom cupboard. It looks like a manicure done by a three year old. Sloppy, uneven. Years ago when the children were small I realized one day in a moment of panic three hours before the fact that John had invited the architectural preservation committee for the City to dinner and we had both forgotten. I phoned Beatrice and told her my situation. "What should I do?" I yelped.

"Paint your nails and act grand," was her reply. So I slapped on the polish and ordered lasagna and salad and rolls from Zarky's. It was a good evening.

SATURDAY, MARCH 17TH, 2018 ~ *"Top O the mornin' to you."* It's St. Patrick's Day today and I'm one-quarter Irish and John thirty percent an Ulster Man. North met South. And married her.

My maternal Grandfather, Francis Joseph Roche,

was from Cork. He died when my mom was not quite two I think. That she never knew him was a great sorrow to her. Jan and Rob were able to find his house at 100 Tower Street in Cork and St. Finbar's Catholic Church where our Great-grandparents were married. Wish mom knew.

A chat with MA. She's been a forever friend. She isn't well. I'm worried and sad.

A quick trip to the Paisley coffee house this morning before some chores (bank, hardware store, Isaac's birthday card.) A large police presence this morning in the neighbourhood, even the two Police horses, in anticipation of the St. Patrick's Day parties that will unfold nearby the university. They start early, end late. Lots of students already this morning with their hair dyed green, shamrocks pinned on their shirts, one tall fellow in a Leprechaun hat. It's my guess that none of them have Irish ancestry.

Warm and sunny and lovely out so why me cranky? I worry too much. Must remind Self that there is One who is in ultimate charge and that One is not me. Worrying is one job that I can safely surrender.

The value for me in writing this is that I've just seen my own solution by that preceeding sentence although it is never as easy as it sounds.

SUNDAY MARCH 18TH, 2018 ~ Sunny! Warm! Church today boisterous. Many people popping into the kitchen with amusing things to speak about and AB in there with me trying to make tea and fill up the trays. It's all welcomed and it's all good. Those people are some kind of wonderful. T told me that he's "saving up to buy a car" when he's grown up. He's seven.

As I sit here this afternoon there's a scoot! scoot! scoot! across the deck. The chipmunk is back. A flash of cinnamon coloured fur and there he goes again.

Note to Self: must be careful when opening this sliding door.

MONDAY, MARCH 19TH, 2018 ~ Beauteous sunshine. Chilly wind. Perfection. To The Second Cup for Skinny Chai Latte this morning with M. Under discussion was the topic of Life in all it's sorrows, joys, frailties. It was a splendid ninety minutes.

This afternoon for cello tuning. A gorgeous day for a drive. Could have gone on for miles and hours.

Funny about the cycles that occur when aging brings back people into our lives from our early years. Recent emails from cousin in Winnipeg and now one

from the other side of the family from a cousin whom I haven't seen since I was twelve. Seems everyone wants to reach back over the years as a way of affirming that those childhood memories were real.

Tonight at the window on the back porch the outline of tall pines against an indigo sky, a silver slice of moon looking down at me.

Spring

TUESDAY, MARCH 20TH, 2018 ~ *"Some Vietnamese authours...write about* Phở *as enthusiastically as if they were crafting poetry."* (The Gioi Publishers, Hà Nội, 2014)

RMB and Self to Lạc Viên for our regular catching-up over a steaming bowl of Phở Gà. Zero degrees Celsius outside so a perfect day for that hot delicious soup. I squeeze lime juice into mine to make it more piquante.

Mostly we laughed. We howled and hooted in fact and didn't get the chance to slurp up all the noodles in our huge bowls because we were too busy talking.

Much of our conversation involved the New Crazy and the upside-down-ness of the world we once knew.

The aging process slips sideways into our conversations too. I told her that I always thought of Old Age as a separate country where other people lived. I was Young and they were Old and that was that. And then suddenly I got through Passport Control without knowing it, crossed over an unseen border and now I'm in!

Home to make a Creamed Salmon And Pea casserole for later this evening. Listened to Bach's Saint Matthew Passion while I read and dozed for the remainder of the afternoon.

An equally lazy evening.

WEDNESDAY, MARCH 21ST, 2018 ~ Happy Birthday Isaac ~ Am sure I heard a Red-Winged Blackbird this morning. They sing the best Spring song. Now I want to see one to prove that they really are back. Must get down to the Point where they flock together amid the sumacs.

A heart-leap over a violet-coloured Campanula which I bought at the grocery store this afternoon. It's in Virginia's blue and white pot on the dining table. I've put the china rabbits and our Hạ Long Bay chickens on the table too for Easter.

Lovely email from LF today wishing us a Happy Easter. We'll arrange a cup of tea in April. She was stuck in that huge snowstorm in Britain which involved buses and trains and back roads through snow-covered villages to get to the airport. I want to hear about it, especially the back roads part. I love back roads. That is where you find life.

Isaac's birthday today so a chat with him. Hayley and kids had a Snow Day due to what they call a storm down there which is not a storm at all by our standards.

THURSDAY, MARCH 22, 2018 ~ An early morning walk to the Point. I was looking for

Red-Winged blackbirds but saw not one. A clear day and lots of bird whistles but they were all hiding.

Dorothy-down-the-street has Snow Drops in her garden; not yet quite open but in full bud. And that lady around the corner who can grow Lupins has Snow Drops too.

Baby Boomer Wisdom says we should walk ten thousand steps per day. Today I tried to count them in sets of hundreds. The hill walk is at the least three thousand steps (rough estimate.) Since up-and-down and to the first bridge takes me thirty minutes that would mean that I'd have to spend ages per day going up and down. And since I was so busy counting steps that might be why I missed the Red-Winged Blackbirds and they were the reason I set out in the first place. I missed the glories of the day. That's the trouble with Baby Boomer Wisdom. They have left out the blissful, carefree piece. Note to Self: Give it a rest. Or get a pedometer which is what normal people would do.

Himself has just come home with some Hershey's Kisses which he has deposited beside me here. What's a girl to do? I'm all for kisses. And I'm all for chocolate. Combine them and I'm all over them like fleas on a dog. Dear Reader, I ate them.

Took Cello to the church for tonight's service and that G string is twanging again like a uke at the Grand Ole Opry. Why? Can play Tenor lines but no Bass.

Jan says that we should "Go Nice". She says we're getting too critical of governments/politicians/ policies everywhere. A world ruled by These Two Sisters might be good we think. I believe that to be true. But then she phoned back to say "Before we Go Nice can I just say this one last thing?" So Going Nice might take us a while.

Managed to play all the tenor lines and the melody lines for the Compline service with MR tonight in spite of having no G string. We practiced the Bach piece for next week. A wonderful season for music.

FRIDAY, MARCH 23RD, 2018 ~ A drive through the bucolic countryside this morning to a sweet small village. I needed to trace the exact route where I will be driving friends tomorrow for the birthday lunch for Joyce. Rich farmland abounds on Highway 5. A treat to see it. Everything else in south western Ontario is being dug up for condominiums and cement shopping malls.

This afternoon two abortive trips to James Street to the Spanish tienda which I love because the owner

blares loud Latin music onto the street. We wanted to arrange something for friends there. No parking spots to be found anywhere. On the second trip we got one right smack outside the store but the owner wasn't there. We decided that our plan wasn't meant to be so we came home, had some butternut squash soup and toast and now in for the night. Himself napping with instructions for me to wake him up in a bit.

Hayley has the flu, poor girl. Wish we lived close by.

SATURDAY, MARCH 24TH, 2018 ~ A stellar lunch party to honour Joyce's seventy-fifth birthday with eighteen of her friends. They represented the various facets of her well-lived life; nursing friends, neighbours, garden club, church. SA and HS planned it at all. I looked down the long table at the group of women and thought how much power is invested in each of them due to their contributions to the betterment of people's lives; medical professionals, educators, a linguist/translator, a Social Worker, people who ran businesses, volunteers, daughters, wives, sisters, mothers, hands-on grandmothers. They all do things to improve society, like VM volunteering at the food bank and MV stuffing hand-sewn bags with toiletries for impoverished Seniors

and JS volunteering at the half-way house for newly-released prisoners.

When I hear about the depravity of mankind at times I'll think about that Long Table Full Of Goodness.

I have developed two theories this past winter;

1. *The Picture Frame Theory*: You're having the perfect moment by yourself, or with a friend or family member so leave it at that. Draw a metaphorical picture frame around the scenario and don't allow any negative thinking or chat to seep through the frame and into the moment.
2. *The Long Table Full of Goodness Theory:* see above. Can be applied liberally everywhere. A balm to the soul.

Must add that I stayed awake in bed to see if I could come up with eighteen friends. I decided that if I were to fly/bus/truck them in from various spots in the globe I might be able to dig them up.

SUNDAY, MARCH 25TH, 2018 ~ *Palm Sunday* ~ A busy morning and a strong sermon including the idea that Jesus didn't make His Triumphal entry into

Jerusalem riding on a War Horse, but rather he came riding on a simple donkey as the King of Peace. Now there's a thought to be remembered.

A quiet afternoon and for dinner the Beef Stew I made yesterday. Enough left for tomorrow.

Leftovers; a soothing thought to help a girl sleep well at night with the knowledge that tomorrow she doesn't have to organize food.

MONDAY, MARCH 26TH, 2018 ~ Another trip to Burlington to get the cello tuned. The fellow explained again what happens when the wood dries and how to keep more moisture in and how to turn those gigantic wooden pegs by also pushing them inwards and then using the fine tuners at the bottom. He knows everything. I'll try to remember how to do it next time. Forced Self to take the 403 home. Feeling more courageous about that small but hideous stretch of highway.

A long phone chat with MA. She's been a terrific part of our lives for over forty years. She's ill. Am sad with her about it.

Himself with me down to James Street to the Spanish store. Found a parking spot that could not be found on Saturday and therefore mission accomplished.

Tonight to Beatrice's to speak to a University Women's Club small group about Lady Harris, Alice Seeley. A nice group of people. I suppose it went alright. Hard to say when it's yourself on tap.

Granddaughter E and her friend want to start a dog walking service. They are hardly tall enough to reach the top of a reasonably sized dog's head. They want posters around the neighbourhood. I wonder wherever they got that grand idea?

My favourite booksellers are closing. We'll miss them. So first one of our favourite coffee shops is gone and now the booksellers.

TUESDAY, MARCH 27TH, 2018 ~ *"Do diddle di do, Poor Jim Jay, Got stuck fast In Yesterday..." (De La Mare, 1958, 31.)*

In the morning newspaper an article about aging and quotes from various people about not being *"stuck in yesterday"*, in our pasts, but rather looking at what we are doing today. Memories have their place but we mustn't let them overwhelm the present. One of the interviewees was a ninety-five year old Physician who has recently returned from a trip to India.

Speaking of aging, our Charlotte is five years old today. Party is postponed for germ control reasons

until after the trip to the Cincinnati Children's Hospital in mid-April for Ms Lucia. They reportedly liked getting their Easter treat in the mail yesterday with the yellow duck on the card.

Rebecca popped in this afternoon. We had a cup of tea and some laughter over our shared grandchildren's antics. The children are on their Spring Break this week. Hayley took them to Mount Vernon this morning where they spent the small bit of Easter money we sent them in the gift shop. E wanted to pretend she was a Tour Guide when they got home. She took her mom on a house tour (of their own house). She spotted a large cardboard tube in the basement; "Ladies and Gentlemen this was George Washington's rake and when he was tired he used it to blow the leaves."

For the third night we had our leftover beef stew. All gone now. It got tastier as time went on.

WEDNESDAY, MARCH 28TH, 2018 ~ A soup-making day. This time I created a recipe for cauliflower/onion/celery/pear for fifteen people for Maundy Thursday Service tomorrow.

Went to the neighbourhood bookshop to say au revoir to the dedicated staff who have sold our family

tons of books for eons. They are closing down in a few days. That is where I bought Hayley's grade eight graduation book, (Lark Rise to Candleford), all the kid's Christmas and birthday books since they were tiny and on into adulthood, books to suit all of my own interests and all of John's and more recently books for our grandchildren. The last two art books we recently purchased there were mailed off to Ibiza for Great-niece Jazmin as she begins her studies at a British school. I was surprised at how emotional I felt saying goodbye to the sales associates. My goodness; how we do impact one another on our journey.

Had a bagel and egg salad for lunch at the Deli at the corner. They were so busy with Pesach orders that we didn't linger. It was a madhouse but we'll go back after Passover for corned beef and a dill pickle which is my favourite lunch of all possible lunches. And later, haddock and asparagus for dinner.

THURSDAY, MARCH 29TH, 2018

I've wondered at my crankiness this past month and have at last figured it out. Fear. I want things to stay the same rather than accept the idea that aging brings a new set of realities. Aging is an integral stage in life, the crowning of our relationships, and so it is vital that we stay our best. Easter gives me another chance to be patient, softer. “New every morning is the Love…”

We went to Shopper’s Drug Mart after lunch to buy the candy for the Sunday School children’s Easter Egg Hunt. Himself loves this event which he organized several years ago. He was a happy shopper in there with his cart full of small chocolate rabbits, colourful wooden wind-up toys, candies in bright foil wrappers.

A Spring rain today and the croci are up but not open. One Muscari plant is poking its head up and the daffodils are gaining strength but no blooms as yet. I see one lone Snow Drop by the old patio stones in the back and wonder how it got there. We might have those old stones dug out. I’ve suggested some pachysandra to fill up that space. Or Snowdrops? Daffs? Muscari? Lily Of The Valley?

When a certain publisher read my manuscript in 2014 for the Alice Harris book they offered to publish it on the one condition that I “remove all the violence”. I told them that I could never give in to lying by erasure regarding Congolese history. Lady Harris spent her career trying to convince people to see things for what they were. It would have unsettled me forever had I caved in to that request even though being published

by an arm of that company would have been a boost. There is no point in being untrue to one's core values and there is no point in keeping a Journal without honesty. So when I said I've been cranky it's the plain truth but the crankiness is based on love. I had thought about not including that cranky/worried piece but then what good is this exercise to me?

Writing is a panacea. It makes me see how to work things out.

The Dawn of La Belle Epoque is a riveting book but I've stopped into the library to pick up The Master Of The Prado for the Art Gallery Book Club in April. Must read it pronto so someone else can have a go at it as the Library has few copies.

MR and I played the music for the last service in Lent tonight. Whoever thought we'd be doing that when we first met with our small children and new babies on the way? My favourite is the Bach piece. It flows well with the two instruments together.

A darksome, rainy night.

MARCH 30TH, 2018 ~ Good Friday ~ I like to think about the thief on the cross saying to Jesus *"Remember me when thou comest into thy Kingdom"* and Jesus answering *"To day shalt thou*

be with me in Paradise". (St. Luke 23: 42/3 AKJV). That short exchange tells the entire Christian story; repentance. forgiveness. *Immediate* forgiveness. No "Why did you do that?" or "How could you?"

Such power there. The actual thief in the story was a bonafide historical character named Dismas. One of the things I love best in Ontario is the sight of the now closed Roman Catholic Church built by prisoners of the now also defunct Kingston Penitentiary between 1892-94. The men quarried the limestone, carted it out of the quarry and built the church, heavy block by heavy back-breaking block. Somebody named it The Church of The Good Thief, after Dismas. I think about those lonely men behind their bars across from the church with their name on it. I hope somebody told them that no matter what they had done their atonement entitled them to the same loving benevolence as Dismas knew, ergo gaining freedom in spirit if not in body. A Priest who was once in charge there allegedly wrote that Dismas *"snagged Heaven in a heartbeat"* with his asking forgiveness.

Am realizing all of these years later that growing up with a father working in the prison system has impacted the way I see the importance of the second chance.

Today the Good Friday Service, a warm and lovely phone chat with Lynn B., ditto with Jan, ditto with Hayley. And after dinner a CBC Radio One program with Inuk Moravians singing German music in Inuktitut. Moving. Stunning Inuk Soprano. Then a drive around the city where we sighted two deer feeding at the University.

SATURDAY MARCH 31ST, 2018 ~ The morning sun has opened up the yellow, purple and white faces of the croci.

Chirping abounds. A bird concerto going on outside our window.

Woke up to an emailed Easter greeting from a dear Muslim friend who exhibits grace at every turn. Her presence in my life is a gift.

A late start to the day. Had my eggs and toast and fruit while listening to Faure's Requiem. It puts me in a seasonal frame of mind as music often does.

We stopped at the bakery after breakfast to buy a cake for Easter dinner at D and E's. A strong sense of camaraderie in the line up; customers picking up small bags of pastel coloured meringues, baguettes, cookies, pies. I thought how sad it would be if they were to close too, like our bookstore and our coffee house. It's these small businesses that lend heart and soul to cities and towns.

This afternoon took Self to the harbour for a short brisk walk in the overwhelming wind. Loved it. It woke up my senses. Thrilled to see those same ducks I see every Spring bobbing on the water. Peterson's Bird Book points to Eider Ducks maybe. I tried to count them but lost track at thirty-five. My estimate is one-hundred plus. They were everywhere I went, even when I walked along the new boat moorings by the coffee shop. They dunk their heads in the water, then bottoms up. Sharp contrast between their coal black and snowy white feathers. Fantailed under-feathers. Frenetic wing beats. Where do they winter? I've emailed Drew to see if he thinks they are Eider Ducks.

I suppose the pink paisley Eiderdown my sister and I slept under in our very early years in that shared four-poster bed was stuffed with the feathers of those duck's Great-Great-Great Grandmothers.

Home for Globe Crossword and the CD of Bach's St. Matthew Passion.

This evening, rain. Lovely rain.

Post Script: Our other Peterson Guide to Eastern Birds says they are Bufflehead Ducks. So much for our childhood Eiderdown.

SUNDAY, APRIL 1ST, 2018 ~ *Easter Sunday* ~ Easter Sunday and our Christmas Orchid still in full bloom, mirroring a piece of theological imagery, Christmas and Easter so inextricably linked, one leading to the other, one the Advent of The Promise, the other the Fulfillment of The Promise, Old Testament prophesies and New Testament realities converging towards Hope.

John's Easter Egg Hunt a great success for the Sunday School with JNR dressed up in her fleecy white Bunny Suit.

A dinner of Butter Chicken, Chana Masala and Basmati Rice at Drew and Ely's with Charlotte and Lucia who were busy stirring things up. Fun to see how rough and tumble L has become. They bounce on the bed, do a crash-landing on top of one another and go back for more. A good evening. Then home to our quiet house which felt just dandy too.

MONDAY, APRIL 2ND, 2018 ~ *Easter Monday.* A wonderful morning walk past the first bridge. The Red-Wings were in full throttle. Their deep throated warble is my pick for Canadian Idol Best Bird Song. Strong sunlight and chilly. The perfect day.

And a general cleaning-up; vacuuming and the

moving of things. Even cleaned some silver spoons that were given to John's maternal Grandmother (Isabel Hamilton Quinn, then Barber by marriage.) Her Godmother gave her one spoon each year and we have ten of them. They were made by Savage Silversmiths in Montreal early on. John says he'll start using them in the morning to make his coffee. Why have these old things and not use them?

Dinner at Lemon Grass with Jock and Ashley tonight. Love them.

TUESDAY, APRIL 3RD, 2018 ~ In TS Eliot's The Wasteland he referred to April being the cruellest of months. Perhaps he was talking about the way in which Spring's glories touch the emotions we may have buried under the snow. At times I do find small scenarios so lovely that they have a shard of pain in them. The mauve lilacs that spread along the railing of our back porch do that to me. They take me back to a drive along a country road with my mom when I was small. She stopped the car to cut some overhanging wild lilacs. That was my first awareness of them, of their perfume, of their deep purple.

TSE also talk about memory and he talks about desire and he mixes them together as one. That idea brings back a sharp remembrance too of finding a patch of violets in the Quadrangle at school. I picked them and left them on someone's study carrel in the library. I must have been twenty. Memories of youth are potent. (Was I meant to be a character in a Jane Austen novel instead of being a real person?)

And because I don't like to think of April as being cruel I bought some red and orange tulips today so that it won't be.

First the head. Yesterday the shoulders. Today the torso. The chocolate Easter Bunny. Going, going but not yet gone.

A surprise visit with friends this afternoon. A.P showed me the photos of her eighty-seven year old mom whom she visited in Hai Phong at Tet; as sweet a face as any woman could have. The others reminisced about how it was when they first arrived. John will perform a marriage for one of their sons come September.

WEDNESDAY, APRIL 4TH, 2018 ~ Like a heroine in a Barbara Pym novel I had a hot milky drink before bed last night and slept like a baby. But if this is to remain an honest Journal then I have to declare that I melted the Easter Bunny's legs in the hot milk. Barbara Pym would never have recognized that chocolaty bedtime repast which for her was usually Ovaltine.

Heavy rain all night. The grass greening. Puddles on the lawn. Early today the sky a ghostly grey sheet lit up from behind. Later, sun. Worrying high winds; the ancient Russian Elms in the back garden are so huge they could take down the fence and the roof if they toppled. Snowflakes coming and going as if they are not sure whether they are supposed to descend in spades or just fool around.

Tea at the coffee house this morning. Just us and the university students. We are now, officially and always, the oldest people there. Everywhere?

I don't like reading The Master of The Prado so I'll return it. It's too mystical for me. But Dawn of La Belle Epoque is full of information about the gift and the building of Bartholdi's Statue of Liberty, given by France to America in 1885. When it was ready to send off it took two hundred and fourteen numbered crates and three weeks to load it onto the train for Rouen. RMB and I have stories about Rouen and the jolly huge French *homme* who gave us a tour and then persuaded us to buy him an expensive dinner. It was the least we could do after him showing us around the city by foot. I digress. After a perilous and almost fatal ocean crossing the Statue of Liberty arrived in New York. The idea of Liberty as a welcoming woman, inviting the world's distressed people into safe harbour, has been a wonderful one.

Granddaughter E has seen a local theatre's production of The Ugly Duckling at school today and was frustrated that the exact production wasn't on youtube tonight. "Just type in the name of my school" she told her mom "and it will come on." There was no convincing her that everything in this world is not on youtube.

THURSDAY, APRIL 5TH, 2018 ~ *Frumious* is today's word on the A.Word.A.Day website. It is a combination of furious and fuming and was the creation of Lewis Carroll in the poem Jabberwocky in his book Through The Looking-Glass.

A walk down the hill. Met there the man I see every time I go; about ninety-five years old, maybe a European accent. We exchanged cursory greetings today. My guess is that he has survived a difficult life which has made him strong in mind and body. He's my inspiration in the way that he walks. I'm a wus.

But since I'm usually wrong in my assessments of

other people he is probably younger than me, is a major violinist in an orchestra and an Orthopaedic Surgeon on the side and lives in a fancy condo somewhere nearby. After all, I'm the one who offered to a help a new neighbour behind me learn English. Left a note in her door to welcome her to the neighbourhood after I noticed her Islamic clothing. She hooted at me over the fence a few days later and said *"Hi! I'm so-and-so. I'm from Chicago!"*

We all do our best.

Is that a nuthatch or a chickadee on our back porch? A nuthatch, the Bird Book says.

The arrival today of John's late brother Garnet's saxophone and clarinet that were shipped from Ottawa by John's nephew Murray caused some glee. Our boys, who are the inheritors of these old instruments, came over tonight to have a look at them. They will need some reconditioning (the instruments, not the boys). A wonderful gift.

Later this evening watched Fake or Fortune on TV Ontario. Last night's episode dealt with an alleged Lucian Freud painting which proved to be a half-and-halfer, some done by him, finished by someone else. Getting more difficult to find worthwhile tv but this is a stellar program.

FRIDAY, APRIL 6TH, 2018 ~ Snow covering everything. Every little thing. It melted by mid-afternoon.

I walked to the bottom of the hill and felt better for doing it. Kept thinking of dad telling me how they had to march for mile after painful mile in the War with the help of the Bag Pipes of the Highland Light Infantry alongside on a flatbed truck now and again to keep both their pace and their spirits going. Had no Piper myself today but could have used one. Am afraid of losing muscle tone as I age so have no choice but to keep at this. Told Jan about this. She remarked that if she had been dad she would have learned to play the bagpipes so she could have been the one riding on the flatbed.

Then to run off some music at the copy shop and to pick up a tin of Habitant Pea Soup to which I added chunks of ham for dinner with a piece of toast. Almost got through the whole of New Tricks but caved at 10:45 and so to bed.

SATURDAY, APRIL 7TH, 2018 ~ This morning to the new grocery store. Decent prices on some items. Smaller than the mega-market where we usually shop. The cashier had copious fake eyelashes and her eyelids were so heavy that she kept opening and closing them.

A long and lovely visit with Jock this afternoon. I gave him some toasted rye with Guacamole Salsa spread. He reminded me that in downtown restaurants avocado toast costs $$$.

SUNDAY, APRIL 8TH, 2018 ~ I have a copy of Edna Staebler's Diaries, (Staebler, 2005, 151.) She said this; *"I must learn to translate my thoughts and feelings to paper."*

She was an Ontario writer and a cookbook writer too. She was singular, a one off, just herself. I liked her.

Sunday School this morning and the Damascus Road lesson. I asked the children what they would do if they were confronted by such a blinding, powerful, light as was Saul. Esther, who is five and fond of her pink, heart-shaped and sparkly sunglasses said *"I'd put on my sunglasses."* She would have looked a treat on the Damascus Road in those.

Wondering if our new sofa and chair in the sunroom is causing us to limp. It felt so comfy in the showroom. This is my new theory about sofa buying; you get out of the car park, walk a mile to get to the store, continue into the vast, over-heated mall, locate the store, walk around in circles until you figure out where the furniture department is, look at all the junk for sale and then you spot a sofa and you sink into it. But because your bones hurt by then it feels like the most comfortable thing on earth; Heaven. So you buy it. You get it home. You wiggle into it to find the Sweet Spot. You get up to get the phone/ to answer the door/to pour yourself a cuppa. You're surprised to find yourself limping. And you realize that the reason the sofa felt like Heaven in the store is because you walked for miles to get there on arthritic feet. Perhaps will get used to this new seating and this crippling business will go away.

Jock sent us the video of his friend trying out Garnet's saxophone which is ninety years old. Emotional to hear that sax belting with new life.

Nightie night.

MONDAY, APRIL 9TH, 2018 ~ The two gardening girls I refer to as Rosemary And Thyme spent the morning digging out the ancient patio stones, raking up the yard, trimming the overzealous boughs of lilac along the back porch railing.

Sent my annual membership fee to The Society of Women Writers And Journalists in Britain this morning. Feeling fraudulent as have not been doing any paid writing for a long while. I wasn't going to rejoin but rethought that. Giving it up after belonging for twenty-five years might be like closing down when at seventy it's healthier to expand. I'll see if my renewal bears fruit in any way. New ideas are my fresh air.

TUESDAY, APRIL 10TH, 2018 ~ The most glorious two hours this morning with Maureen in The Royal Botanical Gardens at Cherry Hill Gate trail. We walked until the trail took a turn and then sat on the bench and chatted. Birds everywhere; Nuthatches, Chickadees, Cardinals, Bluejays, Hairy Woodpeckers, all of them so near by that I could have put my hand out to touch them. I felt like Snow White with birds flitting everywhere and wanting to perch on my hand and the quiet air full of their music. Also, saw a pair of Whistling Swans and a Muskrat who was digging a hole in the mud. He took to the water when he saw us looking at him. The perfect morning.

Made soup with a tin of diced tomatoes, a cauliflower, an onion, celery stalks, vegetarian soup broth, sea salt, pepper, Parmesan cheese.

Spent an hour late today with our little Smiths to

say bye-bye before they leave for Cincinnati Children's Hospital tomorrow. Godpseed, sweet little ones.

WEDNESDAY, APRIL 11TH, 2018 ~ Via email this morning seems we're still working on naming that restaurant north of Toronto which a friend's family plans to open. What's a girl to do Dear Reader, when on a sunny Spring morning she can't think up a decent name for a restaurant specializing in certain types of Chinese noodles? I'm sticking with my original idea of The Dancing Noodle.

Small chores this morning on King Street and a tea and a vegan biscuit at the coffee shop. We are not vegans; the pistachio/coconut/sea-salt biscuit is.

Lynn F. here for tea and raisin bread this afternoon and a catch-up. Was lovely to be together.

In the London Review of Books today an article by one of my favourite of their writers, Rosemary Hill, regarding women's clothing and what Virgina Woolf called *"frock consciousness."* Who knew that the pullover was revolutionary? It was invented just as women started to dress themselves rather than have their maids, or in the case of the poor, a family member, do it for them, with buttons to be done up, hooks to be fastened and corsets to be laced. Soon

women everywhere were tugging those pullover sweaters right over their heads all by themselves. Freedom!

As for me, I have no frocks of which to be conscious.

A phone call from Cincinnati from Charlotte who said this: "Grandma we're at the hotel and we have a red chair that is big enough for two people and we have a great view."

THURSDAY, APRIL 12TH, 2018 ~ To take John's jacket for new zip to seamstress this morning. Have decided that since he (the seamstress) is not female maybe he needs to be referred to as the seamster, sort of like a teamster, only without the Union to back him up. He has recently bought the business from the former owner. I asked him if he was from Iraq. He grinned like a happy kid at Eid. For the first time he raised his head, looked up at me. His smile came from home, all the way from Baghdad, from somewhere deep inside. "Yes!" he proclaimed.

A drive through this socially depressed city this afternoon. If it were mine to fix I wouldn't know where to begin.

Here I am saying the above and yet at the same time delighted that in the mail today came a copy of

English Home magazine. I'm an unabashed lover of floral fabric, bright wallpaper, Chinoiserie, colour. I am my mother's daughter. And a hypocrite by the sound of things.

Drew emailed from Cincinnati to say that the all is ok. Our brave smallest member; what a girl.

FRIDAY, APRIL 13TH, 2018 ~ MH and JB here for our regular cuppa in the back room. In the summer our Porch Parties will resume on our various porches. Dependable types, those two. Solid as Gibraltar. A good morning indeed.

Later MH sent along a new recipe for noodles, asparagus and lime zest. Will try.

A quiet afternoon but a most disturbing evening. The tv news. How to sort it all out?

SATURDAY, APRIL 14TH, 2018 ~ The greyest, windiest day ever. And cold.

This morning to the Women of The Church meeting over tea and lemon loaf. A cosy time with the five of us who braved the ridiculous weather. The Book Of James; full of common sense and the genuine, deep-seated wisdom of the ages. VM pointed out that the words *wisdom* and *understanding* are frequently combined in the passages, that one never occurs without the other in a kind of parallel idea. I told them about my new theory, about finding threads of commonality that bind us to the vulnerable. It could prove a panacea to isolated people and to ourselves who stand to learn much from them. It won't be political posturing or policies that move us forward toward a better society. Only well-founded people policies will make that happen. And people policies aren't made up of endowed committees. They are formed by the small efforts of the Canadian public, one by one. We must progress in our social thinking. There is an ill-begotten idea that throwing money at situations will move them ahead. Tiny actions of friendship, a smile that says "I see you!", not money, will help heal heartbreak.

I've developed three new theories this winter: The Picture Frame Theory, The Long Table of Goodness Theory, The Thread Theory. It makes me feel better about not cleaning the oven. (I'm not really a philosopher. I'm an old snollygoster at heart.)

A long phone chat with cousin Donna this afternoon; both of us wishing we were more mechanically inclined so we could figure out household things and how to fix them.

At 3.30 the predicted ice storm began. The wind as wild as can be. If the Russian Elms blow down they will crush the house, John napping on the bed, me in my new tangerine-coloured armchair, and the radio that is pouring out the loveliest piece of music by Felix Mendelssohn ('Hymn of Praise') on CFMX-FM.

A wild evening, but not in the sense you're thinking, Dear Reader.

SUNDAY, APRIL 15TH, 2018 ~ Ice! Wind! Rain! The doors frozen shut! Two plans: mine is that we keep a hammer nearby the outer glass door in case it needs to be smashed to save our lives. The Bolshevik's plan is that we should keep the wooden front door open and hike up the furnace so that the outer glass door will feel the heat and melt the ice. At about 4 p.m. we spotted our neighbour outside with her shovel. I opened the window and shouted "Diana! Can you clear away the ice from our front door? Can't get out!" So she did, the lovely girl.

This is the first time in my life that I remember Church being cancelled. It makes good sense as I don't suppose God is crazy about the idea of His Peeps at St. George's checking into the Orthopaedic Ward at The General dragging broken femurs along behind them.

We didn't seem to get the same memo the rest of the province got as to the gravitas of this storm and didn't get groceries but don't tell our kids or they'll have us put into a Home.

Just hard-boiled some eggs and roasted two pieces of pork loin in case we lose electric power later. Not a bone of pioneering spirit in me.

Phoned Helen in Dumfriesshire this afternoon to wish her a happy birthday. Had a wonderful chat and with Rob too. Golden friends in them and many happy hours spent together. They thought it funny that we are frozen into our house when they have snowdrops out and the daffs have already bloomed. They await the bluebells in the wood behind their house. Years ago a ticket agent at a castle asked Helen and me if we wanted the senior's rate. Found it annoying then as we were still in our early 50's. Now, we'd go for the discount.

MONDAY, APRIL 16TH, 2018

"Nothing on the grey roof, nothing on the brown, Only a little greening where the rain drips down..." (De La Mare, 1958, 90.)

Rained all night.

This noon-hour an outdoor Memorial Service

and Burial at the old Cemetery where tall Victorian monuments loom in dark granite over the city's founders. John laid to rest the urns of two good souls among bucketing rain, ancient dripping trees, a few mourners under the small canopy. Looked like an episode of Midsomer Murders. We sang their favourite hymn, All Things Bright And Beautiful. And then a funeral tea at their son's house; old-world style. A large percentage of newspaper obituaries today say things like "Come and share some drinks in his memory at Bill's BBQ Place And Bar. Live band. Wear loud colours." We all need different things according to what we know and feel. I'm stuck in traditional mode which can be seen as either fortunate or unfortunate, depending on your point of view. A mix might work.

Marg and I to cello concert downtown tonight. Expected soothing strings. Wondered why ten million young people were crowding in the door with us. Knew that 2cellos does different music (movie themes, etc.) but did not expect Michael Jackson's Thriller, girls screaming "You're hot!", dancing, strobe lights, driving drum rhythms for ninety minutes. Lots of prancing up and down the stage and rolling around on the floor with cello. Who did that sort of thing back in the day? David Bowie? Mick Jagger? Remind me.

The kids in front of us were kissing and lollygagging the whole night through. Who does that at a concert hall? And you can drink beer and eat pizza in there now. Used to be that you got dressed up to go there. I had just finished telling Marg that I enjoyed playing the Bach piece at Easter and before I knew it we were both singing I Can't Get No Satisfaction with the other ten million children when I was expecting we'd be humming along to Arioso. Was all worth the ticket price for the laugh we had at Selves. A very good time for MH and for me.

Got home at ten o'clock from concert and John said he's been dizzy for three days so wanted to go to Urgent Care at The General to make sure it isn't more than vertigo. He insisted I come home at 1.30 this morning from hospital. I can't settle so am writing this. Creepy coming home by cab at that hour in this city.

TUESDAY, APRIL 17TH, 2018 ~ John home at eight this morning with no bad news thank goodness. He has a crystal lodged in inner ear just as I had diagnosed and it should pass within the week.

I slept fitfully and very little. Himself told me this morning that he learned much on his overnight stay.

He related many tales of being on a cot nearby other patients, one of whom screamed from marijuana overdose the entire night.

My letter to The Editor was in The Spectator this morning about the legalization of marijuana which concerns me for the sake of the nation's youth. The new form of weed is reportedly loaded with dangerous chemicals and has been designated by child experts as a gateway drug that harms the developing brain. But nobody seems to be listening. Aging makes you over-think perhaps. Or makes you smarter. One or the other. Will let you know which when I figure it out.

Was out to get groceries early this morning so North Atlantic Salmon for dinner tonight. Some left over for lunch tomorrow, which we'll enjoy cold with vinegar and cucumber.

Granddaughter E pleased that she has two loose teeth and grandson H pretending his are also loose.

God Bless us everyone; especially the young boy with the drug overdose with whom John shared the Emergency room last night.

WEDNESDAY, APRIL 18TH, 2018 ~ Quick trip to grocery store in order to make scalloped potatoes to take to D and E's for dinner later. En route

home stopped at coffee shop. JB/RB were there; an unexpected jewel in the day. Then to library to pick up dvd called Victoria And Abdul with hopes that we can make the dvd player work this time.

L'Assommoir has arrived but not in French. The whole purpose was to give my hippocampus a kick-boxing, neural-pathway-producing workout. But as the time period ties in with my current reading I'll get a better picture of the era.

We had Cincinnati Chili at D and E's tonight. They had a fruitful trip to the USA last week.

THURSDAY, APRIL 19TH, 2018 ~ Little sister's sixty-eighth birthday. I looked in Charles Ritchie's Diary this morning (Ritchie, 2008, 470) to see what he was thinking in mid-April of 1963. Mike Pearson had just defeated Diefenbaker and Ritchie was writing farewell notes to those he had enjoyed working with in Dief's office. He writes *"I shall not be writing to Diefenbaker. I consider his disappearance a deliverance; there should be prayers of thanksgiving in the churches. And those sentiments do not come from a Liberal."*

I read that passage to Himself *after* he'd had his breakfast. When John was a young boy and living

in Ottawa he crawled under Diefenbaker's tent to see what was going on inside. Dief was not yet the Prime Minister. John enjoyed himself and decided that when he was grown up he might like to try the political life himself. So he did.

Years later, we were invited to have dinner with Dief and five other people at The Connaught Hotel. He seemed lonely, broken for his losses, both politically and on a personal level. He talked non-stop but he was a pleasant dinner companion. That is what happens when we wind up alone after a wide life. People's stories of former glory become discounted even though he had been one of the first outspoken critics of Apartheid in South Africa. The fall from political grace is a long one. I mentioned to someone we met soon afterwards in another situation that Mr. Diefenbaker seemed an ordinary fellow, the type you could have for a weekend visit. I had no idea that the man to whom I said it was a friend of his. He called me the following week and said "Mr. Diefenbaker would like me to tell you that he would enjoy a weekend at your home." I had a conniption. We had a tiny house, one bathroom. In no way could I imagine myself schlepping around in my housecoat, Dief brushing his teeth in the bathroom, John wondering where to put Himself. I can't remember exactly how we got out of it but it never happened. A good story and a true one. Saddens me now that I know more about life/aging/isolation to recognize that it wasn't grandeur he was after for a weekend. It was friendship, having listeners. It was people. We learn too late.

FRIDAY, APRIL 20TH, 2018 ~ Sunshine, finally. Wasted (spent) much of today waiting for a phone call that never came.

"Wasted most of the day" is a poor choice of words whereas "Spent most of the day" answers the question "Is any day wasted?" It's an insult to time to say that a day has been wasted. Readiness to listen to time and to the rhythm of the day has turned today on its head, from a discouraging sort of a day into an enlightened one. Time must be valued.

Tonight out for a hamburger with Himself. Always makes me feel like a teenager on a date so it's my favourite thing to do.

SATURDAY, APRIL 21ST, 2018 ~ A musical day. Played the Psalms At Midday Fundraiser over the noon hour; piano, upright bass, violin, viola, cello. Playing in harmony uplifting and fun.

A lazy afternoon listening to CFMX-FM with the Crossword. Heard a lovely piece of music on the radio sung by Josh Groban. It was the Love Theme from Cinema Paradisio.

An evening of better than average British mysteries; Father Brown and Midsomer Murders. The bucolic English village in Father Brown is just the ticket.

The most beauteous fingernail moon looking down at me as I type this missive far too late. And so to bed.

E has lost two teeth.

SUNDAY, APRIL 22, 2018 ~ A large congregation this morning. Today's warmth and brilliant sunshine got people out of the house.

Ashamed to admit that we haven't used the dvd player in two years so had Jock run through it with me this afternoon when he and Ashley popped in. A friend on the other side of the world can get emails from us in a few minutes so why can't someone design a dvd system that doesn't take three converters to work? We watched Victoria and Abdul tonight. I love that she upheld this gentle Muslim Indian man in front of the household staff who were rude and cruel

to him. Who knew she had learned to speak and to write Urdu? I suppose if you're the Empress of India you really ought to. She told Abdul that he was her only true friend.

MONDAY, APRIL 23RD, 2018 ~ St. George's Day and a new Prince, Prince Louis of Cambridge.

An early morning treat; a faun thought he might scamper across the road on the hill until he saw me. Perhaps his mother had crossed into the woods ahead of him and left him to try it himself. I stopped, said "After you" but he scrambled back up the hill. He was frightened, poor thing. What joy for me though.

Lunch today with JS and LM at an Eastern restaurant. Delicious. Will be living with the garlicky aftermath for some time but worth every bite as those two Wonder Women enrichen me at every turn.

Came home to a long phone chat with LB who is planning her garden at the cottage. We talked about how difficult the war years must have been for our parents and we pondered this important matter; why do those rings embed themselves in our flesh for ages when we take off our knee socks?

More reading of my Paris history book, Dawn of the Belle Epoque. Am trying to finish it so I can get

on to other things. If I don't record new learning it flies off. Here is what I've learned. The strange French word (poubelle) for trash can presents a conundrum until you discover that Eugene Poubelle was the Prefect of the Seine who was in charge of garbage collection. Sculptor Antoine Bourdelle taught his students this bit of lovely thinking; "Sing your own song". The Poet Mallarme held literary salons in Paris on Tuesday evenings in 1876. Only men were invited. Not fair.

Note to Offspring: If you care a hoot about salons see my article about same:

<booksbywomen.org/the-literary-salon-and-how-to-have-one> or check the Women Writers, Women's Books website under the article's name.

Salons are worth reviving in terms of the ideas they generate. They were early think tanks.

In an effort to protect new ideas from flitting away, my books are underlined, notated, marked up with marginalia. This is considered infamy in some quarters. But why waste what I've just read and will forget? The man with whom I share my life cries "You have too many books!" and I reply "They mark out my life, inform my ideas, give me new thoughts. I need

them." My notations have turned my books into small personal treasures.

The news out of Toronto is horrific. Won't repeat it here because the world has heard it all day long and nobody needs to read it again. Tonight the world tucks itself into bed with that on their minds.

Bambi on my peaceful morning walk. Friendship in the afternoon. Tonight, that.

TUESDAY, APRIL 24TH, 2018 ~ A funny day. Not much doing. John had a good eye appointment. Was boring waiting in clinic so read the wall charts to exercise brain. I read about Macular Degeneration and I memorized the Hospital Emergency Codes chart;

Code Blue = Cardiac Arrest
Code Red = fire
Orange = outside emergency that will soon arrive for Triage
Silver = active shooter
Aqua = flood
Black = bomb.

Hospitals everywhere should invent a new more uplifting code, like for instance Code Pink meaning "You're in the pink! All better now"!

A soft rain all day. I like this weather.

JB &RB sent us a link to an article about Victoria and Abdul. How could we have missed this fascinating piece of British history?

WEDNESDAY, APRIL 25TH, 2018 ~ A light rain all night through. The grass is greening and the daffodils are up. Tiny blue Scilla all over the front lawn.

CBC interviewed people on the street about the tragedy in Toronto. Every one of them said something positive. An East Indian man said "This has changed my life. It will make me a kinder person."

There was beauty in his statement in the midst of the horror. He could have vowed to get even or to hate the perpetrator or to live in fear from now on in. Instead he has decided to make himself a better man, which indicates that he is a pretty good fellow to start with.

Lucia is in hospital. Code Pink, Sweetheart.

THURSDAY, APRIL 26TH, 2018 ~ John and I for dental check-ups this morning. Per usual our girl at the desk handed us two toothbrushes on the way out with the question "Are the blue and the

green colours ok for you?" It seems that some people complain if the free toothbrush doesn't match their bathroom. Someone's watching too many of those home improvement tv shows.

Charlotte spent the afternoon and evening with us. We played with Rory's Story Cubes, found words that rhymed with hat, drew pictures, made an animal shelter with playdough and some furniture for the Fisher Price people to sit on. Uncle Jock came for the evening and got out the ancient and huge tub of Lego. A hit. Glad we didn't throw it out when we moved down here. They made a two story house complete with a door that opens and a rooftop kitchen. Swanky indeed.

Many memories are embedded in that box of plastic Lego. The one that stands forever is this. Elad was a little boy from Israel who used to come to visit his grandparents next door to us. I best remember the summer he and his toddler brother came to get away from a violent incursion. Our boys and Elad spent hours with the box of Lego. Every now and again an eerie sound would come wailing out of the sunroom via Elad. I asked him if he was ok.

"I'm making air raid siren sounds," he said, "to warn the people to get out of the way."

The three of them, Jock, Drew and Elad, were "building a city" together with those tiny plastic blocks throughout the summer weeks. Their project grew bigger and more extensive. I watched their sweet little heads bowed towards their noble civic project and wondered what happens between boyhood and manhood that makes people want to tear down rather than to build up.

Our Lucia is feeling better tonight.

FRIDAY, APRIL 27TH, 2018 ~ Lucia is home. Happy her. Happy us.

A haircut this morning at the cheap walk-in place. I felt more satisfied than if I'd paid a small fortune.

Once in the extreme folly of youth RMB and I decided to spend a whopping amount of our pay cheques at a chi-chi salon in Toronto. I was going to name the salon here but googled and see that it is still in business so will pass on shaming them. The owner had a reputation for being the best (read *most expensive*) stylist in the city. We made joint appointments. RMB was finished first. When I got out to the car she was behind the wheel, a scarf tied over her head. "You should see what he's done to my hair!" she yelped. I abhorred what he had done to

mine too. That was the end of my expensive hair cuts to date. Snip!

Midsomer Murders good tonight. I think I've seen it before. That speaks to being seventy perhaps, when I think I've seen it before but can't be sure.

SATURDAY, APRIL 28TH, 2018, ~ A quick peek down the hill on the way home from a few small chores this morning. The hillside is clothed in bright moss as are the grey limbs of the pine trees. Nature has its own palette. It knows what to wear to suit the occasion.

Rain and the crossword; almost finished it but always those remaining blank squares stare back at me.

The obits are entertaining. Take for example the one today about a woman of ninety-six. She was still waterskiing in her elderly years, her best trick being that of placing her foot into the handle of the ski tow so that she could wave to people on the dock with both hands. I tried to demonstrate for John how she must have put her foot in that handle while leaving both hands free to do the waving part. We fell into hysterics.

Volume 40 Number 8 of the LRB arrived this week.

The ads speak of a *"Studio for short lets in the heart of Chelsea..."*.

There is also, among many others, an article to cherish about Tolstoy and Tolstaya (Mrs. Tolstoy), regarding the new book, A Life In Letters. From the bits I've read so far I see that Tolstoy wasn't the kind of guy you'd want for a husband. He was a nightmare. He left Tolstaya to take care of their thirteen children, nine of whom survived, while he went off to have a think.

The pine table beside the armchair in the sun room is piled high with good things to read.

SUNDAY, APRIL 29TH, 2018 ~ (Hazel K. Bell, 2004, 12). This, from French philosopher Simone Weil; *"Christianity is pre-eminently the religion of slaves, that slaves cannot help belonging to it, and I among others."*

The idea of early Colonialism begs this question of me and has for a long while; if the system was so disreputable, and it was, (i.e., Belgium's rubber trade for one example), why did the slaves cling to the Gospel message and why do their descendants cling to it still? You'd think they would have spurned it.

Could it be that embedded deep in that message was

their guaranteed acceptance? That their individual equality was ensured? That they connected to the idea of a God of unconditional love? That the one freedom they could grasp in their present physical life was a spiritual one, and that it was theirs for the taking, no strings attached? It's an interesting idea.

The common ground between Pym and Weil was that they were both drawn to the poetry of George Herbert, and Weil was especially drawn to his poem called 'Love'. *"Love bade me welcome: yet my soul drew back..."*

A drive through the city approaching it from a different angle, eastward along York Blvd. It looked much better that way unless you count the Police presence outside of the halfway house standing beside the man with the bloodied face.

Unforgotten is the name of our new favourite tv British mystery on Public television Sunday evenings. It held us both in silent speculation for an hour.

MONDAY, APRIL 30TH, 2018 ~ To the coffee shop at noon to split a toasted chicken sandwich with Himself. We made a suspect chart about last night's tv mystery as we ate, in hopes that we can solve it ourselves before the end of it. Who has what to lose? The teacher who has just been connected to an Escort Service in her youth? The lawyer who is in the middle of adopting a child whom he and his partner desperately want? He has promised ransom money to the putative father of the child. It begs the question as to why he was willing to hand over five thousand Pounds to this *arriviste* stranger. What does the stranger have on him? The ex-cop and wife of the murder victim? The angry nurse who seems to be disconnected to this story; where does she fit? Or is she meant to throw us off the scent?

Charlotte here this afternoon. She focused for four hours on the Lego.

I've been thumbing through Barbara Pym's Excellent Women where she talks about the books by her bedside. She liked reading cookery books in bed and Christian Rossetti. It has made me take a look at the books by my own bedside, all of them poetry books: two books of John Betjeman's poems (my favourite of the lot), Philip Larkin's Collected Poems (borrowed from daughter. Forgot to return), Keats Poetical Works (from my mom, April 1966), Wordsworth (Christmas 2008, from John), Lyric And Longer Poems (Grade 11 English text), W.H Auden's As I Walked Out One Evening (daughter's. Must return), Collected Poems W. H. Auden, (gift from daughter, Oct. 1966. Why? Must ask), Yeats When You Are Old, (bought recently. Title self-explanatory.)

Can't say I've read them all. And no, don't picture me in bed with an erudite book in hand. Head hits pillow; I'm away. But I'd love to *imagine* that I say farewell to the day propped up with pillows reading poetry.

What's on your bedside bookcase, Dear Reader?

TUESDAY, MAY 1ST, 2018 ~ To the mall to buy towels this morning. Now we have new soft blue ones and I can pitch the slovenly ones. Why do I form attachments to inanimate objects, to towels which belong in A Museum Of Antiquities?

Today was as warm as a summer's day. Time to dig out some seasonal clothing. Must I? I'm happier in my cosies, my knee socks, pull-over jerseys.

Cherry Hill in New Zealand sent me a brilliant poem she wrote after I told her that a great title would be Who's Who In The Wop Wops? The wop wops is NZ slang for countryside. Her poem warns of being careful of whom you speak about when you move to a new place, just in case.

Who's who is essential knowledge for anyone

changing locations. I learned that lesson when we moved to a pretty lakeside town when I was twelve. My mom felt scrutinized by some women I think. She missed her old friends but was fortunate to make two very good ones in our new place. (Myrtle. Ethel. Barbara Pym's Excellent Women, both of you.)

The oldest residents of that town, the who's who, were still boasting all of those years later that one of their antecedents had "danced with the Prince of Wales" when he came to open the town hall which was modelled after the Old Bailey in London. This event took place in September of 1860 and yet still they were speaking of it in the 1960's. I can't imagine that the Prince was over the moon about that stop-over. "Who is this woman who wants to dance with me and how can I escape this Colonial outpost?"

And so it goes...

WEDNESDAY, MAY 3RD, 2018 ~ Another one of those beauteous sunny days when we run around getting things done; the plumber this morning to fix the bathroom drain for an enormous sum, to Honda this afternoon to get the snow tires removed (ditto re enormous sum.)

John planted five of the raspberry canes this

morning and I watered them; a joint project. We have another five to plant. The racoons will get to the fruit before the children will I'm sure.

Am preparing for the Jane Gardam Book Discussion group tomorrow night; am interested in the Raj orphans. In an ironic twist the colonizer's offspring often suffered greatly. Gardam's trilogy deals with it in a subliminal way.

THURSDAY, MAY 4TH, 2018 ~ Back to the mall first thing this morning to exchange items that didn't suit. Picked up on-sale shoes that kind of jumped out at me just as I was going out the door. Hope they don't kill my feet but you can only wear orthotics for so long without pining for shoes with pizzazz. Spring Fever is an annual event with me

Had a wonderful time at the library book discussion tonight. Same terrific people from The Pym Reading Circle returned except that JB and RB were not able to come and we missed them. I took copies of an interesting article from The Independent about her writing from September 2009. Have decided to meet three times a year and maybe four so we can cover all of her books. Next book, Last Friends, for September.

FRIDAY, MAY 4TH, 2018 ~ The wind thrashed and rushed in gusts all day pitching everything in its way. I feared for those Elms. But Spring is here, clothed in tiny green leaves on the Dogwood, on the sapling I'm growing from the defunct Amora Maple and on the small tree the city replaced on the front lawn. There are huge buds on the lilacs. Goldfinches swathed in yellow feather's feast on K-and-L-next-door's Niger seed.

This morning a quick whip around the grocery store to stock up. I roasted a plump chicken for dinner but Himself not wanting anything much as he was out for a hearty lunch with longstanding friends. We ate some in a sandwich tonight but I realize that I never like the taste of chicken nowadays. It tastes like wax.

SATURDAY, MAY 5TH, 2018 ~ A long phone chat with Hayley who was thrilled at the turnout at last night's International Night at the local school where their family hosted the Canadian table. E's tiny sweet friend was stunning in her sari. She sent photos of the girls side by side, smiling, excited.

Later to Charlotte's fifth birthday party. Elizabeth made a beauteous birthday table with tiny flowers and pink and mauve treats and small paper lanterns on the ceiling. And strawberry mousse with fruit stirred in.

SUNDAY, MAY 6TH, 2018 ~ This morning we sang He Who Would Valiant Be. It is one of my favourite hymns. It was written in 1684 by John Bunyan et al. It has both a beautiful full melody and determined words. I wish to become valiant as I age. Growing old is a kind of Honourable Mention. It is commonly dismissed as a time when we no longer have a role to fulfill. Aging is as important as the other stages of the human life cycle. You heard it from me. I'll try to make good on it.

Finished reading Lila, by Marilynne Robinson. Was a strange book but am glad I read it.

We waited all week to see the second episode of *Unforgotten.* We sat silent and riveted. The plot becomes further layered. High quality British mysteries are not as frightening as the low-end ones. Better writing. No need to add eerie effects.

MONDAY, MAY 7TH, 2018 ~ (Ritchie, 2008, 192). *"Lunched with Elizabeth in the downstairs grill in the Ritz. There were pink tulips on the table with pinkish lights. It was odd coming into it from the*

sunlight and the wind. We talked as we did when we first got to know each other. It was one of those times which we shall both remember afterward and say to each other, "that fine, windy Sunday in spring when we lunched underground at the Ritz."

That was novelist Elizabeth Bowen about whom he was writing. I don't need lunch at The Ritz, but I'd be fine with lunch anywhere at anytime, especially outside. Just say the word.

My mom was born on this day in 1911 which would make her 107 today.

A morning email from a friend from Saigon with lovely news about a young boy in Quảng Nam province who has won the Gold Medal for his school English tests.

Beautiful weather. Have just been to the Garden Centre at the grocery store. Came home with two four foot cedar trees in pots (two trips) which I lugged to the back porch using the baby stroller as a dolly. Also bought some hot pink bougainvillea and plant food to feed it. Brian and Gail have bougainvillea vines of orange and pink blossoms floating down from the rafters of their front porch. Since we are not living in a Mediterranean clime as are they I must remember to bring it in tonight in case it's chilly. Swept off the deck, washed the outside

windows, set up the outdoor furniture and put up the turquoise umbrella. Have created the Sweet Spot where we can sit, read, think in peace with our bird friends and where we can have lunch out of doors. The Mister must be persuaded to join me in these pleasures. Perhaps this could be the year for it.

TUESDAY, MAY 8TH, 2018 ~ Alan Bennett; what would I do without his humour? He wrote (Bennett, 2016, 307) in May of 2013 about the starlings in his garden that *"have the look of a threadbare maitre d' who hangs up his tailcoat shiny with age in his cheap lodgings every night."* I can't say I'm a lover of starlings but John is keen on them.

Cracked my egg this morning to find twins. Twin eggs. Double yolks. The next one was the same. And the next. Oh yuk. That's not natural. Somebody's been modifying the genetic code of the chicken's laying habits and I don't like it. I have adorable twin great-nephews so human twins are all good but I don't want to see double-egg yolks sizzling in the frying pan.

Only Canadians could sit on the porch with their winter jackets on but that's what we did this morning. Anxious us, pretending it's summer. John drank his coffee and I my tea and we each enjoyed a heated up mini croissant chocolat. I read the Alan Bennett quote (above) to John regarding starlings. While we drank our coffee/tea he told me the story of his love of them. It relates to him being in Grade three at Muchmore Public School in Ottawa. They went to The Museum of Natural History and saw a Diorama with real garbage cans with fake garbage spilling out of them and a few taxidermied Starlings. It struck him that those birds had figured out how to stay alive all winter by eating garbage and he has admired them ever since (whereas many wouldn't.) I, too, tried to remember a school lesson of greatness but couldn't come up with much other than the Geometry Tutor I had in grade ten in the person of retired Collegiate Principal, Mr. Roamer Mackenzie, who sat me down in his brown living room at a card table. He had sharpened pencils laid on the table in a precise geometric line-up. He was an excellent teacher in spite of his neurosis over the pencils. He made Geometry as easy as pie (or pi r squared) and after a few lessons from him it all made sense. My dad worked with me too at the kitchen table when I was at a very young age. He chopped up oranges and apples and had me repeat the fractions back to him. It was always a battle between myself and math. Wonder why?

A funny email from RMB about how she inadvertently erased the first episode of Unforgotten that I have been begging her to watch so we can discuss clues/possible outcomes. I replied to say "Wouldn't it be funny if we forget to discuss Unforgotten?" Could happen.

I planted many giant sunflowers after lunch using the ancient wooden yardstick as a dibble stick, a la Margaret Meade. If the squirrels don't eat the seeds the gigantic sunflowers will be nodding at us right up close to the porch, along the back fence, at the front window come August.

John to the ESL program and the Vestry meeting tonight. I'm deep into Emile Zola's L'Assommoir. It's as tragic as can be like most of the French books of that era (mid-1800's). Life was a series of sorrows for the poor while the wealthy danced it up. It still is. And they still do.

WEDNESDAY, MAY 9TH, 2018 ~ Up early to stay with Charlotte for a couple of hours. We played a card game, watched a cartoon, pretended we were fairy godmothers which involved performing feats that proved my failings; "Twirl around fast Grandma! Now hop on one foot." What with the

Dermatologist this week remarking that every little spot I revealed to him was "age-related" and our five year old asking me to perform contortions, well, it could get a girl down.

At the grocery store this afternoon I got out my list. I read "top of nose, right side of face, left hand, front right ankle." The flip side read "sliced ham, havarti, croissants, bananas, tabouleh, garbage bags." One list for the dermatologist and the other for the grocery store.

I love keeping lists. They tell us much about how we live. My favourite list of all time was my dad's weekly drugstore items. In his precise blocky printing it said "Gold Bond Powder, Hall's Cherry Cough Drops, Colgate Toothpaste, Wurther's Butterscotch candies." The list was the same every week for about three years. He was approaching ninety-three during on our last trip to the drugstore and I sensed we might not be doing it again. Dear Reader, I kept the list and glued it into one of my journals.

Laurie who lives in my favourite Massachusetts village has sent me a copy of an anthology with her article in it about being a single mom with a new baby boy and wanting to create a garden, a task which at first glance overwhelmed her. She wrote this: *"Step by step, flower by flower, and day by day, I kept at it."* Therein a healthy bit of imagery for living; *flower by flower.* It was her lovely article that caused us to meet at The Red Lion Inn in Stockbridge for lunch. Laurie's writing and her garden nourished more than plants.

The Baltimore Oriole is back flashing his orange and black feathers against the lime of the new leaves. We wait for them every year. Where's his wife?

THURSDAY, MAY 10TH, 2018 ~ This morning's newspaper ran this advert entitled *"Gifts she'll love this Mother's Day"* from a local hardware store. The gifts she'll love include a *"slicer and shredder for food and dessert"*, an ice cream maker, a copper cooking pan, an *"acrylic beverage pitcher".* Happy Mother's Day to all those of you who are lucky enough to end up with those flashy kitchen items. Must remind self to see what the ad says for Father's Day. Golf clubs? Tennis racquet? A lounge chair?

A wonderful lunch here today with MR. We had much good conversation over our Red Pepper soup and croissants. Laughter too. Always that.

My freelance article off to Strings magazine today. I'm trying to prove a point to myself that everything is worth a try.

An early start to my summer routine of this: sun out so put up umbrella on porch, set out cushions on chairs. Clouded over and windy, looked like rain so put down and tethered umbrella, brought in cushions. Sun out again. Set up umbrella, brought out cushions. Canadians are suckers when it comes to outdoors. Anything to be outside. We are a desperate people.

FRIDAY, MAY 11TH, 2018 ~ A coffee house visit at The Mulberry with JB/RB. To the tienda afterwards for Western Union purposes. The woman who runs it warned me thusly; "Sorry to have to say this to you but old people get scammed by people posing as Western Union agents so don't answer any of their questions."

On the way back to the car a teacher had a group of children on the sidewalk and said this; "Old people approaching boys and girls so make space for them to pass."

That was us of course. The old people. We are now seen as defective in some way. We looked a bit like Moses and Mrs. Moses at the parting of the Red Sea as all those ten year olds melted away to the edges of the sidewalk to let us through.

Lucia and I walked hand in hand back and forth

tonight. A first. And because her legs are strong enough now I showed her the joys of standing on the living room sofa and looking out the window. She put her hand prints all over the glass and I might never wash them off. Love makes you feel that way.

SATURDAY, MAY 12TH, 2018 ~ Just realized that I've been writing this Journal for nine months, the same time it takes to grow a human baby. I was crazy about our newborns but this project has offered me more time to sleep.

The women's meeting this morning continued with James Chapter Four; discussion re motive, humility, double-mindedness. A small group with warm hearts and sharp intellects.

Wonderful visit here this afternoon with friends. S is involved in a project towards her PHd which will involve interviewing a variety of people on the topic of how faith may/may not affect cognitive function in aging brains. I've volunteered. She told me that for her a favourite piece of music is Amazing Grace which I thought interesting coming from a young Islamic woman. I told her the background story of the slave ship and John Newton who wrote the text to that hymn after he had a mid-Atlantic a-ha moment about the evils

of slavery as he himself was a slave trader. Her mom's great question then was *"So what did he do about it en route? Did his enlightenment last?"* I pondered her idea for hours. The strength of his words will be rendered useless and will die to me if I discover that he'd carried on with his human cargo and delivered them to England. Many things to think about on what looked like an otherwise quiet Saturday afternoon.

Tonight an Indian dinner and down the hill on the way home to be greeted by seven wee goslings with their mom and dad walking alongside them.

The big news for today is that Lulu (Lucia) got her groove on. She has been walking solo all day; the very best Mother's Day gift for her mom and dad. Look Ma! No hands!

SUNDAY, MAY 13TH, 2018 ~ *Mother's Day* ~ A jazz pianist for Morning Prayer today. Funny that he should have rocked Amazing Grace after the discussion we had with our friends about it here yesterday. Later this evening Jan found evidence online that Newton actually did turn his ship back to Africa to set the people free. He joined Wilberforce et al in the quest to abolish slavery.

A wonderful afternoon BBQ at the Hội Thánh

Tin Lành and a long chat with three of the daughters whose mom and dad came to Canada thirty-five years ago. They have grown up here and are all at university and college and they are curious. The adult offspring of refugees want to know things now about their parent's immigration experiences. They seek answers now that they have time to reflect.

When we got home our little Smiths were waiting for us with some mango cheesecake. Jock has had Strep all week so they will visit later in the week. Hayley and Isaac and children were visiting family today to the south of them.

MONDAY, MAY 14TH, 2018 ~ *Common Goldfinch song. Long-sustained, clear, light, and canary-like. In flight each dip is punctuated by a simple ti-dee-di-di,"*(Peterson, 1934, 167.)

Set out for my walk this morning, tripped and pulled a muscle at the back of my leg so came home to the Voltaren.

That was followed up by a futile trip downtown to a shop that we hadn't realized had left that location thirteen years ago. So that was two failed *"trips"* of differing sorts. It was the kind of a morning when the Smiths batted zero while the world watched.

Home to type up John's sermon for next Sunday's Evening Prayer on Submission and Freedom and how in Christian theology they are a holistic concept in spite of their usually opposing natures.

Goldfinches, often four or five at a time, dancing at the fence to get at K-and-L- next-door's Niger seed. A sighting of the female Oriole. Greening everywhere.

His Majesty's Loyal Opposition tried his new walker for the first time after lunch. He got halfway around the block. He's not liking it one bit but I'll keep badgering him. That's my job.

The LRB has arrived with a review of a new book about the now old struggle for co-education. It tells the tale of one man, a graduate of an elite school, who returned his rowing jacket once women were allowed in. (I *do* say!)

Our new plants are thriving out there in the sun on the porch. The Jade has shot up two or three inches and the bougainvillea overflows. The cedar trees sit complacent, en garde at their respective posts.

TUESDAY, MAY 15TH, 2018 ~ Heavy rain all night so a lime green morning. Downtown early to buy the pansies we noticed yesterday in a parking lot plant sale. We'll plant our window boxes when the weather clears.

Practiced some music tonight. Was terrible. Need a new teacher as my Bravo one isn't able to play along with me due to an injury. Mustn't lose interest. It's a heavy instrument and difficult to lug around. A quiet evening with CFMX-FM and a bit of reading about Wystan Hugh Auden. Googled him so I could see for myself his craggy, rut-infested face that, other than this poetry, was his hallmark.

WEDNESDAY, MAY 16TH, 2018 ~ A funny morning thinking about life and how it works. We drove through our old neighbourhood. Passed the house in which we raised our three children and a few dogs. It was that house to which my mom and dad came every Friday afternoon for a visit, for Christmases, for birthdays. John's mom and dad's house was three doors away. Our former red brick family home has transmogrified into a palatial mansion that no longer looks like anything to do with our past. The house across the street, ditto. The election signs were out blooming on the lawns declaring the homeowner's affinity to whichever political party they will vote come June. Once upon a time (seems not all that long ago but it was) those same lawns were sprouting signs with Himself's name on them. That little toot through our former lives this morning proves how quickly one's personal history dissipates, ergo the need to cling to that which is lasting. Often feel a jab of sorrow for missing people when we take that same route but then, on coming back to the place we've called home for the past eleven years, we find trees, birds and peace.

Something exciting this afternoon. A young woman friend wants to know the personal history of her early years when she arrived in Canada at age four. I've put her in touch with CBC as a documentary was made about her family by journalist Hilary Brown at that time and that has led to our reconnection to H.B. who says we should meet for coffee after our thirty year hiatus. Life and its circles. They do spin.

Planted the window boxes this afternoon. I've given the pansies some plant food to spur them onwards. And Jock came and fixed the vacuum cleaner and took us for Indian food. How good could a day get?

THURSDAY, MAY 17TH, 2018 ~ An early morning run to the grocery store as holiday weekend ahead. Wanted to avoid crowds. Was home by 9:15.

Picked up Love's Civil War (letters between Charles Ritchie and Elizabeth Bowen) from the library too this morning so that I can scan it. It was Beatrice who put me onto this book a few years ago. We've had lengthy book discussions by phone over the past forty years. I have Beatrice to thank for many of the wonderful books I've read.

Charlotte this afternoon. We strung the Union Jack bunting along the porch railing for the Victoria Day weekend and for the Royal Wedding on Saturday. I worry about the cost of that wedding cake. If it were me I'd go without the expensive cake. But I'd insist on white satin shoes with huge silk bows. Although I could be accused of name dropping here I'm going for it anyway as it's a good story. John and I went to the Olympics in Montreal in 1976 just after we were married. He was representing Ontario with another fellow whose name I will omit. We attended The Queen's Reception in a large and crowded room. The young man in front of me turned around and said, "Have you seen my parents?" "They are right over there in that corner," I told him. It was Prince Andrew.

Charlotte, who has learned to wink and did it at me all day long, picked dandelions. We put them to float in a bowl of water with the fuchsia blossoms that had dropped. We picked Bleeding Hearts for the tiny vase. We made a Lego fairy house with pirates on the roof top. I never remember buying our sons those Lego canons and Lego swords. We made a Lego lake with boats and more pirates on it. We made a Lego-something-else about which I stand perplexed and another Lego thing too. It was a complicated structure and she was using her new big word "obbortunity" but that didn't help explain what we were building. The Imari bowl has been removed from the dining nook table and replaced by the Lego buildings in an honouring of our five year old craftswoman's work today. Her mom and dad and sister came for dinner after their appointment at the Children's Hospital where they met the Wonder Woman Dr. from Montreal. A happy day.

Later, bed felt like a good place to be. In Ida John's letter to her friend Rani in May of 1905 she describes her fatigue this way: *"You know, I was very near the laudanum bottle."*

FRIDAY, MAY 18TH, 2018 ~ Spring's beauty startles after months of wintry landscapes. Windy, sunny, chilly; a gorgeous day. To Dam Seeds this morning out on Highway 8. Came home with packets of dull brown seeds that will grow into these wonders: Lupins, Bachelor's Buttons (John wore one in his lapel on our wedding day), Calendula, Cosmos, Zinnia, Larkspur. I saw a picture of a Gertrude Jekyll style garden this morning on a blog. The lupins! Couldn't leave Dam Seeds without them even though they won't bloom this year and Himself says they won't grow in this soil at all. I must keep trying. Just in case. Lupins are something I've wanted forever. They were $2.75 for the pack so no loss if they won't grow. But I'm so sure they will grow.

Sat outside for an hour on the back porch this afternoon in my quilted winter vest and woollen jacket, the wind whipping my hair into a bird's nest but I was in the fresh air so didn't care. I looked over the Ritchie/Bowen letters.

A long phone chat with Hayley who is home with little E and her sore throat. Miss them.

SATURDAY, MAY 19TH, 2018 ~ Soft, silent rain on the gardens. A televised wedding this morning for Prince Harry and Meghan with words about love being the agency of change for the world. The Commonwealth looked today as it was meant to, a reflection of the ethnicity of the constituents.

A sweet email from NW at The Mount. She is on to a new career now but says she will never lose interest in Edith Wharton. She has sent me her email address so that we can stay in touch. Young friends are gemstones in our aging. I learned that bit of magic from John's cousin Virginia when she was in her nineties.

Watched a bit of Hercule Poirot whom we love but it was complicated tonight and nearing the end we turned him off. Au revoir, Hercule! That's it for you, mon ami! Your plot was tres difficile ce soir et nous ne la comprenons pas. (Thank you both, RB and JB, for helping me with the long-forgotten verb form of comprendre.)

SUNDAY, MAY 20TH, 2018 ~ In May of 2015 Alan Bennett (Bennett, 2016, 355) heard this tidbit from a friend whose intelligent four year old son Wilfred was learning to play chess. The boy had been taken to a Confirmation service and was introduced to the Bishop. The young boy asked his father *"Does that mean he can only move diagonally?"*

A quiet afternoon. Read a bit. Chatted with the neighbours who were having a car-wash fundraiser and they cleaned our car inside and out so that it looked brand new.

John was supposed to preach at Evening Prayer but he was too fatigued so I went alone and the Rector read the sermon in his stead.

MONDAY, MAY 21ST, 2018 ~ *Victoria Day* ~ A beauteous day and a walk down the hill first thing. Birdsong. Violets, Periwinkle on the hillside. Forget-me-nots under the overhanging shrubbery. At the bottom the Willows are dripping into the water. Passed a few walkers and a couple of runners. Most of the time just the birds et moi.

Only a few pages left of the Paris book. Emile Zola was the hero in the Dreyfus affair of which I knew little before I started to read this book. The story of Zola's bravado in the face of criticism/banishment to England showcases the importance of standing up for the innocent, even if our own reputations suffers.

Rosemary & Thyme, the women who come to help with the gardening, were here today. The result of their labours is a lovely little ribbon of colour along the fence. It's the prettiest garden. John and I like massed colour plantings but they have interspersed the colours and it's more interesting this way; pink Petunias and purple Muscari beside clumps of Marigolds snuggling up to softer pink and white

Snapdragons. They have seeded the Cosmos and the Zinnias. They did all this on hands and knees in the hot sun non-stop, not even to visit the loo, which to me proves the miraculous nature of their work. I made a pot of tea but they wouldn't have a salmon sandwich.

The raspberry canes are growing and the roses that have survived (one suffered winter kill) are doing well. We'll enjoy sitting on the porch surrounded by this quiet beauty. Gladys Taber once commented on how the light on May evenings is soft, tender. I'll watch for that.

TUESDAY, MAY 22ND, 2018 ~ Rain all night on our new garden. A quiet day. Read a bit, dozed a bit.

This evening Drew dug out some of the many daffodil bulbs at the front. He scattered the Lupin and Larkspur seeds where the bulbs had been. We'll see what happens. I made hamburgers. Lucia vry busy now trying to reach the Lego from off of the dining table. Now and again she'd score a piece. Charlotte building a Lego bakery with an oven. I promised her that next visit we will finish it.

John at ESL tonight so a chat with Isaac and then Jan and finished the last few pages of my book. I can

put that one up on the shelf for now if I can find a space. It's a wonderful reference book.

I'd say I need another bookcase except that might make His Majesty's Loyal Opposition suggest I get rid of a few more books. Not happening.

WEDNESDAY, MAY 23RD, 2018 ~ In May of 1972 Elizabeth Gray Vining wrote this in her Journal (Vining, 1978, 141), ***"Today we live in today's sunshine, today's rain, today's love, today's service."***

Saw something this morning on my walk that I haven't seen since childhood; a robin's egg. It was smashed upon the sidewalk on the hill. Forgot how beautiful that colour is; a decided turquoise. And beside it was a tiny feather, like a signature, a fare-thee-well note. The contents of the egg would have been bald at that stage I assume, so no feathers, but I speak the truth. Someone's wee feather was fluttering in the breeze.

This afternoon drove to Bronte to sit on the harbour and watch the sailing vessels that are moored, waiting to get out onto Lake Ontario. Could have sat there forever. I grew up on Lake Ontario. I love being near water. A sleek, brown mink scampered along the front.

On the way back home drove through my favourite streets. What annoys me about the wealthy are not the people themselves but their perfect gardens. When we moved in here we planted an Eastern Redbud tree on the front lawn. It grew into a huge pink balloon every Spring. Five years ago it split down the trunk, filled with ice in the winter and went feet up and had to be taken down. But the Eastern Redbuds we saw today on the manicured lawns of mansions were works of art, soft pink blossoms ready to burst, every limb stretching and reaching in the most artistic of ways. Elizabeth Bowen allegedly referred to the small annoyances of the wealthy as their *"Fortnum And Mason sorrows."*

In the same vein, John said to me "Not sure if that animal we saw was a mink or a weasel."

"Trust me," I said. "It was a mink. We get the weasels. In Bronte they get minks."

Bird count today in the yard: goldfinches, Mr. and Mrs. Oriole, one purple finch and the swallows hovering over the lake.

Came home, re-heated the chicken. Sat on the porch with Penelope Lively's memoir, 'A Life In Gardens', and then I watered our own garden.

Felt merciless and terrible for spraying the

hundreds of huge, winged, swarming ants on the porch tonight with a powerful ant spray. There is a nest under our porch we assume. They staggered, fell over, died.

THURSDAY, MAY 24TH, 2018 ~ Why can't I apply the quote from E.G. Vining of yesterday to today? In fact why can't I apply anything of wisdom towards today? Feeling some unsettledness, but life can't always be about Baltimore orioles and larkspur.

Charlotte here this afternoon; loving and sweet. She's still practicing her winking at me. Her eyes are as big and as black as hockey pucks.

"I think ants are lovely" she told me as we sat on the back porch. (Oh dear. See entry of yesterday.)

We worked on our Lego Bakery which turned into both an emergency ward and a restaurant before you could say "Bob's Your Uncle."

FRIDAY, MAY 25TH, 2018 ~ Sitting on the pine table is this; a bouquet of Lily Of The Valley in Virginia's blue and white milk jug. Their frilly cups are as delicate, as beauteous as any flower could ever be. JB gave them to us this morning after a splendid cup of tea with her homemade Rhubarb-Apple cake.

We had a tour of JB/RB's neatly laid out and thriving garden, the vegetables penned in against the rabbits, the hedge of old Peonies ready to burst, a garden corner at the back under the Copper Beech with Lily of the Valley, Columbine, a strip of Solomon's Seal.

Lunch; tomato on English Muffin for me, Peanut Butter and cheese sandwich for Himself. (I *know!* A revolting combo, isn't it?) Very hot to sit out as it thirty degrees Celsius today but I did for a while anyway.

An evening visit on the porch with Jock tonight. A light breeze and the orioles.

SATURDAY, MAY 26TH, 2018 ~ In my book by Ruth Hayden, (Hayden, 1980, 110), there is a picture of Swallow Wort which Mrs. Delany (1700-1788) crafted with her tiny scissors from fine paper into a work of art in her eightieth year. She did this scores of times and became famous for them. They are housed in The British Museum. She didn't start until she was in her seventies, which should bring hope to the hearts of so many of us except that I'm not clever with scissors so would have to come up with Something Else.

A drive to Bronte again this morning for lily of the valley plants.

Tea with K and R this evening on their patio. A beautiful twilight with their flowering trees dropping their petals, pink confetti on the cobbles.

SUNDAY, MAY 27TH, 2018 ~ The beginning of The Pilgrim's Progress, John Bunyan's classic allegory in children's version for the next thirteen weeks at Sunday School this morning. A's parents who are visiting from China for the summer asked if they could sit in.

Otherwise a quiet day. Political tv debate tonight which seemed to me to have been about nothing. So few concrete plans and no mention of where the money will be found to enact the vague ideas they do have.

MONDAY, MAY 28TH, 2019 ~ Robert Louis Stevenson wrote this: *"Our England is a garden and such gardens are not made, By singing "Oh* how *beautiful!" and sitting in the shade."* Often wondered if he had me in mind. I am a fake gardener. A phoney. For weeks I've been talking about plants as if I have a Post-Doctorate in Horticulture. What I am is a lover of plants that other people put into my sightline by their own labour, not so much by

mine. My love of plants comes from visits to gardens and plant nurseries, from thoughts of Sissinghurst whose creator, writer Vita Sackville-West, is in a framed postcard above my desk, from pictures in English magazines of country gardens filled with variety, colour, height, and from every mention of the sacrosanct names of David Austin, Sir Edwin Lutyens, Gertrude Jekyll. Until this past hour none of it has come from my own toil digging up the soil or from the sweat beading upon my own brow. But because John Glenn went to space at age seventy-seven I thought I should at least try digging, creating, planting a lily of the valley garden today without falling over.

As I weeded I remembered reading The Poisonwood Bible by Barbara Kingsolver. It was, among other things, about an American family in Congo who tried to make a vegetable garden by struggling to tame the encroaching jungle. Never would they accept the fact that the jungle was more powerful than were they. It made me wonder why anybody gardens at all as weeds will always win.

I used the shears to snap down the sapling offshoots at the bottom of the Amora maple. I raked. I snipped off the overreaching branches of the Lilacs. Raked again. I dug a trench like John taught me to do

and watered the empty trench after I shook out the clumps of dirt in the oversized brown bag for garden trash. I placed the plants in the damp trench, banked them up, watered again. I could hear my Dad urging me to "put a little gumption into it Judith!" So there you have it. Full disclosure. I'm a failed gardener. I want pictures of and books about gardens, I yearn for fresh flowers on the pine table in pots. I want the results but not the sweat. But I enjoyed myself out there this morning. I might find myself doing it again.

Shared a toasted cheese sandwich at Paisley coffee house at noon with JRS after his Physiotherapist left. His new walker has arrived and the loaner has gone back to the drugstore. Walkers are a wonderful invention. I hope he uses it. His Physio loves him. He loves her. It's all good.

This evening spread a bag of topsoil on lily of the valley garden and filled in the hole where the old maple tree was dug out. Two new badges of honour tonight as the sun wanes; dirty fingernails and my first bug bite of the season.

TUESDAY, MAY 29TH, 2018 ~ Jan sent me an article entitled 'A New Stretch of The River' by Mary

Pipher who is a Clinical Psychologist in Nebraska. The article can be found online at 'Psychotherapy Networker, Mar./Apr. 2018.'

Pipher herself is seventy. She quotes Austrian novelist Marie von Ebner-Eschenbach who wrote *"Old age transfigures or fossilizes."* Must remind Self not to fossilize, but to transfigure.

An email from Diane in Mahone Bay was waiting for me this morning. We've been friends since toiling away in the university library trying to sort out the fourteenth century Sir Gawain And The Green Knight. I remember this much only: *"Men wondered at the hue, That in his face was seen. A splendid man to view He came, entirely green."* In spite of the mileage between Nova Scotia and Ontario we continue along life's journey together. She and L are fine. We'll plan a phone call soon.

The best visit on the porch in the breeze this morning with a wonderful young friend whom we haven't seen for a long time. We talked about cultural issues and her PHd studies. She was born in a refugee camp and came to Canada a few years afterwards. It was a morning of reconnecting infused with new ideas, warmth, memories.

Sitting on my kitchen shelf are two angels that

Helen mailed off to me from the gift shop in Paisley Abbey. They arrived today; one blonde, one redhead. She says they reminded her of our friendship from the time we were twenty-two when she came to Canada to work. We shared a hot, crummy room one summer under the eaves in government housing where we were bored out of our minds on stifling evenings. In the outpost where we were stationed there was nothing to do, nowhere to go. It led to hilarious conversations that we remember still. I tell her that she was the most wonderful outcome of my four year spell there. Since that time I've tracked her around the world and John and I have had many splendid visits with her and Rob.

An evening on the porch with Jan on the phone.

WEDNESDAY, MAY 30TH, 2018 ~ Rosemary & Thyme showed up again today. What workers they are! They remodelled the funny little garden I made the other day. It looks more as I intended it to now; tidier, and more woodland-like with the ferns and the hostas moved.

I made ahead a dinner that I hope will do us for three nights. MH gave me a recipe for lime and asparagus on a bed of pasta and parmesan.

This afternoon a breeze, the sun, the porch, my

books. And a thirty minute nap which I feel I deserved after hauling eight bags of topsoil into the car.

A visit tonight from our little Smith girls.

THURSDAY, MAY 31ST, 2018 ~ A humid morning on the porch with Lynn F. and a cuppa; a hearty catching-up and a few laughs, most of which were aimed at ourselves. A gust of wind blew our new striped umbrella right out of the hole in the table and up into the air it flew like Mary Poppins and landed with the utmost grace at Lynn's feet.

Too hot. The weather-woman has been promising a major rain. Hasn't happened. The window-box pansies have their little heads bowed. They're thirsty even after I water them. I'm doing the Rain Dance before I go to bed.

FRIDAY, JUNE 1ST, 2018 ~ *Sarabande* ~ *"In its darkness of melodic design it is so unusual that it resembles contemporary music."* (Mstislava Rostropovich from Siblin, 2009, 200.)

A cello lesson this morning. The lovely young woman teacher showed me how to get more sound out of the body of the instrument. She was able to feed her baby and teach at the same time without missing a beat; the consummate professional. Happy baby, happy me. The mention of theory still sets me on edge; a mental block I've been hauling around since childhood. She helped me to get started on Handel's Sarabande. And I'm free to book lessons often/infrequently/anytime. How to rid oneself of a mental block? Anybody?

The much needed rain trounced down for fifteen minutes and then out came the beating sun.

SATURDAY, JUNE 2ND, 2018 ~ On the porch this afternoon with both the crossword and Penelope Lively's book Life in the Garden.

Gave our flowers a good drenching late this afternoon. The poor things thirst. I used both watering cans. Hector's (John's dad) huge watering can is ninety years old and is made of steel. It's a thing of dented and bashed-up beauty. We had a vegetable garden plot at The Botanical Garden when we moved down here eleven years ago. The fellow who gardened beside us came over to us in the coffee shop this Spring and said "I remember you! You're the people with the antique watering can." Our other watering can is a lightweight plastic model. It's easier to carry but I like to think that Hector's masses of gladioli were

the result of the water that poured from the spout of his sturdy steel one. Using it connects us to the past.

Tonight we watched Andrew Graham-Dixon's tv show about the Royal art collections. Have gone online to order his book on Caravaggio from the library.

Time for Bedfordshire.

SUNDAY, JUNE 3RD, 2018 ~ Service of Holy Communion this morning and post-service lunch with HD who came to visit. I pointed out that the words from The Sarum Primer for God Be In My Head which we sing at the end of service were written in 1558. It's a beautiful piece of poetic writing and is enough to carry anyone through the week. It's remembering to let it that's the trick.

On the porch chatting with John this afternoon in the sunlight. A drop in temperature and a sudden rush of cold air. I threw the cushions into the sunroom just as the rain pelted down. I can see a difference already. The Persian Lilacs are opening. I swear the flowers have popped up another inch. We're surrounded back there with green. Can't see the neighbours behind us. It's as if we're sitting in our own private jungle. Poet May Sarton (Sarton, 1984, 114) refers to the *"thick*

green world of August". I'll change it to the *"thick green world of June".*

That bit of Glory was followed up by a bit of Un-glory. Music practice was horrible. Had trouble unravelling the chart she gave me for Chromatic Scales which by this time shouldn't take any thought at all. I'd never seen the chart before however and must learn to be less hard on Self. Went to bed discouraged.

But on a more pleasant, pre-practice note, we spent much of this quiet afternoon before the rain with six goldfinches and a purple finch. Nice company, I'd say.

MONDAY, JUNE 4TH, 2018 ~ A good way to begin a new week. I woke up at 6:30, showered, got out my music, sat down and said to Self "You are going to get your head around this Chromatic Scales chart and you will learn them."

Dear Reader, it worked. Such a tiny, wee thing in the end. I had built a wall around it the size of the dike in which the little Dutch boy had to stick his finger. Mom used to read that book to us when we were tiny. The finger in the dike story was popularized in the book Hans Brinker And The Silver Skates, written in 1865; wonder wherever that little book got to?

The fact is that I have often built walls around

things that I didn't take to. From now on, no more walls. As May Sarton says in her Journal, At Seventy, *"the wind is rising in my sails."*

And a phone call from MA with some hopeful news.

A Sunflower is coming up under the front window. The rest of the greenery is weeds. It's like a scene from 'The Day Of The Triffids' around here with weeds overtaking us. They will crawl in the window and wrap themselves around the furniture, pin us to the sofa, grow down into the drains. Our descendants will someday discover us wound into a mass of leafy greenery in our own home.

JRS and I have decided to keep a list of obsolete expression and words, words that were used when we were kids. Tonight's offering is "isn't that a corker?" My mom used to say that situations/people who were problematic were "real corkers." But according to the online dictionaries it means "something that is better than the best." I think the online dictionary is wrong. John's dad used the word "nincompoop" which I think was reserved for those whom he thought had done something wrong. "She has more brass than the British Navy" my mom used to say about people she thought were "nervy" (i.e., bold.)

TUESDAY, JUNE 5TH, 2018 ~ ***"In the midst of winter I discovered that there was in me an invincible summer." (alleged to be a quote from Albert Camus).***

During the night the raccoon knocked over the cedar tree in the pot. There is no way you can outsmart a raccoon. We know this wily, lumbering fellow; bold as brass he is. He once came onto the porch in daylight and didn't move until we stamped our feet and looked daggers at him. Soon this battle will become Man Versus Nature. Nature will win.

RMB for tea and strawberries outside this morning although we both needed our winter vests. We reminisced about our visit to her family in an Oxfordshire village when I pushed their baby in his pram down the pathway to get to the tiny stone church with our hostess. The baby would be fifty by now. All of these remembrances help us to rekindle that ***"invincible summer"*** **part of us.**

I'm trying to partition my days into this: a jolt of music, a smattering of reading, human connection, a modicum of exercise for my body and a bit of something for my spirit. In this way I feel I make the best of the gift of time. ***"I think the main thing, don't you, is to keep the show on the road."*** **(Alleged to be a quote by Elizabeth Bowen.)**

Just so my children know, I did do some housework this week. But I try to keep it to a minimum.

Typed up John's sermon for him for Evensong in two weeks time; this time about God as Agency in His role as the Good Shepherd. We got first hand information about being a good Shepherd from his cousins in New Zealand. They told us this: *"You shouldn't be a Shepherd unless you love your sheep."*

WEDNESDAY, JUNE 6TH, 2018 ~ (Sarton, 1984, pg 306). Poet may Sarton wrote in her journal At Seventy that she sometimes misses her youthful face but this is what she decided: *"An old face that looked too young would be troubling."*

Now there's a philosophy of aging that I can take to. No botox; just hard won crinkles and wrinkles. The trench between my eyebrows showed up on every single face in a family reunion photo several years ago. That's how I know to whom I belong. It's the family talisman, although I would have been fine with them having high cheekbones instead.

Finished Penelope Lively's book. She describes various rose gardens. We tried to make one happen here when we moved in. We'd planted several varieties but most of them succumbed to Black Spot or winter

frost. Five bushes remain. Our friend Helen nearby us had a small rose garden and every June she'd invite all of her friends, via stamped invitations, for "An Evening of Roses". She served drinks, put out her garden picture books and her books of floral poetry. She'd lead us once again around her small patch to show us the scented abundance. Perhaps there were fifteen rose bushes. She had named each of them after one of her friends. That is what I liked most about it. Helen was a creative woman. Her home was humble but filled with art, books, ideas and those roses in her small garden. The way she lived inspired me.

Crossed my mind that a stone wall with roses tumbling over it would be the perfect backdrop to this garden of our own. We're not stone masons so we never managed to get that built. We did have a New Dawn Rose of the palest pink that climbed over the wire fence but it grew out of control and we had to take it down. Wire fences are never to be compared to the beauty of stone anyway. Most of the David Austin roses have died. The Canadian breeders produce the hardiest bushes for this climate (i.e., Morden in Manitoba) but in my imagination that little stone wall scenario lives on. Perhaps that is enough. My imagination is portable. It goes where I go.

Good news came via email. The article I submitted to Strings magazine about learning a new instrument as an adult will be published in the August issue. I sent it on a whim. It worked. So whims count.

Plus this: I caught the elusive fly that has been buzzing around us inside the house for days. Do you know how hard it is to catch a live fly?

THURSDAY, JUNE 7TH, 2018 ~ The Globe today features the Obituary of Jill Ker Conway, the first woman President of Smith College in Northhampton, Massachusetts. I salute her accomplishments. Hayley spent one month at Smith the summer between her grade twelve and grade thirteen years reading Emily Dickinson *et al* at a summer school for girls who hoped to pursue English studies. On campus at Smith was a Japanese Tea house and a small lake. The romance of that stands out in our joint memories. I read Jill Ker Conway's The Road From Coorain at the time. She is remembered as being a feminist but The Globe credits her as a cheerleader for both men and women having equal opportunity, which makes the best sense to me.

Jan and Rob arrived early today. We had lunch in Bronte. John had Duck soup, like the Marx Brothers movie. He wants to go back for more. I don't like eating duck at any time let alone when they are waddling around across the road from the restaurant. We stopped in to see E and D and the girls and then came home for a late dinner in front of the television so we could watch the election results. The voters have kicked out the current government and replaced it with a vast majority of another stripe. Next round we'll kick this one out and replace it with another majority and then we'll do the same to that one. On it goes.

As Edith Wharton would declare, *"Unberufen!"* May nothing evil befall us.

FRIDAY, JUNE 8TH, 2018 ~ Jan and Rob left before noon. They are fresh air, those two. A quiet day afterwards. We had leftovers on the porch for dinner. I read some Caravaggio with bits about the Counter Reformation before the sun went down.

SATURDAY, JUNE 9TH, 2018 ~ A trip through my early childhood this morning. The farmer's market in Galt (Cambridge) began in 1830 and is one of the oldest farmer's markets in Canada. I think my mother used to take us there when we were small.

Sometime I'm not sure that I remember things accurately. Perhaps I *think* I do. Today we bought freshly picked strawberries, rhubarb, asparagus. We sat on the patio outside the market building for a cuppa. Everybody spoke to everyone else in that kind of old-world friendliness.

A lofty old church that sells Apple Dumplings and coffee opens its doors onto the market square. There are forty farmer's stalls outside and inside the market building are the cheeses, meats, jams, jellies, baked goods.

Afterwards we drove through Preston, past my grandparent's house and the house (two doors away from grandma and grandpa's) that mom and dad bought post-war and where we lived until I was ten. We drove past the house at the confluence of the Grand and the Speed Rivers that they built to retire to when they returned to Preston. We passed the Tudor style Baptist Church that my dad had helped to create by digging out the basement for the building in his young years. It was created by then recent immigrants from England, Scotland, Ireland, Wales, the majority of whom were my direct predecessors on both sides of our family, both by birth and collaterally via marriages. Their chosen denomination signified that they were a part of the historic British Chapel movement which was a direct reaction against the Church of England, ergo an early form of separation of church and state. They were Anabaptists. I was taken there as a newborn. It is where I first was taught the amazing piece of information that God loves the people of the world and went to great lengths to prove it. The supposition followed was that we were meant to love the people of the world too, of every creed and race. That's the kind of information you tuck into your back pocket in case you need it someday.

A quiet afternoon with CFMX and the crossword which I could not solve.

Charlotte phoned us tonight to say that she wants me to help her "make goodie bags for hungry children." It's quite complicated, her plan. It involves dropping things off from airplanes and us "knitting blankets". Ask somebody else's grandmother about the "knitting blankets" part Sweetheart but I'd love to help you out with the airplane part. Her mother has been spending time with her talking about children who have nothing.

SUNDAY, JUNE 10TH, 2018 ~ This morning there are eight blooms and two buds on our Morden

Centennial Rose. Something I have never noticed in other years is this; they start off the palest pink and then darken to crimson. Is there a change in the soil chemistry? Have they always put on this little magic show and we've failed to notice? They are beauteous swaying out there in the morning breeze.

The Jazz pianist was back for Morning Prayer this morning. At the end he played Mercy Mercy Mercy inspired by the Cannon Ball Adderly Quintet. I could have stayed there all day, listening.

Sat on the porch in the breeze this afternoon and watered the garden tonight. Takes six trips with two watering cans. We seem to do everything the hard way. Not sure why that is. Normal people use hoses.

MONDAY, JUNE 11TH, 2018 ~ I found American Erma J. Fisk's book after weeks of trying to locate it. (Fisk, 1990, 8). She wrote it in 1990. I love it. It's homey. She infuses the daily grind with meaning as did Barbara Pym. Her friend, Bob Hale, who wrote the forward said this lovely thing; *"What she does in her book is poke around the closets of her life, muttering, remembering, reflecting, sorting, throwing some things away, treasuring others anew."* That is what journals make you do.

In 1988, when Jock was three, I started keeping journals. In a huge plastic tub and on one shelf of the bookcase there awaits twenty-five hard-covered journals for our offspring who might like to have a poke around at their own pasts someday.

"Don't throw them out," I tell our children. Tucked between those handwritten pages is every adorable thing they ever said, everything we ever did, every bit of love we have for them. I chose to write them in hard-covered books on purpose as they plead to be taken more seriously than mere notebooks which have a disposable look about them. I've dug out the following journal items from various spots and laughed aloud: We had a burial service in the garden for a bird where we sang All Things Bright And Beautiful. Drew dug up the bird days later to show his friends. He was eight. Both Queen Beatrix came to our city and Princess Margaret. Hayley (twelve years) presented flowers to HRH Margaret. She was wearing a pink dress and had her hair in braids. (Hayley, not HRH.) And I wrote about Jock falling asleep in the back seat of the car, rosy cheeks, ink all over himself as he'd got hold of a pen and played Tic Tac Toe on his arms and crossed off the results to show how he'd won every game. He was five.

This morning to renew my Health Card after a bureaucratic boondoggle the other day when I tried. It resulted in me having to return with either my passport or my car insurance form. More and more I see how the term 'privilege' applies. The man ahead of me told me things that indicated homelessness. His health card expired and he needed hearing aids. The clerk asked him several questions and one of them was "Do you have a library card or something with your address on it?"

Her question is embedded with these assumptions: that he can read, and, that if he could, he would feel at ease checking books out of the library and that he has an address. He went stomping out the door spewing curses at the system. I can't blame him. I felt like cheering for him. Here I was with my passport and car insurance forms which meant that I both travel and own a car. He went out unable to get his hearing aids. I felt guilty being me. He told me he'd been waiting outside since 7:00 a.m. It opens at 9:00.

Lots of cool fresh air outside all day. Sleepy tonight.

TUESDAY, JUNE 12TH, 2018 ~ Today is our forty-second anniversary. We were married in a fifteen minute ceremony in my parent's living room

at 11:00 in the morning. Present were our parents, Jan and Rob, John's brother and sister-in-law and niece, the Minister and his wife. Met John at a Christmas party, got engaged on Easter Monday, married in June. I found my dress for forty dollars and spent another seventeen on a white feather boa. The masses of mauve lilacs in the hedge across mom and dad's back garden were in full bloom. We had lunch on the deck, left right afterwards, drove to Cape Cod for the week. We spent Honeymoon-Part-Two a few weeks later in Povurnituk, Eastern Arctic where we stayed with Abelie and Lucie Napartuk and their five children. We went fishing on the river, watched the Mayor of 'P.O.V.' skin a seal at the water's edge, visited several homes, watched Joe Talirunilik carve a soapstone figure, went to an Inuktitut Service of Morning Prayer at St. Matthew's Anglican Church where Abelie was the Rector, carried their new baby in a plaid shawl on my back, went with the children for a walk on the tundra where we picked wee, colourful flowers. Forty-two years has sped. Grateful hearts.

To celebrate this event a baby-pink New Dawn rose opened today and more large blooms on the Morden Centennial. Am tempted to pick some for the house but seems unfair to the flowers.

We had lunch on the patio at The Rock, the new restaurant at the Botanical Gardens. I notice this about eating out with my husband; we don't chat much unless there is something specific happening but focus on what's going on around us. But if you see a couple in the throes of newly-minted love they stare at each other and talk non-stop. It was a perfect spot to be today, in the sun and looking at the huge pine trees, silent and with him.

Stewed the rhubarb tonight with the strawberries we bought at the market. I've thickened it with Corn Starch. It will add a bit of zip to John's morning oatmeal.

Ten bells and all is well.

WEDNESDAY, JUNE 13TH, 2018 ~ *"Tôi biết nói tiếng Việt, ít ít." ("I can speak Vietnamese a little.")* Found that in my Journal from 1988.

A wonderful lunch time reunion at Lạc Viên with Hilary Brown and Huyên. We talked for three hours over mango salad, rice, fresh spring rolls and Vietnamese sweet iced coffee. Hilary, who made the CBC documentary in a refugee camp with Huyên's family twenty-eight years ago, reminded us of things that we had forgotten. Huyên filled in the blanks. We

poured our own memories into this recipe of human stories. And we all stirred.

Circumstance cuts a swathe through various lives and pitches them together. It bound the four of us and created ties that I believe were pre-designed. Thirty-eight years later I can still only speak Vietnamese *"it, it,"* (a little.) But there we were over lunch drinking our Cà Phê Sữa Đá; four people, once strangers, tied together by history, by a political mistake of epic proportions that changed our own small world and shook the lives of others inside-out and upside-down.

That coffee is keeping me wide awake at 11:30 p.m. Also seems to be a diuretic. My hands look thinner. (Always my hands.) Must drink more of it.

THURSDAY, JUNE 14TH, 2018 ~ In the summer of 1971 Charles Ritchie wrote this in his journal (Ritchie, 2008, 561); *"Lunched with the Queen Mother. On the dining-room table great silver bowls of outsize sweet peas breathing life over us..."*

Come now, Dear Reader. Does this make me a sham? A Material Girl? I can't help loving the idea of silver bowls brimming over with giant sweet peas.

K-and-L-next-door have sweet peas. And the good

news is that they are growing like mad up our side of the fence.

Not sure why we are so lazy today. We've sat out all afternoon, me with the Caravaggio book, Himself with peanuts for the birds. They flocked to the garden for them. Himself is tickled pink with it. I believe that these activities, or whatever you call doing nothing, do make us officially Ancient Peoples.

FRIDAY, JUNE 15TH, 2018 ~ A vry funny thing. On JRS's Ancestry website, about which we are delinquent in every way, there is new information. Seems he had relatives back in the day by the last name of Flocker. Jock says "That's why Dad loves birds."

Why did it take me all morning to make a pasta salad? Shouldn't the chopping, mixing, boiling of the dressing be quicker than that?

Spent much of this afternoon/evening with Caravaggio. Am determined to get him finished. The agonizing medieval religious art reflected the way the fellow named Borromeo wanted faith taught to the masses. They were to imagine themselves as witnesses to the actual Passion scenes and to internalize those ideas, to breathe them in, to become one with it

all. The theory was that this would impassion the population. It was a distinct Counter-Reformation effort to restore the faith. The artists followed that lead and produced their tortured paintings.

SATURDAY, JUNE 16TH, 2018 ~ This morning's news concerns the devastating fire at the Glasgow School of Art. John's grandparents both attended it as did his Uncle John. John took both our boys there on separate occasions and we went together another time. A huge loss to Glasgow. The building was designed by Charles Rennie Macintosh whose unique architecture is irreplaceable.

The evening here with Jock and Ashley.

SUNDAY, JUNE 17TH, 2018 ~ Steaming hot today. A music practice before we left for Morning Prayer. I taught the Sunday School chapter of Pilgrim's Progress about the potential risks of taking short cuts in things in which we want to succeed. What important things do we leave out? Which path takes us to where we aspire to end? The kids acted it out as we talked and then they all got a box of raisins since the last line in the chapter says *"So she gave them a drink, bread and raisins and sent them on their way."*

Wasted much time this afternoon looking through years of old journals. What to keep? What to toss?

Tonight John's sermon at Evening Prayer and the soothing line from The Day Thou Gavest about the rotation of the earth as it moves towards daylight. The Service of Evening Prayer seals off the week and opens onto the new one.

MONDAY, JUNE 18TH, 2018 ~ Ida John wrote to her friend Mary Dowdall in the summer of 1904. (Rebecca John And Michael Holroyd, 2017, 172). ***"Your letters make green places in my arid life."*** **Poor Ida would have been struggling with babies, poverty, fatigue, loneliness, while Augustus was off painting in the beauteous countryside for weeks on end.**

Contacts via emails, calls, the odd, and now unusual, letters from friends make green spaces in my own life. In that vein, in my inbox this morning an email from LB with many interesting items. LB and AB tread gently upon the earth. They leave goodness in their tracks.

An early morning haircut back at my former downtown place. I get used to people and places and miss them when I switch. So now I have two good places to go for a quick haircut.

The little Smith girls arrived for a visit tonight. I was in the back room and heard the front door open and noticed two pigtails bobbing on somebody's sweet little head as she made her way straight to the dining table to try to grab some of Charlotte's Lego creations that are still there. She was all smiles. She never sat down for a second. Jan says she reminds her of our mom who was always on the move. Charlotte's new and constant game is to ask me "Would You Rather?" Tonight's first question was "Grandma would you rather skip and hop all day long or sit on the sofa and feel stiff?" She must have overheard me.

And H has a lovely little report card from his Pre-K day school which says he is a good listener. Now that they've both graduated from their Kindergarten programs I've promised them a trip to The Dairy Godmother in Del Ray when I visit them this coming week.

TUESDAY, JUNE 19TH, 2018 ~ (Sarton, 1984, 58.) In June of 1982 May Sarton wrote about her friend Eugenie; ***"She sowed light in all her friends… and in the children she taught, sowed light like some miraculous seed."***

Which of my teachers sowed light? I'll think upon that. There were several.

At noon, mango salad and iced coffee at Lạc Viên with RMB while we sorted out the human condition once again. Much to talk about these days including how to sow light in a complex world. The many positives go under-reported. We have to clear the woods of the tangled undergrowth, then look at the new life springing up on the forest floor under our feet.

Strings magazine has sent me the PDF for my article which will appear in the August edition.

WEDNESDAY, JUNE 20TH, 2018 ~ Early morning to the grocery store for ground beef and chilli sauce. I'll make a meatloaf for Himself to enjoy while I'm away.

Home to a surprise visit from Ms. Lucia, her first visit to us without her sister. She headed straight for the Lego the minute she hit the front door and then for the toys in the bottom drawer of the chest. She has almost figured out how to get that wee leg high enough to get herself up onto the sofa (it's much higher than the one at their place) and she likes to touch the buttons on her Granddad's shirt.

Tuning cello a challenge today. Kept at it until I got it right. I messed it up badly and thought I'd never

get it right again for the rest of my life. Persevered; a tiny progress.

Learned today that Tantalus was a son of Zeus but that fact is debatable. He lived in the underworld and did awful things. 'Nough said about Tantalus.

Tonight Thiến dropped in with Spring Rolls and sausage, made by his kind wife.

Summer

THURSDAY, JUNE 21ST, 2018 ~ *National Indigenous People's Day* ~ A walk down the hill this morning to where the Princess Point people once lived. The view from the first bridge over the marsh is a treat; the copper dome of the Sisters Of St. Joseph's Mother House in the distance, the willow trees across the way dripping into the water, the thick border of greenery from end to end encircling the vignette. Chilly and a breeze

Although I'm not a fan of siblings fighting I have to say that I was thrilled to hear that Lucia and Charlotte have had their first set-to over a Barbie doll. That places Lucia smack in the mainstream of life. It's wonderful. She's showing her stuff after all those months of lying on her back in hospital waiting for her world to open up.

Porch Party at JB's this afternoon with MH before JB gets off for the summer. We drank lemonade with mint and strawberries floating in it, chatted about MH's bike ride for miles and miles through Holland (ouch) and JB's upcoming course on quantitative/ qualitative research (ouch again) and other items.

Tonight to a contentious city meeting about transportation in our area of the city. (One more ouch.)

Home to see a peaceful show on TV Ontario called Our People Will Be Healed regarding Indigenous culture. We emailed Pond Inlet.

FRIDAY, JUNE 22ND, 2018 ~ from Frome, Somerset today an email from CM about her second play regarding Lady Harris, Alice Seeley. She has called it The Meddling of Mrs. Harris which is the perfect title. I love to think of Alice as a meddler. If meddling is done in the right spirit it can change the world. The emphasis in the play is on King Leopold this time. Last year she held the play in the Dissenter's Cemetery where Sir John Harris and their daughter are buried. I always admire people who are Dissenters if they've had good reason to be one.

CM claims that the famous camera was given to Alice Harris by Harry Guinness of the Congo-Balolo mission before she left England (same Guinness as the brewers. The other half were Anglican clerics, or so I've read.) It was Mark Twain who referred to it as the *"Kodak"* in his writing King Leopold's Soliloquy. CM claims it was a Goerz-Anschutz Folding Camera. Must keep that info.

Spent much of today fiddling around with the details of packing my solitary carry-on bag to get to Hayley's tomorrow.

SATURDAY JUNE 23RD to Wednesday June 27th in the USA ~ Had the best few days with our family to the south of us. E and H are fun and busy little people. She is thrilled to have four more loose teeth and he longs for a few for himself.

We spent some of Sunday in Georgetown walking along O Street with me admiring the gardens, the front doors, the architecture, while my forehead streamed with humidity. We walked over to Georgetown University, that place that was built by slave labour for the Jesuits (can't connect that one at all) and where my own grandchildren were free to kick a soccer ball back and forth on the green lawn. Not until recently did they offer free tuition to students who could prove their lineage to slaves. We walked past The Church of The Holy Trinity where a plaque on the outside wall declares that it was there that JFK, the President whose legacy was his attempt to end racism, attended his last Mass on November 1st, 1963, three weeks before he was executed. Under it is the inscription *"Home is the sailor, home from the sea..."* (Robert Louis Stevenson, Requiem.) Housman also had a poem with those lines which are said to be in tribute to Stevenson. I stopped to read it and found it tear-worthy. We trod up and down small hills and a few cobbles down to King

Street to that now famous Georgetown Cupcake chain that was built by two sisters from Hamilton, Ontario. We tasted the wares and went on our way.

Over the next two days we went to a splash pad where the children played while Hayley and I sat under a shade in the breeze (utopia). We fed a multitude of ducks at the waterfront which caused maximum excitement. Had it been registered on the Richter Scale it would have zipped right over the top. After The Feeding of The Five Thousand Ducks we stopped off at Pop's Ice Cream Shop, as you would. Hayley and I went to Blackwall Hitch Restaurant on the harbour in the evening for tea and raspberry sorbet where we sat on the patio with a breeze (more utopia) off the Potomac. I made a BOO! sign for the children's lego haunted house and we watched two animated movies: 'Monster University' and 'The Beauty And The Beast'. I loved 'Monster University' and Grandpa would have loved it too. E has been reading a Madeline book and told me she wants to travel to Paris when she grows up. I told her I'd find some of those pastel-coloured Parisienne macarons to feed her when she visits.

And home to the news that the robin whose nest is in the ivy has hatched her babies. Missed John. He missed me. All good.

THURSDAY JUNE 28TH, 2018 ~ Spent today with Charlotte here while they took Lucia to Sick Kid's Hospital in Toronto. They had a helpful, informative appointment.

FRIDAY, JUNE 29TH, 2018 ~ Went with John to the Ophthalmologist after lunch. He needed another needle to his right eye so no driving until he sees the Dr. next week.

Too hot for words. Too hot in fact to do anything other than stay indoors. The new copy of The LRB has arrived and I read about George Bernard Shaw, his Fabianism, the possibility of him being a eugenicist, and the fact that he wrote a speech for Sir Roger Casement to defend himself in a British court. Casement decided not to use it and was subsequently hung for treason. Casement's role in the Congo Reform Association comes into play in the Lady Harris, Alice Seeley story.

An email from Jeremy Yudkin's listserve today as a result of our attendance at a talk he gave in Stockbridge, Massachusetts a few summers ago. He teaches Music at Boston University. The talk we heard was about both Beethoven's Fifth and the Beatle's tune Eleanor Rigby. This year his talks celebrate

Bernstein's one-hundreth birthday anniversary. Our kids were impressed that we had heard a lecture about Eleanor Rigby. But don't ask me what it was about. I forget. Totally.

Long phone chat tonight with cousin Donna. We go back a long way, to our newborn selves.

SATURDAY JUNE 30TH, 2018 ~ On June 30th in 1978 Elizabeth Gray Vining wrote this in her journal; (Vining, 1978, 154).*"I got a letter from my Crown Prince yesterday and answered it at once."*

If a Crown Prince were to write to me (he wouldn't) what would he say? *"Dear Judy, Thank you for the description of your small garden, of the new salmon recipe you are going to try and of the sweet bunting you've strung up across the back porch. How very quaint. Yours, The Crown Prince."*

It's Canada Day weekend and is too hot for any sort of outdoor activity. I went at eight this morning to get the groceries as I didn't want to wait until the crowds grew and the heat with it. Afterwards I set up the Parish Hall for the post-service lunch tomorrow and home to listen to CFMX and read The Globe.

Some people think that a female MP should not breastfeed her hungry baby in The House of Commons.

A short article about it in the paper. Consider the fact that this woman returns emails at midnight and reads every tweet at every hour of the day, goes through heaps of papers, messages, complaints on a daily basis from sunrise to sunset and never misses a picnic, a rally, a hockey game or a neighbourhood shindig in her Constituency. Shouldn't it be ok to let the woman feed her baby at work, since she does her professional work 'round the clock ? Poor baby. Poor mama. Poor misunderstood biology.

Out to get gas, more chores after dinner. Still very hot.

Almost 8 p.m. and will not move another bone until it's time to go to bed.

"Night 'y'all." A woman in Virginia who was letting the kids pet her dog last week said to us *"Have a good day, y'all."*

Remedy for arthritic feet. Rest your tootsies on an ice pack when you sit down for the night. Magic. Yes, I know. Seventy.

JULY 1ST, 2018 ~ Happy Canada Day ~ *"Be not discouraged, brave emigrant. Let Canada still remain the bright future in your mind, and hasten to convert your present day-dream into reality. The time*

is not far distant when she shall be the theme of many tongues, and the old nations of the world will speak of her progress with respect and admiration." **(Moodie, 1989, 21, from her 1853 quote).**

It's not until I look backwards that I realize the fortune that I was handed at birth by way of citizenship. This is a brilliant, shining, exemplar of a country in most ways although historically it wasn't that way for everyone. My thankfulness quadrupled ten times over when I began to meet people who had to flee their own beloved place on earth.

Morning Prayer. Everyone sang the National Anthem with gusto. Old friends showed up and A.B. and I did the lunch.

We drove to Brantford late in the afternoon to ER and MR's Annual Canada Day Party. It was cooler there. We sat in the shade under their huge trees with old friends (BD/JD and ML/AL) and I made a new friend too who had provided the gathering with the best raspberry punch ever made by womankind. The true value of friendship can never estimated. Try imaging life without it. It'd be like living atop an arid mesa with no green and shady spots upon which to rest. Aging is the crowning of those friendships I think. So this evening was full of verdant spots, both

metaphorically and in reality with delicious food in the mix. The drive back along Highway 99 was a treat. It's the yet undeveloped Ontario with fields of corn and rolling hills; *"glorious and free…"*

MONDAY, JULY 2ND, 2018 ~ Spent most of the day stirring and chopping and tonight the kids came for a salmon and salad dinner with the honey-mustard sauce recipe from H. I was hoping to send some leftovers home for Ashley but alas, all was consumed.

Toopsie has taught herself how to get up on the blue sofa and the blue armchair. We clapped.

And if you count the rain that bucketed down for 15 minutes in early afternoon it was a wholly good day.

TUESDAY, JULY 3RD, 2018 ~ K-and-L-next door's-sweet peas have climbed the fence and popped their huge, pink blooms over to our side. I know K-and-L wouldn't mind if I snipped some but I suppose the flowers are happier *in situ.*

The little Thai boys who fled deep into a cave last week to avoid the heavy rains when they were playing soccer have been found alive. This piece of

news brought joy to a news-weary world. Now, to get them out of that misery.

I am ever aware as I write this journal that as I'm rattling on about sweet peas there are little boys stuck in caves, frantic parents, bombs falling elsewhere, people rioting, general suffering. It forces me to look into the mirror. I have taken so much for granted for seventy years. My year of note-keeping is beginning to take shape as a worthwhile exercise.

In the extreme heat of this July morning I bumped into a man we know when I was headed for the drug store. He asked for money as he always does. JRS and I have had an on-going conversation as to whether it is helpful to him or not to be handed a few loonies upon request. I don't think he needs the money as much as he needs us to stop and ask him about himself and to call him by his name. As we headed back to comfort and a tuna sandwich at lunch he headed back to his loneliness.

Charlotte stayed with us over the early afternoon while her sister was at a check-up at the Children's Hospital. Success; good weight, good height. One thing leads to another. Several babies here are now benefiting from something that D and E discovered by a phone call they made after meeting strangers in another situation. The story is a wider one than this but it begs the questions "Is anything random? What is coincidence?" Although many may see this through a different prism, for us it is another example of Providence.

Lucia was wearing her Colombian tee shirt today from her Abuela in South America. The World Cup game this afternoon was between England and Colombia. We were hoping for victory for Colombia but England won 4-3. Imagine me, turning my back on the Motherland? Dear Reader, I did it all for love.

Charles Ritchie in his journal spoke of a July day when he met a woman he refers to as D in the park for lunch. She came all dressed up and he felt she didn't appreciate his simplicity of thought for the event. *"She had dressed for The Ritz and was not too pleased at my enthusiasm for the simple life."*

My heart goes out to D. A few summers ago Himself told me he was taking me on a surprise anniversary afternoon to Niagara-On-The-Lake which is a local beauty spot. In N-O-L there rests a bounty of restaurants and George Bernard Shaw live plays. There are cafes, a pretty hotel and lovely views of the waterfront. There are shops with small items in them, bakeries, art galleries.

Himself couldn't have surprised me more with his planned outing; we stood in a field for a re-enactment of The Fenian Raids in which his Great-Grandfather Edward Quinn had been engaged in Pigeon Hill, Quebec. It was followed by a nice meal out.

The Princess Diana Clematis has bloomed and is laden with buds ready to burst. It climbs up the side of the porch and along the porch floor. Because its beautiful pink cups open upwards it can be also be used as a ground cover.

WEDNESDAY, JULY 4TH, 2018 ~ A warming visit with MA. Can't hug her due to germ control but told her my heart is hugging her's.

Email from A.M. in Frome, Somerset, who was such a help to me when I needed information.

Our Mother Robin in a panic today when a cat stood on his hind feet on our front windowsill trying to reach the babies in the nest. She flew to the telephone wire to watch over the scene and then flew after him like a mad hen until it ran off. Poor thing. Nature can be so cruel and the Bolshevik loves his birds. It's wonderful to have a nest of fledglings right over our front window. I'd hate for the cat to get the birds but I'd hate for the cat to be hurt too.

We once had a cat we loved as children. His name was Caesar. He'd been given to our family by the men in the Guelph Reformatory where we lived at the time.

I had two cats when I was single; Abelard and Heloise. I named them that after seeing the stage production in London's Wyndham Theatre as I was so taken with their love story. But I'm more dog than cat, as is Himself.

And have we had dogs. John went to the bakery years ago while we were visiting with my sister's family and emerged with a dozen Chelsea buns and a Springer Spaniel pup. We took it home but it kept knocking over the baby so we put a bow on his neck and gave it to Jan for her birthday. They loved him for years.

On another occasion he took Drew for a haircut when D was tiny. They met an elderly woman at the barber shop who was moving and wanted somebody to take her miniature white poodle, Brandy. They came home with haircuts and the dog. Brandy spent the next few days either baring his teeth and growling at me when I tried to get upstairs or galloping through the neighbourhood. He went back to his owner who found him another family. (Editor's note; this did not make me cruel. This made me annoyed.)

One Christmas John emerged from the car with a huge, galloping Airedale with a red bow on his neck. He bought him from a farmer north of Toronto. I forget the dog's name. Freudian Slip perhaps. My parents arrived on Christmas Eve. The dog jumped on my tiny mom and put his paws on her shoulders, face to face. I put him in the basement for the night but he found a way to open the door and ate the Christmas treats from off the counter. The neighbour, who fancied herself a dog trainer, said she could calm him down so she took him out in the snow and he bit her in the bumpity. John phoned the farmer and said "I'll pay you to take him back." The farmer said "It's a deal." So the farmer got paid both to sell him and paid to take him back. After our National Lampoon Christmas the dog went home.

We got two King Charles Cavalier Spaniel pups from a breeder in Oshawa. Bertie and Monty were ours to enjoy for years. Monty had too many toes. Overbred.

Niko was an Airedale pup offered to us by a friend who raised them. He was wonderful, crazy, loveable, hyperactive, half-human. We had him for years. Himself was so broken-hearted when he died that I vowed we would never go through this again.

Watched The Capitol Fourth tonight on WNED. I love Bernstein, Gershwin, American musicals. I can see no sense in the harsh feelings that are spewing back and forth across the border just now. It is no solution. We've witnessed how that has worked in other countries throughout history until it deepens into a crevasse that cannot be bridged. Better to bide our time. A lovely American woman asked me last week, "Do Canadians hate us?"

What hard-edged words. What a sorrowful thought.

THURSDAY, JULY 5TH, 2018 ~ John has re-broken his toe so we spent the morning at the local clinic.

This was a crabby day for me so I don't want to dress this entry up to showcase Sainthood because I've run fresh out of it.

Just before bed tonight some relaxing CFMX and a bowl of cereal; two of my fond pleasures. Fell asleep in armchair holding Caravaggio. Have renewed him online again but much left to read before renewals run out and overdue fines kick in.

FRIDAY, JULY 6TH, 2018 ~ John's appointment at the eye clinic. No driving yet. Patience. A virtue.

Lunch at The Paisley where we bumped into JB and RB so sat together. Shared a toasted cheese sandwich.

Home to the back porch and my book for the first time in two weeks. The humidity has lifted.

Wonderful third birthday party for Lucia. A pink cake and pink everything else. She goes into the bottom drawer and takes out a book and sits with it and looks at it.

Her mom is the best birthday party planner. I have to say that this is what she did; she went to a thrift shop and bought two glass candlesticks and two white china plates. She glued the plates to the candlesticks et voila; two pretty cake stands on which were the chocolate cupcakes she made which she piped in white icing and dotted with pink crystallized sugar. Lucia was a happy little Birthday Person.

SATURDAY, JULY 7TH, 2018 ~ A morning walking/ driving around downtown trying to locate someone who has gone missing. I had only his photo and his name. There are many good people in this city several of whom I met this morning. Am hoping this story has a good outcome. In this huge, wide, caring city I met two strangers in a bakery, both of whom knew him by his photo. We live in a big-small city.

The 4 p.m. shadows remind me of late summer in the way in which the gold of the sun traces the outlines of the old elms and elongates them across the lawn.

I picked up two cold coffees for us late this afternoon. As a result I'll never sleep tonight. It was a summery treat. Have decided that I'm not going through life regretting these small things on the basis of "a waste of money" or "too late in the day" (too latte in the day.) No. Enough already! Shush. Not another word out of you. It was fun and we enjoyed chatting as we sucked the cold liquid up through the straws. Take your pleasures where you find them.

SUNDAY, JULY 8TH, 2018 ~ Taught Chapter Six in the children's edition of Pilgrim's Progress this morning. The emphasis was on the main character's concerted effort to keep on the right path no matter how challenging it became. I let them act it out. They are very good at it; Oscar-worthy actors, you might say.

As evening sets in again the world thinks about the little boys in Thailand. How many will they get out of the cave tomorrow when rescue efforts resume?

MONDAY, JULY 9TH, 2018 ~ The first morning at Vacation Bible School was wild. Alison and I have five active boys ages nine to twelve in our group. They have named themselves The Jack Rabbits. I reminded them that Jack Rabbits are fast, smart and quiet. The quiet part will prove debatable but it is summer. The lessons this week are geared to the stories of the children of the Bible and their importance in the grand scheme. The action songs (piano, banjo, guitar, cello) are loud, fun, melodic.

STRINGS magazine arrived today with my article smack in the middle. It's included in a section about adult learners. Other features are about Joshua Bell (hear 'Ladies in Lavender' on youtube) and a tribute to Leonard Bernstein due to this being the 100th year of his birth and another one about Sheku Kanneh-Mason, the young British cellist. The fact that my own piece is in there is proof that you should never say "no" to yourself when you get an idea and that everything is worth a try. In a billion years, never did I imagine...

Our friend Roberta, who lived in Thailand for many years, forwarded me an email from her friends there about the Thai boys currently in the news. I'll share it with our five boys in the morning so they can think about them.

There is nothing like a life story in real time to connect learners to their task. One of the little cave boys is named Abdul. The naming of names is important when something or somebody is lost. It gives them life. It's a good idea to lift Bible stories out of the history of the time and place them in the light of the present. Easier for children to think in terms of what they already understand and can visualize and then translate that into positive action for today.

TUESDAY, JULY 10TH, 2018 ~ Lucia's third birthday! All of the boys are out of the cave. This is a story of mercy in a world that often does not practice it. It is the result of a global brain trust, of people of various creeds and nationalities who came together to save the lives of strangers. It underlines the uniqueness and value of each human life.

Our five boys, the Jack Rabbits, this morning were wide-eyed and even quiet for a few minutes when I told them about the importance of knowing Abdul's name. Tonight we saw Abdul's face and heard his name on the CBC news. His parents sent him from Myanmar to Thailand to school which means he is undocumented in both Myanmar (as a member of a persecuted group) and Thailand. But he's not

undocumented in terms of the world hearing his story now nor is he unrecognized to his Creator. There is power in the naming of names.

The sunflowers I planted all around the porch so they could look at us? Lack of rain and extreme heat equals nada. Too hot to sit outside but that sweet garden gave me such pleasure when it first went in...

A quiet evening. Early to bed so we can get up at six.

WEDNESDAY, JULY 11TH, 2018 ~ My mom loved these lines from Robert Browning's poem Rabbi Ben Ezra; *"Grow old along with me! The best is yet to be, The last of life, for Which the first was made..."*

I have it in her handwriting in her notebook. I love the concept of the plan of life and how the first was meant to link up to the last and vice-versa. Although our family had moved to the other end of the province and back again my parents died in the nursing home in their original town right across the road from the house they had built before the war, the same house that they returned to post-war (they had rented it out, during) and the house where I lived until I was one year old. The circuitous nature of that...

Growing old is often not easy but the circle of our lives does make sense to me. A strengthening thought with which to begin the day.

Another busy morning but a good one with an effort to get the kids to dig deep with regards to the lesson. I took along my much enlarged copy of the postcard I bought at The Montreal Museum of Fine Arts of Jairus' daughter. The artist was Austrian Gabriel Max and he painted it in 1878. I taught them what ululating is (tried to demonstrate it; failed. See youtube) and how the reference in the story to wailing would have been in fact ululating, just as Eastern and African cultures still do in times of grief and joy, and I taught them the Aramaic words that Jesus spoke to the girl *("Talitha cumi." "Damsel, I say unto thee, arise."* Mark 5:41 AKJV*)* We took a long look at the artist's work, at the shadows and the light, at the meaning of the fly on her arm and the significance of the fresh rose at the other end of the picture with the sunlight shining on it and at the tenderness in the hand that was holding hers. We talked about where this lesson leads us in a world when many people are fearful and in need of a hand to lift them up.

Was pleasant enough to sit out for a while before dinner tonight.

THURSDAY, JULY 12TH, 2018 ~ (Pym, 1952, 1978, 84). ***"You look like a wet week at Blackpool."***

A successful morning, this time with the emphasis on the news of Peter's escape from prison and the little girl named Rhoda who opened the door to greet him. The kids love music and they sang with gusto.

MR is teaching a group of much younger children. She came for lunch afterwards. We sat on the deck in the heat and had ham on a croissant, a lemon tart with blueberries on top and big mugs of tea. We are both, as they say, knackered. The above Pym quote describes me well.

Charlotte was here for an hour too and after she left John and I had another ham sandwich which we christened 'supper'.

We're both enjoying this week. John does the opening exercises. I'm re-thinking old stories and am sucking the marrow out of them in both the traditional way and a new-learning way.

Nodded off on the deck after dinner so had a shower and came awake. Before bed listened to a bit of Joshua Bell's violin and to Bernstein conducting Gershwin's Rhapsody in Blue. I figure I owe it to Lenny, as they called him.

FRIDAY, JULY 13TH, 2018 ~ *"From my fathers perspective, the cello spoke from the heart more than any instrument."* That is what Jamie Bernstein said in her interview with STRINGS magazine, page 21, August 2018, about her father, conductor Leonard Bernstein.

Whenever we play the children's songs this week and they sing it out with joy I feel as if I'm playing with my whole heart. The music does the talking for me.

Today was the last day of the kid's summer program. It was an opportunity to validate the children and their faith and to think globally.

Extreme heat again today. Thirty degrees Celsius and humid.

E and H spent the morning with their mom at The National Gallery in Washington at the Art Investigators program for children. Last year they learned about Georgia O'Keefe and this year it was Van Gogh's painting of roses which he did immediately before his release from the asylum at Saint-Remy (1890).

Himself suggested we go to The Snooty Fox for Steak and Guinness Pie tonight. It proved too heavy, too rich and too heart-burning.

When we came out a street musician was playing and singing 'Killing Me Softly' originally by Roberta

Flack, 1973. He did it well except that I think it was intended as a woman's song. He stopped for a minute and said to a little boy, "You don't know this one. You're too young."

Then he spotted me and said to "But I bet you know it."

SATURDAY, JULY 14TH, 2018 ~ Thinking about the importance of names. John and I were remembering this morning our friends who became separated due to circumstances as they fled their homeland. Neither of them knew where the other was. Because of that, the others in her encampment where they had washed ashore told her that she would be the last name to be called out for resettlement if ever they were found. But the plan for their lives was far greater than that. Due to the diligence and caring of the then Prime Minister Joe Clark she and her children were the first names called once the group was located. That family became a part of our blood and huge gift to Canada.

Our names are the one thing that nobody can take from us. In times of crisis they are often all that remains; our mother's gift to us. And we might be called first!

An early morning with three loads of laundry in before another quick drive over to Burlington to sort out the cello.

A quiet afternoon with Gershwin again and Samuel Barber's 'Adagio for Strings', Copland's 'Appalachian Spring' and the Saturday crossword. It's fun to imagine what story is being played out inside the music. And the Saturday crossword used to be much more interesting. Somebody please fix it.

Have been waiting all day for lightning and rain. Nothing. Everything is sere. Small leaves drift off the elms, turn brown, curl up on the porch and wait to be swept away. White flowers are out on the Dogwood and the Amora Maple is full of keys. Is summer on the wane?

Jock's phone call this evening startled me into wakefulness and I realized it was only 9.00 p.m. I was watching Inspector Barnaby. Was so tired from the week's vigorous activity that I missed most of the episode. We chatted for a bit. I told him about my plans for a French Tea Party for the children when H and E visit. E says she has plans to go to Paris when she grows up. I'll buy French macarons and serve tea in the tiny china cups.

To bed at 9:30.

SUNDAY, JULY 15TH, 2018 ~ *"Summer's lease hath all too short a date."* (Shakespeares's 'Sonnet 18, Shall I compare thee to a Summer's Day?')

This mid-summer business is a puzzle. It takes forever to get here, then it pops like mad into breathtaking beauty and just as you start the revelling it starts packing up for the season. I see small hints of it. John says the plants have reached their full bloom.

A good service this morning with the children singing their happy songs from last week and John's sermon about bearing fruit and are we doing it?

Too hot to be outside so the rest of the day inside reading and doing nothing much.

MONDAY, JULY 16TH, 2018 ~ Our Ely's birthday today. She is one terrific mommy.

RMB and I to the hospital this morning to visit our dear MA. Am calling today by its name; sorrow.

TUESDAY, JULY 17, 2018 ~ *"...bicycling...has done more to emancipate women than anything else in the world...I stand and rejoice every time I see a woman ride by on a wheel...the picture of free, untrammelled womanhood."* (Susan B. Anthony,

Quaker, Abolitionist, American Women's Rights advocate, 1820-1906.)

Two of my favourite real life vignettes could have been lifted out of a Barbara Pym novel. This afternoon was one of them. I was waiting for Marg on the bench outside the coffee shop. I caught sight of her a block away on her bike, her helmeted head bent to the task and her skirt flying in the breeze. She glided past me through the green light, held up her finger and yelled "One minute!" With that she dismounted, dashed into the bakery and emerged with a raspberry scone for us to share on the patio with her coffee and my chai.

The other scenario I love to think about is the story my friend Jill told me about her long ago trip to Malta which included a visit to the Sisters in a then cloistered Convent. For entertainment the nuns stood on the rooftops to watch the planes landing and taking off. Those silver wings must have represented a form of freedom. Everything inside their walls was the same colour scheme; black, white, grey. Drab. Lifeless. The Nun's habits were black and white. White sheets were on the bed, their knife-pleat edges folded over grey woollen blankets. White walls. Black chairs. It was a trifecta of dull. At the end of the visit one of the Nuns asked her if she would like a cup of tea. Jill took her up on her offer. The Sister brought out the tea pot; it was cherry red.

Although I wasn't at that Convent I was on the patio sharing the scone and drinking the Chai Latte with Marg. We covered most every topic that needed a thorough dredging and had a catch-up that was perfection-on-a-summer's-afternoon. And then she hopped back on her bike and pedalled for miles to get home.

Doesn't life make you take a second look?

WEDNESDAY, JULY 18TH, 2018 ~ Another long morning at Honda. Although I feign interest in things automotive the process bores me no end.

Rosemary And Thyme came to clean up the weeds. We look forward to the blooming of the cosmos next month. They have good height already. Everything else looks destitute. Even the roses, which were perfection when they did blossom, are wan. No rain all summer so the land is thirsting.

The prettiest road in our city is Beckett's Drive where the shade of the forest covers two lanes of traffic all the way up the hill and all the way back down. There were spots of sunlight waving back and forth through the shadows today. It's a little trick of nature to make you think that for three minutes you are in the bosom of the pastoral but in a wink you are thrust back into the snarling traffic. The bright sky startles after the darkness of those deep woods.

Sat on the back porch briefly this evening. John announced this; "The robins have all left." Seems to me they just came back but Himself notices nature's cycles like no one else I know.

We've had sad news from New Zealand. Cherry and family, Ted and Mary are in our hearts. ("A good shepherd loves his sheep.")

THURSDAY, JULY 19TH, 2018 ~ Dear Caravaggio, I'm sorry that our relationship had to end this way. When I dropped you off at the library early this morning I wondered if I was doing the right thing but I felt that our relationship had come to an end, for now at least. That doesn't mean we won't get back together at some point. It's just that I've renewed us twice and still we didn't get anywhere. For now, just give me some space. You could have taught me so much more had I been patient. It's not that I wasn't taken with you. I enjoyed the ideas you introduced me to but the following factoids annoyed me no end:

1. **the sword you carried to use on people you dislike. Who does that?**
2. **the treacherous crowd you hung out with,**
3. **the fact that you murdered somebody.**

But still, perhaps someday we can finish what we started.

Yours, with every turn of the page of which there were too many, JS x

Returning unread books gives me a slight feeling of having failed.

Awake far too early, at 5:30 again, this morning. When I'm awake, well, I'm awake. So up to do some laundry, water front porch plants, breakfast.

After lunch I sat outside and read The Arctic News from The Diocese of The Arctic. The new Rector of St. Jude's, Iqaluit, is Rev'd Methusalah Kunuk. John went, years before I knew him, to the opening of St. Jude's Cathedral. (Iqaluit was formerly Frobisher Bay). St. Jude's burned down a while ago and has been rebuilt. It is a famous Canadian church building as it is in the shape of an igloo. Many interesting articles in the small magazine including the sorrowful news about men trying to get to the hunting grounds and falling through the ice due to the warming climate.

This evening sat on the back porch with JRS sorting

out life. Resolved: we can't change what we *cannot* do, but we can focus on what we *can* do. Attitude is all. I'm the talker. He's the listener. I think.

Perfect peace out there tonight. Nothing but beautiful birdsong. Bird count: three goldfinches, one purple finch, one hummingbird and a robin that John thought had already left for southern climes.

FRIDAY, JULY 20TH, 2018 ~ *"It is not enough to reject this courtyard – you need to have a vision of the meadows with which you want to replace it."* (Mernissi, 1994, 215).

Fatima Mernissi was a Sociologist at University Mohammed V in Rabat, Morocco. I read her Globe And Mail obituary in 2015. She grew up in a harem that was filled with legalities designed to regulate the lives of the women within its walls. The book is a wonderful metaphor for both imposed and self-imposed barriers, fences, gates and getting up and over the things that hold us back. Ergo the above wondrous quote from her mother. And this one on pg 214; *"The main thing for the powerless is to have a dream."* The women in her harem became embroiderers par excellence. They were instructed to sew only the approved designs. But in the secret and unseen corners of the harem what did they weave into glorious being? Birds; free-flying, large-winged creatures in vermilion, turquoise, gold. Birds that could fly up, up, up and carry their dreams over the walls.

Makes me think about the nuns in my July 17th entry. We all of us need to imagine what it is to soar, to leap over fences

H took the children back to the National Gallery this morning for a children's presentation about artist Mary Cassatt. Her soft palettes have made her art a favourite of my own. These small experiences build confidence, help children, help all of us, to scale the ramparts if and when we choose to.

SATURDAY, JULY 21ST, 2018 ~ According to today's paper I'm an endangered species, and, like a rare bird, am destined to become like the Great One-horned Rhino, the Beluga, the Dodo. As birth rates sink to two children per family, those of us who are the middle kids might have had our day. We're on our way to extinction.

Downtown for haircut and lowlights. My white hair too Andy Warhol so needed toning down.

After hair I sauntered a bit. Went into the shop called

Chocolat (like the French movie) and ordered four tiny mint chocolates, two to take home for John and two for me. She totalled it to $8.17. A shocking amount for those tiny mints. I said politely that I'd decided against them. I felt emboldened. If not now, when? Then I went into the shop called STORE and bought a small clay mug which will be perfect for tiny leaves, flowers. I went into the artist's co-op and tried to understand the gist of the show but didn't. I felt surrounded by its anger. But as Jock reminds me, "That's what art is, mom. That's the purpose of it. To express."

I did another bold thing today. I sent an email about something that I need to know and will see if that leads anywhere. Endangered species perhaps, but this *rara avis* is envisioning meadows.

Bold felt good today. It's only taken me seventy years to try it out.

SUNDAY, JULY 22, 2018 ~ Rain all night long. Opened wide the window and let the soft sounds lull me back to sleep. Nothing more soothing than the sound of rain tapping out a message on the rooftop.

Morning Prayer and a nap (not in Morning Prayer. Waited until I got home.)

A chat today with LB regarding memories of the

Saturday night Coffee House in our town when we were in our late teens. It was held in the basement of the beautiful old Anglican Church. (I once read that Susanna Moodie worshipped there.) People strummed and sang protest songs and covers from Bob Dylan, Pete Seeger, Joan Baez, Gordon Lightfoot. We grew up with strong, definitive music that blossomed between 1960 and the mid–1970's. It was music that kindled the hearts of a generation. It informed our future mindsets about peace as the way through. It was the panacea for Saturday evenings in a small town. It connected us not only to friends but to the wider music world and to new thoughts. After LB and I spoke tonight I listened on youtube to some of that same music. Am wondering how it is that I so easily conjure up the strength of the emotions I had from fifty plus years ago? With what did I replace them? Pragmatism, I suppose, the pragmatism that is needed to make life work.

A visit this evening from friends whose son and fiance have asked John to conduct their marriage ceremony. He does that with joy considering that we have known the boy (man) since he was tiny.

Otherwise, quiet. An overcast evening. Am hoping for more rain in the night. The garden smiles.

MONDAY, JULY 23RD, 2018 ~ A sad phone call about illness. Friends have no price. I'm sifting through a trove of memories; the day we tried on her mother's box of old hats when she was sorting out their house, getting soaked when she sped us across the lake to get to the mainland in a downpour, walks on wintry evenings when our daughters were at their Highland dance lessons, the way she belted out MacNamara's Band along with her ancient recording of it every St. Patrick's Day never missing a word; *"and Hennessy Tennessee toodles the flute and the music is something grand..."* When I first met her she was hugging her ten month old against her hip in their back garden. It all comes tumbling out. We sort through the stories of a life, empty them out, sift them, lock them up within.

My grandmother told me that God gives us *"dying Grace."*

TUESDAY, JULY 24TH, 2018 ~ Some new growth on the zinnias this morning. Although they are small there are a few open now; red, gold, orange. I love the glow of them. They look as if they're leaving for vacation with their tropical clothes on.

Had a conversation with LB the other day about

why we don't feel old on the inside. We asked ourselves what happened to the strength of the emotions we felt long ago. I came upon two appropriate quotes from 'Last Friends' today (Gardam, 2013, 150). This, speaking about the elderly Dulcie; *"They could not see the imprisoned girl in her"* and this regarding our more placid emotions now; *"It's the cooling of the blood."*

Tonight John at the English Language Conversation Group with the Chinese Grad students and me doing this. Have made him some oatmeal porridge and set it out for the morning. Hector, John's Greenock-born dad, told me to make it at night and let it sit in the liquid so it's creamy the following morning.

Violence once again in Toronto. Maybe Canadians have a tendency to be smug about how wonderful we are. Hello world; we're not perfected yet. Working on it.

Light rain. More to follow, they say.

If I have cooling of the blood then why am I so hot all the time?

WEDNESDAY, JULY 25TH, 2018 ~ I love the porches of my life. Our grandparents had a generous one across the front of their house. At least it seemed generous when I was small, but looking back maybe it wasn't. Life takes on assumed glories in retrospect. My grandparent's porch had Dutchman's Pipe vine growing on netting right up the sides. We played there in rippling light, shady patches intertwined with shards of sunshine, the shadows dancing and trading places according to the whims of the breeze. I loved being out there when it rained. It meant that we were safe but not quite. There was a slight tension to that because we were also just feet away from getting soaked. And they had a porch swing. It was green and white striped canvas, a sofa on chains. It produced a back and forth squeak.

We had a front porch when we lived on Highway 2 in our lakeside town. It was a long way back from the highway but it was close enough to watch the traffic growling at a snail's pace on hot summer evenings before the major highway was opened.

The Red Lion Inn in Stockbridge has the best porch in the world, with wicker rockers and chintz cushions and people who will bring you things to drink. Nobody rushes. You can rock away the entire evening, chatting or not, dozing, reading or watching Jane Jacob's street ballet. The small back porch we have now suits us well. It doesn't have to be large to be enjoyed. We all share the same sky, the same roses, the same July.

Our long awaited patio door went in today. Took four hours. It gave me a chance to clean behind things that got moved to make way for the workmen. This door is guaranteed to keep the cold air out in winter along with stray humans like the young man who ended up on the porch at 5 a.m. one pitch dark Autumn morning, begging to be let in. Now we have a double-locking system plus the old hockey stick that gets put in the doorstop at night. As it turned out the young man was a freshman at the university who had had too much in the way of things that weren't good for him and wasn't sure where he was. And out of all the thousands of homes in our city he picked us. I did feel for him. He had his jammies on. He was somebody's baby boy. I didn't let him in and the police came and drove him home.

Tonight we sat on the porch listening to the Cardinals as they performed Choral Evensong in the elms.

THURSDAY, JULY 26TH, 2018 ~ Jock is thirty-five today. He arrived at one in the morning at ten pounds four ounces. We were thrilled with this round, fair-haired baby whose arrival the obstetrician announced with "This one is as big as a Christmas turkey!" And now he is a good, kind man and not one bit a turkey.

A microburst this afternoon when I ran into the bakery to get a chocolate birthday cake. Wet to the skin. It only lasted for a few minutes. That seems to be the new pattern for rain; five minute deluges that look like Noah's back in town and then, done. I miss proper rain, the kind you could count on for two day stretches.

Another blast of rain late this afternoon and again this evening. I love thunder, the noise of it, the darkening sky. The threatening rumble calls for listening to the powerful Rachmaninoff Three, or The Rach Three, as they say. I find it on youtube as I don't have it on a cd. Yes, I know. I should be saying "I stream it." Have a listen if you have time. Pump up the volume. It'll make you want to hear it every time the weather is rough. Promise.

A birthday dinner here for Jock with our little Smith girls too.

Jock called when they got home and said "Thanks for having me."

I replied "It was fun."

To that he replied "No, I mean, thanks for *having* me."

And now for a quiet sit in front of the tv.

FRIDAY, JULY 27TH, 2018 ~ In Edith Wharton's fine book The Age Of Innocence, Ellen and Archer meet in the museum in a room of antiquities. Ellen considers the small objects from days gone by and muses as to how objects and the people who owned them are forgotten over time.

It was a comment about the changing kaleidoscope of the Golden Age social group to which Archer belonged but it also provided a description of the small items in our own house that we've held dear as being specific to people whom we love.

I was putting things away in the cabinet drawer this morning when I found a silver spoon I've never seen before. I suppose it's been hiding in there for years. I showed The Bolshevik but he had no idea how we came by it either. It is a dessert spoon with a delicate, twisted handle. And on the back, engraved in a pretty scroll, it says "Lizzie, 1888." Who was she and how did we come by her spoon? I often wondered why my mom, an antique lover, wrote down the provenance of everything she owned in a notebook.

Jan has the notebook and sometimes reads it to me over the phone, item by item, and we howl. Mom would laugh with us for the fun we've had with her lists. But I wish I knew who Lizzie-of-the-silver-spoon was and I wish Lizzie had kept a notebook and I wish I had it.

On our front door is a brass nameplate that was once attached to a doorknocker. The plaque says, in a graceful flow of old-world etching, *J.R. Smith.* It belonged to John's paternal Grandfather, John Roxburgh Smith, and was on their door in Glasgow. It was brought to Canada and was on their son's door in Montreal (also John Roxburgh Smith.) The knocker and the brass name plate were stolen right off the door. JRS, the Bolshevik's Uncle, found the name plate in the pawn shop but the knocker was gone. He took the nameplate home and put it on his apartment door on Peel Street in Montreal. And now we have it on our door. It will be passed along and treasured.

We did have an item which we've sent to the Textile Museum in Glasgow for safekeeping. It was a huge linen tablecloth that belonged to John's Great Aunt Jessie and Uncle James Murray Smith when they lived at 11 Butte Gardens, since torn down for the Adam Smith building at The University of Glasgow.

Jessie had embroidered it with acorns and oak leaves. Hector's cousin in Greenock passed it along to us. We know that the tablecloth often had an interesting group sitting around it for dinner, including Scottish writers, Neil Munro for one. The man who invited us to the Glasgow Arts Club several years ago for an evening has since died himself. He was a fount of historical information and knew things I'd like to ask him about now. I used that cloth one Christmas and spent the meal making sure that nobody spilled gravy on it. I vowed never to use it again so we had it cleaned and packed it off back to its Glaswegian origins. And to our offspring, if you ever want to see it contact the Textile Museum. The stories that unfolded around that tablecloth in their Hillhead house would make a book. I wish they had kept notes. These stories may seem inconsequential to others but to me they are precious. It's saddening that those memories get washed away over time.

If this journal makes me look like a materialist I'll have to accept that fact about myself. I love old everything.

A reheat of yesterday's dinner and a sit on the porch. Two downy woodpeckers.

What makes me the Keeper-type, the collector

of memories, things? I'm exactly like my mom in that way.

SATURDAY, JULY 28TH, 2018 ~ A phone chat this morning with Diane at a cabin somewhere near Mahone Bay, Nova Scotia. They have loons on the lake and one of them carries her baby on her back.

Diane said this; "I used to think that when I reached seventy I'd be able to sit back and say well, I've got it all figured out now."

And now that she is seventy she sits back in this world-gone-mad and says to herself "I don't understand a thing."

Spaghetti sauce made, laundry in, window boxes replanted with Autumn colours. I planted Fountain Grass, red begonias and coleus vines. Stuck together the broken clay window box and am hoping it holds. Tossed a bag of soil on the front garden. The muscari bulbs have been dug up again; squirrels. JRS instructed me from his perch on the front steps. He's a good teacher re gardening. There are some benefits to be found in our new situation. He is passing his knowledge re plants onto me. I'm learning new tricks. We have also developed a new form of 'I spy' to see where in this vast city we can find the best free parking spots for disabled people since he now has a car sticker. He doesn't use a wheelchair, but a cane. In fact, I see that he uses his new walker (which he keeps in the garage) to hold the garbage bag off the floor so the mice can't get at it. If this journal is to be about aging, then there's a piece of advice for you.

I love seeing dirt under my fingernails; it's my new look. There once was a time when I had nails painted with Pink Pearl. I've had a slothful history and now here I am, at seventy, with dirt. It is alleged that Virginia Woolf mentioned the *"chocolate earth in our nails"* when she wrote about gardening with Leonard.

Chickadees in the lilacs, their thin cries piercing the breeze. Baby Baltimore oriole at the feeder. Hummingbird flitting around with fifty wing beats per second. (saw that factoid on the huge tv screen at Tim Horton's.) Baby blue jays squawking at John for treats.

SUNDAY, JULY 29TH, 2018 ~ Our grandchildren have arrived. They were here this afternoon until early evening when they went back to their other grandparents. They will be back tomorrow. E built a Fairy House in the garden with twigs, pink rose petals, a clear plastic lid for a pool, a bachelor's button over the front door and a clematis bloom for a broom. H played with the lego and emptied out the bottom toy drawer. He was thrilled with what he called his "laptop", a disconnected computer keyboard I use to help Charlotte practice numbers/letters. We played a game I made up called Art Clues. We guessed which painting the other person was thinking about. I got John's cane, (it was my grandmother's first, then my dad's, now ours), and another cane we have and told them to use it as a prop for improv. H used it as a rake, an airplane, a hook, many things. E used it with vigour and athletic prowess which she might have inherited from her other grandmother but not from the one who is writing this missive.

E was anxious to get back into John's Grandmother's wooden box that we looked through at Christmas. She was keen to find a mystery. And we did. She found a yellowed business card that says this on it; *"1776 House ~ Major Andre Prison, Tappan NY."*

The card had belonged to her Great-Great Auntie Gertrude. She was excited about the word prison and knew it meant jail. She asked me to google the words on the yellowing card. So I did and up it came. Before we knew it we had a story that was indeed a mystery, involving George Washington, The American Revolutionary War and Major Andre who was imprisoned in that house and hung as a spy. She is keen to come back tomorrow to discover more dreadful things in that box and laughed her tiny socks off about this new story. She wondered why her Great-Great Aunt had the card in the first place. And so did we. It had been turned into a public house but was a long way from Montreal in those days.

And so to watch Endeavour on PBS and have a chat with Jan.

MONDAY, JULY 30TH, 2018 ~ On a tv episode last night one of the characters talked about moving away from the bleakness of his childhood English village for a bigger place elsewhere. He compared it to stepping into a world of technicolour after living in a world that was painted in black and white.

Living in technicolour; you don't have to move to a bigger-and-better anything to get it. Technicolour comes from within. It's right there waiting for us to knock on its door. Hello? Technicolour? It's me!

The children had a wonderful day out at The Lion Safari with their other grandparents which left a chunk of time for us to be with our girl, their mom.

Chat. Chat. Chat. You could hear us from here to Madagascar. The children came back for the late afternoon and evening. We fed the birds their bread crumbs on the porch. H's bird-feeding style is unique but not uncommon for four year olds; one bit for the blue jay babies, then one bit for himself. Cooler now and time for some tv.

TUESDAY, JULY 31ST, 2018 ~ An early morning visit to the hospital to find that M.A. has been moved to specialized care.

I could write about the Fairytale Version of the French Tea Party I've been planning for a month or I could give you The True Version. I'll go for true. I used the Blue Mikado tiny espresso cups and saucers. I bought what I thought were macarons when what I bought were meringues. They look alike. I set the table on the porch. The kids love weak tea and when I go to their house to visit they always have a tea party. I set out the teapot, the milk and sugar jugs, flowered napkins, tiny spoons. I told them the French word for bakery is "boulangerie" but Edwina said it was "patisserie". I was beat before I began and I knew it. They liked the colours of the meringues (pink, mauve, yellow, blue, lavender), which in no time

melted and became microscopic bits that clung to the sweat on their sweet thin arms and made a crumbled pastel kaleidoscope on the table in the style of the Impressionists. Appropriate when you think about it. The tea party lasted for eight minutes. The wisdom to be found in the Tea Party Experience is this; never over-plan. In fact, never plan a thing. Wing it. Once the meringue crumbs were wiped away I bought out the tray with various objects on it to play Kim's Game (thank you Rudyard Kipling.) That last moment idea and the further story telling about each object that evolved lasted for well over an hour. Lovely dinner at K and R's tonight.

WEDNESDAY, AUGUST 1ST, 2018 ~ Early this morning to different hospital to hold M.A.'s hand, the hand that has performed so many kindnesses over the years, for her family, for others, for me.

A wild day. The children wanted to put on a circus. We got it half organized but a friend dropped in who distributes great dollops of excitement wherever she goes so she stirred things up a bit. Chaos reigned afterwards. Will try again tomorrow re circus.

In early evening I delivered them to their other

grandparents. And then here all was quiet. And quietude is what you think you need until they're gone. And then, missed them.

At dusk, cicadas thrumming in the trees, a herald of Autumn's approach.

THURSDAY, AUGUST 2ND, 2018 ~ A fun day with Charlotte while Lucia visited Sick Kids Hospital in Toronto. We took her to Tim Horton's for lunch. She was proud as she sat at the table with her bagel.

A glorious thing happened when they got home. Drew said *"Watch and listen."*

He rocked Lucia in his arms through the air, up high and back again, back and forth, and we heard soft but audible syllables of little girl laughter.

And if a girl is going to wait for three years to make her first vocalizations it may as well be laughter!

FRIDAY, AUGUST 3RD, 2012 ~ Daily events need a place to settle and become a part of our consciousness. Too easy to let them slip away, unnoticed. We have to suck the marrow out of our moments.

But today did not slip away unnoticed. Our circus unfolded in the garden with acts concerning a hula hoop and a broom which doubled as a tight rope. K-and-L-next-door sent us a bowl of popcorn over the fence as no circus is complete without it. We had intermission and I made chocolate milkshakes.

Kim's Game again, this time with boy's items (a hammer, wrench, screwdriver, flashlight). I know how politically incorrect I stand on this one but as Neville Chamberlain said *"Peace in our time"* and I'll do anything to achieve it. A friend brought nail polish for Edwina the other day and Hamish has since been wanting a surprise too. I've told him he can keep the flashlight in the kitchen drawer forever although he had his heart set on that large, dangerous hammer. We played Kim's Game again with girl's items from my top drawer (fake pearls, bracelets) and she got to keep the wedding favour we got in October. More Kim's Games unfolded when their Mom was out for a while with Granddad. When they got home we all returned to our senses, which two of us had quite lost during the interval. Granddad took himself off for a nap.

They went to other Grandparents for dinner whereupon Himself and I fell to dozing in the breeze on the porch. Then inside for jammies and tv.

SATURDAY, AUGUST 4TH, 2018 ~ A scorching hot morning in the Fairy Garden at The Royal Botanical Garden with the children. Extra bonus was meeting the curly haired little granddaughter of MH/AH. The Fairy Garden has it's charms; young women volunteers dressed in metres of pastel tulle skirts, pink and mauve fairy wings, silk butterflies glued to their cheeks, crowns of twigs on their heads intertwined with flowers. The heat unbearable. E and H wrote out their secret wishes on long ribbons of cloth and tied them to the Wishing Bridge and walked up and down the pathways in the rock garden looking for Fairy Doors and did small crafts. They were at the last activity (filling up biodegradable cups with dirt for Fairy Gardens) when I espied two red Muskoka chairs on a small rise. Thank you for your largesse Parks Canada. I sat for ten minutes overlooking a small hill that showcases hundreds of huge trees in the foreground. My idea is that come Autumn I will return to those chairs to overlook orange, yellow, red foliage. Home this afternoon for some quiet time. Jock came in and shared our dinner.

Was ready for a soft evening. Crossword. My new non-fiction by the late Moroccan sociologist Fatima Mernissi. Plans were skewed when I put on the tv and Inspector Barnaby appeared. He had me locked in the case room with him for an hour while I helped him figure out which of the villagers did those wicked things to people.

SUNDAY, AUGUST 5TH, 2018 ~ Morning Prayer. Scorching hot outside; the poor animals, the poor people who live in downtown rooms with tiny windows, the poor people who need cold liquids and can't get at them, the poor hot fish in RMB's lake.

The children here late afternoon and evening. They had McDonald's Happy Meals which I have renamed Unhappy Meals. Those prizes. They always want the one they didn't get. Marketing at it's most annoying. They had a long phone chat with Charlotte and Uncle Jock came to play. They love it when he does the tricks for them that my dad did for our kids when they were small and for us before that. Jock drove them back to the other grandma and grandpa's home and now I'm in my housecoat.

I was re-thinking the idea of getting a Fit Bit, one of those things that counts your daily footsteps. If I'd had it this week it would be worn out due to my lack of sitting down.

Hi there CBC evening news which I will watch if I can just limp into this armchair...

MONDAY, AUGUST 6TH, 2018 ~ All of the too-muchness of this past week led to a general unravelling in the Department of Childhood today. We aspire to make the visits memorable when the best thing for kids is sometimes unstructured play. So from now on they play. No more tea parties, no more fairies. Play.

The sky turned the colour of pitch, the wind blew and it rained for five minutes. I wish we could have a true rain storm. Sometimes I think our emotions are tied to the weather and a downpour releases and cleanses something within.

It's only just gone 7 p.m. but I need my housecoat and my book. And honestly, I could do with a pacifier.

TUESDAY, AUGUST 7TH, 2018 ~ Wicked heat again. An eye appointment for JRS this morning and another coming up next week.

The children are with their other grandparents today so all too quiet. I'll miss them when they leave. Saddens me to think about them driving away next week, their trusting little faces looking out the car window as we wave them off.

A pleasant evening with a PBS show about the ten best cities in the USA, all of them planned around

a grid system of some type by the architects of the day. Some good ideas in there for post-war affordable housing all built with the front doors facing the back onto a common green space. I asked the Bolshevik "Why can't they make that happen now?" Seems like an easy solution for the masses who are shut out of the housing market. Why isn't some hotshot planner who has just watched that show sitting down this second with a pencil stuck behind his ear and thinking up ways to make attractive and affordable housing with green space behind so that every child has access to an outdoor play area?

Listened to Joshua Bell's sweet violin; Ladies In Lavender theme and Meditation From Thais. MASSENET

Read much of my new Mernissi book which is interesting, informative. I'm underlining, making margin notes so I can refer to it later.

My next plan is to read Dinner with Lenny by Jonathon Cott which was the last interview with Leonard Bernstein. This will be my salute to his one-hundredth birthday anniversary.

WEDNESDAY, AUGUST 8TH, 2018 ~ In August of 1943 Ira Dilworth wrote to Emily Carr about his desire for a place of his own; *"...just a garden*

which would not be a fancy one, and a small house where I could have my pictures, my books and my piano. Everyone should have a place for his household gods." (Morra, 2006, 222).

I love that quote. It's comforting and cosy, and appeals to me no end. After declaring myself to be a materialist (see entry for July 27th) I like to think that other people enjoy their "household gods" too. Our bits and pieces are imbued with memory and stamp the space as our own, our feeble anchors to the world which in the long run aren't worth much at all. They rust. But let me have my fun.

A noisy, crazed afternoon with all four of the children here. Hamish has lost his cough so it was possible to have Lucia in the same company. Madness reigned. The three big kids (six, five, four years) shut themselves in the back room and told me to stay out. "No adults allowed. This is a kid's club and we are evil." Edwina made them all name tags. Lucia comes to us now for hugs and for besitos (kisses) and for tickles which she demands by putting our hands on her tummy and making scratchy motions with her own fingers.

Such awful world events. It's not just the kid's club members who are evil.

THURSDAY, AUGUST 9TH, 2018 ~ A crazy way to start the day. Looked at our morning city newspaper, noticed a full page ad for a sale of handguns, wrote a joint Letter to The Editor and cancelled our subscription which we have had for forty-two years; a sort of panacea.

The children here today. They were enthused about the children's collection at our library this morning. We came home with a huge bag full of things including a dvd about a Golden Retriever which is the dog that E has her heart set on. Later this afternoon they went off with their other G and G to Cherry Hill Gate to see the wildlife.

The LRB has arrived. *"Marleybone spacious sunny ensuite room with use of kitchen/diner in quiet street three minutes from Baker Street Station and Regent's Park..."* and many articles to look at.

A quiet sit on the porch tonight. A blowsy evening and twilight early. The leaves were showing their silversides so showers perhaps in the night. I watched Andrew Graham-Dixon's TVOntario show on the art heist that involved skilled thieves getting away with two of Van Gogh's paintings within three minutes and five seconds from the Van Gogh Museum in Amsterdam.

And to think I found it challenging to plan a successful backyard circus for two of our Little People.

FRIDAY, AUGUST 10TH, 2018 ~ A breeze today. Sunshine. No humidity. We sat on the back porch this afternoon chatting with Hayley when a cheery voice called over the fence. Isaac had left home at 5.30 this morning and was here by 3.30. I offered him lunch but he only wanted a cup of Typhoo. With thanks to JB and RB I have addicted family and friends to this tea. The children were at Bronte Park today with K and R.

And a trivia quiz emailed to us by Lynn and Andrew which I failed with flying colours. If someone were to ask you to name a famous North American landmark that is always moving backwards wouldn't you say the Reversing Falls in New Brunswick? Nope. The answer is Niagara Falls as the rim erodes two and one-half feet backwards every year due to the pressure of the water.

American friend Laurie's First Person essay in The Globe today. A most soothing summer read right when we need it most. As I read her article it dawned on me how good writing can help people in a real way, by diverting their attention to something gentle thus taking their minds off the harsh stuff. Have mailed her the front section so she can see the setup.

SATURDAY, AUGUST 11TH, 2018 ~ I find little jewels in other people's days. For example, when LB said she'd gone to the Mennonite Plant Sale to pick up some hydrangeas I was imagining the bonneted women, the tables of colourful plants, the garden lovers picking over the wares and the joy they had in finding just what they needed to glorify their gardens.

So when I read this quote from Charles Ritchie's 'Undiplomatic Diaries', (Ritchie, 2008, 396) I wanted to share it. Charles Ritchie was visiting Stonington, Connecticut in August 1959 and this is what he found there: *"...eighteenth century white clapboard houses with fanlights over the doors. In one Mrs. Carlton Sprague-Smith practices chamber music and collects white Wedgewood stone china. On another Miss Bull perfects fine book-binding in a pre-Revolutionary hideout in her herb garden. We dine on terraces here and there..."*

I remember many things about the neighbours of my early childhood. When they knocked on the door to borrow a cup of sugar or to share some rhubarb or in hope of a chat my mom invited them in and put on the kettle. When was I about eight my mother ironed a shirt for the husband of Hannah the hairdresser next door. He had died and it seemed that the neatly

pressed shirt was going to accompany him to the next world. I thought it was peculiar then but now I see the caring in that small act. We have formalized our lives now, have shut ourselves away. So while Mrs. Sprague-Smith in Connecticut is practicing her chamber music the Mrs. Smith at this address is much of the time unaware of most everything outside of Dove Cottage.

My current Intelligence in Britain informs me that a certain, admirable film star has gnomes in the front garden of her London home. No saying who told. But there's a bit of neighbourhood trivia for you.

Sat with The Globe crossword this afternoon waiting for the children to arrive after their playtime at the park. The thing I notice most about aging is the loss of control over planning. We wait for others to tell us what comes next. The reason for that is because the others have more to consider than we do; children's schedules, errands, nap times, jobs. I remember my mom and dad saying the same thing.

I have sliced some watermelon, put out a few small squares of pizza toast, cut up tiny blocks of cheese and the old Bunnykins mugs are ready for a drink.

What are your neighbours up to? Any idea?

I suspect that ours think we've been noisy this past two weeks.

SUNDAY, AUGUST 12TH, 2018 ~ An early morning phone call to Rob at their hilltop home in Scotland that overlooks both the egg man's cottage at the bottom of the gate and their tranquil village. His birthday today, (Rob's, not the egg man's.) I've been urging him for years to write a book of his memoirs (R, not the e.m.)

Morning Prayer and home to spend the rest of the day here with the children before they head back home tomorrow and with Charlotte and Lucia too. L grows stronger every time we see her. She lets me cuddle her now providing I'm very rough about it and will hang her upside down; my little possum.

Have closed the blinds, turned down the bed, watered the hostas in the front garden, the Fountain Grass and the window boxes. Kitchen is clean, have tidied up the porch and put the house to bed. Soon will go ourselves.

One yellow rose bud out in the back garden ready to flower.

MONDAY, AUGUST 13TH, 2018 ~ A visit here this morning with our eastern friends. They bring us fun, good conversation and an understanding of new things. We cherish them.

The children had a good trip back home and phoned to say so when they got there.

Tonight to the hospital. M and I held hands and talked for ten minutes. Her sense of humour intact. She made me smile when we talked about my maternal grandfather being an Irish Catholic and her huge family comprised of same.

"Do you think your Nana would let this Anglican sing with the Irish up there?" I asked her. She grinned, gave me a thumbs down, murmured "no" and closed her eyes to sleep. And that is how I left her, with the grin that I've seen so often.

We're all judgemental in some way; religious, political, status-wise, whatever. We all of us want to rise like cream to the top of the milk jug.

We're such a bunch of coconuts, we humans.

TUESDAY, AUGUST 14TH, 2018 ~ To the ophthalmologist with Himself this morning. Still no driving. I tell him to be patient. Must go back in eight weeks time.

A longish day which started at 5:30. Nap in the p.m. Phone chats with Hayley and Drew and Jan. A piece of salmon for dinner and a salad with cucumber, avocado, a friend's garden tomatoes, red onion. When we sit down for dinner at night we say how lucky we are to be eating at all, let alone something delicious.

WEDNESDAY, AUGUST 15TH, 2018 ~ In the cartoon called Rhymes with Orange in this morning's newspaper, (which we cancelled but still seem to get), is a sketch of two elderly men in wheelchairs, wearing berets, sitting on a balcony overlooking the lily pond at Giverny.

One says to the other *"Which one am I? Manet or Monet?"* The other replies *"I always get us confused."*

I've clipped it out and taped it in the front cover of The Art Of Rivalry. I've read the book, have seen their paintings, but still can't remember who painted what, whom, when, how. Will remind Self with this: Monet is the Giverny fellow. His name starts with the same three letters as does Moniaive, where his friend James Paterson lived and painted.

Housework this morning just to keep up my reputation.

I've been glancing through Alison Light's book, Mrs. Woolf & the Servants, (Penguin, 2007.) My grandmother was a servant in London pre-immigration, in the kitchen of what she called "a great house." And how I wish I could remember the name of that family for whom she toiled and boiled. (Yarborough is the name we think we remember but that might be wrong.) So my own grandmother was a part of the Downton Abbey scenario which helped fuel the class system in Britain, with her at the bottom of that social heap. I don't know how old she was when she entered 'service' as she referred to it. I found a census at her family address in Shoreditch when she was young and still living at home, but after that who knows? I picture the Countess going over the weekend guest list while Grandma cleaned the parsnips below stairs.

On page 281 of her book Alison Light indicates that oftentimes retired servants in their elderly years looked back with anger about the demands of the jobs and the rules and regulations to which they were expected to ascribe. But not my grandmother. She talked about those days often. I had the impression she was happy with her lot in life. She told us several times that when the grandees gave a party she and the other girls were allowed to sit on the top of the stairs to watch the ladies and gentlemen arrive all dressed in their finery. I wish that I had written it all down. But who's to know when you are ten, fourteen, twenty that someday you will lust to know every detail in sparkling clarity and then record it. Who's to know?

The Selwood sisters were servants for Bloomsbury households for several years; Marion, Beatrice, Daisy, Elsie, Mabel and Flossie Selwood. They had lovely names.

After dinner I clipped a red zinnia, two pink cosmos, orange and maroon nasturtiums for my small clay vase. And tonight our favourite comedy; Boomers. BBC.

News from Julianne in Warsaw. A Chopin concert today including an amazing cellist.

THURSDAY, AUGUST 16TH, 2018 ~ In 1943 Emily Carr wrote this to a friend; *"These little pauses in life and artistry must be for a purpose. I'm trying to use them to creep towards something bigger.* (Morra, 2006, 195)

I like Emily's idea there. This journal has been an engaging writing project and is almost finished. Creativity often takes a break until the next idea comes creeping along. But wasn't Emily wise to think about the pauses in our lives in that way, that they serve a purpose? It is alleged that Marcel Proust, too, reminded us that it is the fallow periods that *"most often fructify into art."*

A stellar lunch outdoors with E and M on their

patio. There was a breeze and light showers danced on the awning overhead. We talked about our favourite artists. E has visited, with some success, all the galleries he can where he can find Caravaggio's work. M has done same for Vermeer's art including their recent trip to The Frick. I love Augustus John's portraits if not the way he treated his wife. First saw a small one titled Poppet of his young daughter when I was twenty-one at The National Portrait Gallery, London. John likes many things including Japanese woodblock prints and Canadian artists (Maurice Cullen, Robert Pilot *et al*) and those others among whom his Uncle JRS thrived.

I like portraits as they tell much about the times and the sitter, excepting I hope the one of me by Scottish artist Rosemary Beaton with a bright pink face and green hair. Our grandchildren find it frightening as do I. Our offspring will have to fight over who *will not* inherit it. People talk about their bucket lists. Just drop me down into The National Portrait Gallery for a month and I'd be dandy.

Home to a long phone chat with M.S., one of my university roommates. My heart did the happy dance for the entire evening after that wonderful time on the phone with her. The years between then and now haven't gone anywhere at all. Same Marie. Same me.

Aretha Franklin died today. R.E.S.P.E.C.T. That's what the world needs. A good dose of it for everybody.

Is watching the Weather Network a sign of the aging brain? Wondered, so switched to TVO's program on Alberto Giacometti.

FRIDAY, AUGUST 17TH, 2018 ~ A cup of Typhoo and walnut loaf here this morning with JB/RB. They have lent me a copy of a P.G. Wodehouse book. RB has joined The Wodehouse Society in England. Their newsletter is called Wooster Sauce. If you know who Bertie Wooster is it's a perfection of a title.

A few chores in the village (eggs, laundry detergent, condensed milk for the Vietnamese iced coffee which I will try to make soon.) Was making a salad dressing from a new recipe just as a visitor popped in to chat with John for a bit and then Charlotte came for a short visit. We played with the lego. We made a school. As her dad buckled her into the car later she said, "Grandma please don't move our lego off the little table, even in the night."

SATURDAY, AUGUST 18TH, 2018 ~ A different shape to our world this morning. Margaret-Anne's lovely face was in the newspaper this morning.

She died yesterday. I was on my way to the hospital and happened to glance at the page that had fallen open on the kitchen table. I'm thankful for her presence in my days for the last forty-two years; a warm, fun-loving, intelligent friend. So many times over the years I've heard her say "When I meet God I'm going to ask Him about..." and she'd finished it by telling me whatever was on her mind.

She has inherited peace.

But that doesn't meant that I'm not missing her already and forever.

SUNDAY, AUGUST 19TH, 2018 ~ Morning Prayer. The words of The Te Deum were just the thing for me this morning; *"...let thy mercy lighten upon us, as our trust is in Thee."* It's the *"...our trust is in Thee"* part that carries me. That is what I need. Something stronger than myself.

A friend's birthday party this afternoon and a pleasant reunion with many old friends. I thought how like life it is to have such sorrow and a birthday party co-mingled; *"a time for every purpose under Heaven"* as Pete Seeger wrote in his song To Everything There Is A Season. He borrowed the words from Ecclesiastes 3.

The events of these past few days have reminded

me that the soul is the only part of us that was made to last forever.

MONDAY, AUGUST 20TH, 2018 ~ I've ordered two slim booklets on writing biography. I want to see what I did/didn't do properly with my Alice effort and how I could try it again if another idea comes my way. One booklet is by Nigel Hamilton, the other by Hermione Lee. I sat in the breeze and finished Fatima Mernissi's book.

I follow a blogger who uses the name Autumn Cottage Diarist. She is based in North Hampshire, England. On her post today is a photo of her writing room, the shelves spilling over with her books and onto her desk. Between the shelves is a window dressed in maroon and cream curtains, a pelmet across the top. I love it. She ends her posts with a question to her readers. Today's was this: Is it *"time to write about those things close to your heart, from which you will never part?"*

I've been writing about them for an entire year.

There is a flash-mob of baby Blue Jays squawking for JRS on the porch railing. Himself is the super-hero of the bird world. I had wondered how we went through a loaf of bread so quickly. Now I know.

Spoke this evening to Jock. Am relieved to know that the black bear that spent the weekend thirty feet from their tent in Algonquin Park did not eat them nor the baby in the tent beside them. Never email your mother a picture of the black bear outside your tent right before she goes to bed.

If ever I need new curtains they will include a pelmet.

TUESDAY, AUGUST 21ST, 2018 ~ (Morra, 2008, 90). Emily Carr compares joy to *"the long good sucks of a candy- if you swallow it holus bolus it may satisfy your stomach but you want to keep the flavour of the very stuff it was made of on your tongue..."*

Holding onto joy takes work. It takes intention, focus, determination to seek the positive in order to be the people whom we were created to be. But we can't smile our way through every single day. That would be fake joy. Grumpy and down-hearted have their place in the spectrum of human emotion too.

Rained in sheets overnight. This heat requires more patience than I have.

Dinner With Lenny by Jonathan Cott has arrived. It's a slim volume. I started it this afternoon. As it happens, Bernstein was seventy when they did the interview.

Sweet corn and salad at dinner. Can't let August pass by without celebrating the fruits of the season. John can't look at corn due to his remembering a babysitter giving him a cob to suck on. Early memories; their power. He ate the salad instead.

WEDNESDAY, AUGUST 22, 2018 ~ At last. A garden. The rain has turned that arid patch into a riot of colourful bloom. The zinnias are taller than the bird bath. Red roses and yellow, soft pink. The window boxes at the front spill over, drip with maroon coleus and lime green. The one huge sunflower, the only one that grew from all the seeds I planted, stretches up to the front window. It was worth the wait.

This afternoon a medical appointment for John confirmed that we have a new situation to deal with. There is relief in having an answer. Hayley and Jock called. Lucia and Charlotte came over tonight and brought along a bucket of cheer.

When Elizabeth Grey Vining closed off her journal (Vining, 1978, 194) she said this; *"Tomorrow I shall be seventy-one."* It's my turn to say the same thing.

Earlier (pg 137) she commented *"I think perhaps there is no one trait quite so satisfying to oneself and*

to the people around one as joie de vivre. An old lady who has a genuine joy in living is an old lady who draws people to her. She is sufficient to herself..."

Would that I can grow into aging as positively as all that but there must be made room for honesty too. Truth is the underpinning of our most genuine selves.

Elsie, one of the characters in Jane Gardam's novel (Gardam, 2013, 198) viewed aging as *"a slow pavane"*. Instead, I see life reflected in the three parts of a concerto; first the fast part, then the slow, then a return to a quicker tempo.

It's the same with the seasons. I've today noticed how the leaves shrink back, take up less of the sky with Autumn's approach. They flourish and withdraw in timed stages. We're all of a bundle with nature and music.

In my daily jottings I notated many things. On January 24th I purchased the new moisturizer that promised to make my skin rosy. It didn't. From Edith Wharton I learned the wonderful word *"unberufen"*. The new restaurant I named in Markham has come to fruition as 'The Dancing Noodle' where we are scheduled to eat lunch within the next two weeks. The man who went missing downtown has been found. Our tiniest family member is making rapid

progress thanks to superb medical treatment and the loving kindness that surrounds us.

We can face today's medical news by drawing on The Well that is deeper than ourselves. *"Deep, deep as the ocean..."* I sang in my childhood. There was sound reasoning and solid truth behind all of those lessons and all of that music. It is my manna.

At the beginning of this journal I dedicated my year's worth of words to Hoàng Thị Lan Phương. Where our love lives so does Beautiful Orchid, the little girl whom we never had the chance to meet.

Journals teach us to name the names of the dates and to preserve the events within them. They help us to treasure the gift of time and the people who make the journey wonderful.

Psalm 90 is the oldest of the Psalms. It is known as the prayer of Moses. Verse 12 says this;

"So teach us to number our days, that we may apply our hearts unto wisdom."

With thanks

I would be remiss if I omit mention of the people who cared so much about those who were fleeing for their lives and their futures during the postwar exodus out of Vietnam. They willingly gave their time and advice as active members of The Mountain Fund to Help The Boat People committee for the years circa 1980 and forward: Dr. Do Trong, Mr. and Mrs. Jack Smye, the Late Ms. Georgina Matheson, the Late Marge and John Nicholson, the Late Ms. Ruth Pearce. Former CBC Journalist Hilary Brown must be thanked for her hands-on compassion and her professionalism in bringing the story of the Đam family to the public in her award winning documentary. There were countless others who helped in a variety of ways.

But most of all I pay tribute to those of you who arrived on these chilly shores, often in midwinter, carrying nothing more than a plastic bag with your documents in it. You, all of you, have exceeded yourselves. And you, all of you, taught me most everything I know. This small journal is one way of showing that we are all immigrants in the remarkable journey called 'life.'

The addition of the Vietnamese diactricals in this manuscript are due to the diligence of my friend Phương My Hoàng (Kimmy) and I thank her for her help. Kimmy calls the time we've spent together "our laughing days". She is right!

Bibliography

Athill, Diana, 'Instead of a Letter', Granta, 2001

Athill, Diana, 'Yesterday Morning', Granta, 2002

Barron's 'Spanish the Easy Way, Fourth Edition', Barron's, 2003

Bell, Hazel K. editor, 'No Soft Incense: Barbara Pym and the Church, Ann Brown Associates, Hove, BN3 2Wg, 2004

Bennett, Alan, 'Keeping On Keeping On', Faber & Faber, 2016

Bennett, Alan, 'Untold Stories', Farrar, Strauss And Giroux, 2005

Beston, Henry, 'The Outermost House' – A Year of Living On The Great Beach of Cape Cod', Henry Holt And Company, 1928

Delafield, E.M., 'Diary of a Provincial Lady', Prion, 1947

De La Mare, Walter, 'Peacock Pie', Faber And Faber, 1958, The Cupboard, pg. 34

Fisk, Erma J., 'A Cape Cod Journal', W.W Norton & Company, 1990

Gardam, Jane, 'Last Friends', Abacus, 2013

Gardam, Jane, 'Old Filth', Abacus, 2004

Goldman-Price, Irene, 'My Dear Governess –The Letters of Edith Wharton to Anna Bahlmann', Yale University Press, 2012

Greene, Graham, 'A Life In Letters', Random House, 2017

Guo, Xiaolu, 'Nine Continents', Grove Paperback, 2018

Hayden, Ruth, 'Mrs. Delany, Her life and her flowers', British Museum Press, 1980

John, Rebecca and Holroyd, Michael, 'The Good Bohemian, The Letters of Ida John', Bloomsbury, 2017

Larkin, Philip, 'Letters to Monica, Edited by Anthony Thwaite', faber and faber, 2010

Larkin, Philip, 'Collected Poems –Edited with an Introduction by Anthony Thwaite', The Noonday Press, Farrar - Strauss - Giroux and The Marvell Press, 1988

Lee, Hermione, 'Edith Wharton', Alfred A. Knopf, 2007

Light, Alison, 'Mrs.Woolf & the Servants', Penguin, 2007

Lively, Penelope, ' Life in the Garden', Viking, 2017

London Review of Books, 28 Little Russell Street, London, WC1 2HN, UK, (various issues, 2017-2018)

Marks, Leo, 'Between Silk And Cyanide – A Codemaker's War, 1941-1945', Touchstone, 1998.

McAuliffe, Mary, 'Dawn of the Belle Epoque', Rowman & Littlefield Publishers, Inc., 2011

Mernissi, Fatima, 'Dreams of Trespass - Tales Of A Harem Girlhood', Basic Books, 1994

Moodie, Susanna, 'Life in the Clearings versus the Bush', M&S, 1989

Morra, Linda M., 'Corresponding Influence, Selected Letters of Emily Carr & Ira Dilworth', University of Toronto Press, 2006

Newman, Lucy, 'William and Dorothy Wordsworth – All In Each Other', Oxford University Press, 2013

Ngọc, Hu, Lady Borton, 'PHỞ, A Specialty of Hà Nội', The Gioi Publishers, 2014

Nguyễn, Ngọc Bích with Burton Raffel And W.S. Merwin, 'A Thousand Years of Vietnamese Poetry', Alfred A. Knopf, 1962

Peterson, Roger Tory, 'A Field Guide To The Birds', Houghton Mifflin Company, 1934

Pym, Barbara, 'A Very Private Eye –Edited by Hazel Holt and Hilary Pym', Vintage Books, 1984

Pym, Barbara, 'Quartet in Autumn', Penguin, 1977

Ritchie, Charles, 'Undiplomatic Diaries 1937 – 1971', Emblem M&S, 2008

Sackville-West, Vita, 'All Passion Spent', Virago 1983, Hogarth Press 1931

Sarton, May, 'At Seventy', W.W. Norton & Company, 1984

Shapiro, Laura, 'What She Ate', Viking, 2017

Siblin, Eric, 'The Cello Suites', Anansi, 2009

Smee, Sebastian, 'The Art of Rivalry – Four Friendships, Betrayals And Breakthroughs In Modern Art', Random House, 20016

Staebler, Edna, 'Must Write - Edna Staebler's Diaries', Wilfrid Laurier University Press, 2005

Taber, Gladys, 'Book of Still Meadow', Harper & Rowe, Publishers, 1948

Vining, Elizabeth Gray, 'Being Seventy - The Measure of a Year', The Viking Press, 1978

'The Book of Common Prayer', 1962 edition, Toronto Anglican Book Centre

'The Book of Common Praise', 1938 edition, Geoffrey Cumberlege, Oxford University Press, Toronto

Authorized King James Version of The Holy Bible, Collins' Clear-Type Press, 1958

Blogs ~

My thanks to Roz Cawley, for her lovely blog 'Autumn Cottage Diarist' and her permission to quote from her words of August 19th, 2018.

Other Sources ~

With special thanks to the warm and wonderful staff at Edith Wharton's home, The Mount, in Lenox, Massachusetts and to Ms. Mary Ellen Warkentin for supplying The Mount with the order from Kiley's Butcher Shop for Henry James' last visit to Edith's home.

Thank you to Nicole Williams, formerly of The Mount, for the information she sent from time to time on her friendly emails.